Rethinking Lawrence

Rethinking Lawrence

EDITED BY

Keith Brown

Open University Press
Milton Keynes · Philadelphia

Open University Press
Celtic Court
22 Ballmoor
Buckingham MK18 1XW

and
1900 Frost Road, Suite 101
Bristol, PA 19007, USA

First Published 1990

British Library Cataloguing in Publication Data

Rethinking Lawrence.
  I. Brown, Keith
  823.912

  ISBN 0-335-09387-6
  ISBN 0-335-09388-4 (pbk)

Library of Congress Cataloging-in-Publication Data

Rethinking Lawrence / edited by Keith Brown.
      p.   cm.
    ISBN 0-335-09387-6—ISBN 0-335-09388-4 (pbk.)
    1. Lawrence, D. H. (David Herbert), 1885–1930—Criticism and
interpretation.   I. Brown, Keith, 1931–
PR6023.A93Z8536   1990
823'.912—dc20   89-49164
                                                          CIP

Typeset by Rowland Phototypesetting Ltd
Bury St Edmunds, Suffolk
Printed in Great Britain by Biddles Ltd
Guildford and King's Lynn

For Keith Sagar

Difficilis, facilis, jucundus . . .

Contents

Notes on contributors

Janet Barron is a freelance writer, contributing frequently to the *Literary Review*, *The Listener*, *New Statesman and Society* and kindred publications. Her study *D. H. Lawrence: A Feminist Reading* will be published in 1990 by Harvester Press.

John Bayley is Warton Professor of English Literature at Oxford University, and a Fellow of St Catherine's College. His many influential books and articles include *The Short Story* (Harvester, 1988) in which the discussion of Lawrence's short stories may especially interest readers of this volume.

Keith Brown teaches English literature at Oslo University. He edited *Hobbes Studies*, is the author of numerous articles on Shakespeare and on the modern novel, and has been a frequent contributor to the *Times Literary Supplement*.

Jane Davis dropped out of formal education in her mid-teens, and did not return until her mid-twenties, ultimately receiving her doctorate from Liverpool University. The author of one novel, she is at work on a second.

Paul Eggert teaches English at University College (Australian Defence Forces Academy), Canberra. His publications include articles on D. H. Lawrence and on editorial theory, and the edition of *The Boy In The Bush* for the Cambridge University Press Lawrence series. He is currently working on an edition of *Twilight in Italy* for the same series.

Avrom Fleishman is Professor of English at the Johns Hopkins University. His six books include studies of Conrad, Virginia Woolf and the English historical novel.

Roger Fowler is Professor of English and Linguistics at the University of East Anglia. Among his many books on linguistics and literature, *Linguistic Criticism* (OUP 1986) would make the best further reading for those wishing to follow up the style of approach of his essay in this volume.

Jeremy Hawthorn is Professor of Modern British Literature at Trondheim University. He has written books on Conrad, Virginia Woolf and Charles Dickens, and edited a volume on the British working-class novel for the Stratford-on-Avon Studies series, of which he is also General Editor.

Christopher Heywood retired recently from the staff of Sheffield University. He is the editor of *D. H. Lawrence: New Studies*, and his other publications include *Perspectives on African Literature* and *Aspects of South African Literature*.

William Larrett teaches in the German Department of University College, London, but has worked in the fields both of German and of English literature.

David Lodge, celebrated as a novelist, has also written several books on literary theory. He is (now Honorary) Professor of Modern English Literature at Birmingham University.

Malcolm Pittock teaches literature at Bolton Institute of Higher Education and at Salford University. His numerous publications include several articles on D. H. Lawrence.

Christopher Pollnitz teaches English literature at Newcastle University (NSW). An active editor and student of new Australian poetry, he is also co-editing D. H. Lawrence's poems for Cambridge University Press.

Rick Rylance teaches English at Anglia Higher Education College. He has published on nineteenth- and twentieth-century literary topics and is editor of the journal *Ideas and Production*. He also edited *Debating Texts: A Reader in Twentieth-Century Literary Theory and Method* (Open University Press, 1987).

Acknowledgements

Thanks are due to the Editor of *Essays in Criticism* for permission to reprint the articles by Malcolm Pittock and Keith Brown, and to the Editor of the *D. H. Lawrence Review* for permission to reprint the article by Christopher Heywood.

References to Lawrence's works in this volume

At the time of writing, the Cambridge Edition of Lawrence's works is incomplete, while the old Penguin texts of Lawrence's novels are in the process of being replaced by a new series, in which some of the volumes have a different pagination. This accounts for what, to some readers, may at first appear to be occasional false references in this volume.

Introduction
Keith Brown

No one would deny today, at the close of the twentieth century, that the works of D. H. Lawrence have won a permanent place, and a significant one, in the history of English literature. And he has achieved this while remaining alive as an author, still read by many people who would never think of taking a 'course' on his work. Explore the shelves of paperback bookstalls, and you will usually find copies of one or two of Lawrence's works, competing for sale on equal terms with the plethora of contemporary fiction. Apart from Virginia Woolf and E. M. Forster, who occasionally also put in an appearance, it is hard to think of many other British authors of his generation of whom the same could be said. As a poet, too, his stock has risen remarkably in our own times: who, once, could have dreamed that some of the articles that in 1985 marked the centenary of his birth would even rate him higher as a poet than as a novelist?

Moreover, Lawrence is not just a still widely read classic: he remains a writer capable not merely of touching hearts and minds, but sometimes of altering lives. (Not necessarily always wholly for the better, but then there is inherent danger in all power and any medicine can be misused.) Again it is hard to think of any other British novelist who today manifests a similar power to any comparable degree: in Lawrence, it is a gift to which some of the most unpretentious publications that commemorated his centenary bore moving witness.

None the less, for private reader and literary student alike, the Lawrence one sees necessarily depends in part upon the frame-of-reference within which he is seen – and the times they are a-changing. The private reader who experiences the kind of intensely direct, profoundly personal response to Lawrence's work reflected in the envoi to this volume, is less likely these days, for instance, to want to turn him into an institutionalized Messiah complete with gospel, attendant earth-goddess and crucifixion myth. Not that such a reader's response is therefore necessarily any shallower – indeed it might even perhaps be thought truer – than those of earlier generations of devotees; it is only that as the world changes, the nature of the perceived debt to Lawrence changes too. Thirty years ago, for example, the present writer can recall hearing the voices of middle-aged English friends literally shake with feeling as they spoke of their gratitude to Lawrence – a gratitude which, they took it for granted, they shared with thousands of others – for freeing them from guilt about the physical side of their nature. It is unlikely that most admirers of Lawrence today need liberating in the same way and we have Lawrence, partly, to thank for that too.

In university English departments the Messianic phase of Lawrence-promotion was virtually over by the time of the death of the immensely influential critic, F. R. Leavis, in 1978. But of course the novels remain firmly on the map of literary studies, and scholars have gone on steadily doing what scholars ought to do. Keith Sagar's big books, combining a certain underlying Leavisian fire with deeper Lawrencian scholarship than the great doctor's, have continued to appear; massive endeavours on the text, under the auspices of Cambridge University Press, make Lawrence the most *edited* of modern novelists; a big biography is due out soon; the edition of the letters has further increased Lawrence's already massive presence on library shelves . . . it is all, you may say, satisfactory; yet it still leaves a gap, a problem. It has become clear, as this volume has slowly taken shape, that many teachers and tutors today are uncertain what to offer students who demand, in effect, to know what all this effort is *for*, what there *is* about Lawrence that justifies such an investment. Simply to send them back to the texts, unaided and with their reactions confused by half a dozen as yet only half-assimilated literary theories, is not enough; yet most 'classics' of Lawrence criticism are products of a mental world which intelligent 20 year olds today simply do not recognize as their own, and which even the middle-aged are beginning to find somewhat remote.

For the Lawrence who has emerged after the intellectual deluge of the past twenty-five years is not only 'post-Leavis'. He is also 'post' the so-called student revolution, with its shifts, partly permanent, in all our perceptions of paternalistic authority; post the sexual revolution and its aftermath; post the feminist (or what was known at the time as the 'women's lib') explosion; post the revivals of more traditional radicalism, left and right; post the realization that British culture is part of the culture of Europe and often best understood in that light; post the recognition that in discussion of poetry New Criticism is not (always) enough; post the incursion into our literary discussions of French and Russian literary theory; and post (which is where we came in) the acceptance of Lawrence as a figure in literary history, repaying investigation of textual history and source and influence in all the usual ways. None of which means, of course, that we cannot make use of the critical discussions of previous generations. But if student readers, in particular, cannot also be offered discussion of Lawrence that – to borrow the jargon of the times – situates his work within the context of *currently* competing critical modes, then their confidence is going to be badly undercut. It is that gap that this volume sets out to fill: offering a reasonable map, it is hoped, of current approaches to Lawrence's work on the premiss that it is generally best to see where you are, before trying to get there from here.

*

Rethinking Lawrence: the title of this collection of essays is thus not a boast but an invitation. When applied to the individual contributors, it has to be taken in varying senses. John Bayley's graceful and tentative exploration of Lawrence's comedic stance, for instance, is patently the work of a critic feeling his way towards a 'rethinking' of Lawrence even as he writes. Janet Barron, by contrast, would seem simply to be reviewing successive feminist rethinkings of Lawrence that have already taken place – until a few quietly made comments in her closing paragraphs force us to look again, and from a most uncomfortable angle, at certain aspects of the debate she has just described. Both Christopher Pollnitz, on the poetry, and Keith Brown, on *St Mawr*, seem to show that we have clearly underestimated Lawrence's concern with technique, and thus by implication bring him more into line with the great modernists of his period.

Fresh facts, too, enforce fresh thinking, or should do so: Paul Eggert points out how our 'increasing understanding of the many-layered compositional history of Lawrence's . . . evolving works' makes nonsense alike of old-fashioned simplistic assumptions about the nature of his authorship and of extreme deconstructionist re-readings of his texts. (Dr Eggert's asides should also be chewed and digested: see, for instance, Eggert on Serendipity, p. 39.) Similarly, anyone who has ever puzzled over the way the familiar analytical tools of 'new' criticism often somehow fail to *grip* on Lawrence's verse, may perhaps be helped by Christopher Heywood's information about Lawrence's debt to Bushman poetry. (Behind this essay may be glimpsed, too, a wider possibility: that Lawrence's own poetry may repay study not merely in relation to individual exotic source-texts, but in relation to the whole discipline of oral poetry studies, as explored in the work of modern anthropologists like Ruth Finnegan.)

The tools or concepts of new disciplines can also sometimes secure the insights of the past, making them less hit-or-miss for the future: Freud, for instance, acknowledged that all his major insights had been anticipated by the great nineteenth-century novelists, but no one would suggest that his own labours were therefore redundant. Similarly, some readers – those especially whose own formal training was completed before modern linguistics had impinged much on higher education – may be irked by Roger Fowler's application of discourse theory to *The Lost Girl* because, they will insist, it tells them nothing that they could not have seen for themselves without the help of his apparatus! To which the short answer is, of course, 'Possibly. But would you have done so?' For the fact is that, willy-nilly, the incursions of linguistics into literary studies in recent years have little changed, even its opponents' mode of attention to texts.

Scepticism will also be aroused in some breasts by the inclusion of two essays (by David Lodge and Avrom Fleishman) on Lawrence and Bakhtin. Bakhtin, I have been cheerfully assured, is merely the currently fashionable guru: our 'flavour of the month'. But that, I think, is substantially to misunderstand the situation. The present rather selective interest in some aspects of Bakhtin's work is not a cause but a symptom, a reflection, of a general shift in our notions of human consciousness that has been silently in progress for some time now. Put briefly, it is a shift from the 'layer-cake' model of the mind (the subconscious sandwiched between consciousness and instinct) to an image of something more like a cluster of consciousnesses. Clearly such Bakhtinian notions as 'polyvocality' (see p. 55 below) fit well with this trend and are thus likely to be carried forward by it into the future, even while his name itself becomes less prominent. (Who now speaks of Sartre? Yet one meets his ideas everywhere.) In much the same way, the intense efforts in some circles during the late 1960s and 1970s to achieve the total politicization of literary studies have made possible Jeremy Hawthorn's and Rick Rylance's contributions to this volume. And William Larrett, too, carries forward a trend already under way, as he increases the difficulty of believing that Lawrence can ever be seen clearly so long as there remains fog in the Channel.

Malcolm Pittock's article, here reprinted, has provoked senior Lawrencians into some splendid rages. But the truth is that Dr Pittock asks questions about the moral considerations inherent in the genesis of *Sons and Lovers* that trouble every thoughtful reader, and are too often felt to have been either swept under the carpet or evasively answered. Whether the answers offered here are the right ones, I do not know; and in a way it does not matter. What does matter, if the moral claims still generally made for the study of literature – and not least of Lawrence's own works – are to retain any credibility, is simply that such doubts should be openly aired. It is a poor tribute to Lawrence himself, with his appalling, exhilarating, total articulateness, to hedge about discussion of his work with protective taboos.

*

It was said above that this volume is intended as a kind of map of current styles of approach to Lawrence's work. But a map does not merely locate areas of settlement. It also sketches the network of highways, bye-ways and streams that interconnect them; and if you really wish to know where you are, then some at least of that network has to be explored, though people will differ in their preferred route.

So too with this collection. Some natural preliminary pairings of the four-teen articles it contains have been indicated in this introduction. But others will vary with the reader's own interests. 'Lawrence's politics' links less inescapably with 'Lawrence and working-class fiction' if your prior interest is in 'Lawrence and feminism': which itself forms a tacit dialogue with John Bayley's explora-tion of 'Lawrence's comedy' (although the latter can also be read as part of a sequence that includes Roger Fowler's essay and those of Lodge and Fleish-man). The opening of the second section of Paul Eggert's essay, too, has obvious relevance to Malcolm Pittock's forceful attack on Lawrence, as do some comments in Jane Davis's 'Envoi'. But such permutations are best left to the individual reader to explore: they are indeed part of the point of the book, and of the basis on which these essays have been commissioned or selected.

1 Lawrence's comedy, and the war of superiorities

John Bayley

... the little driver, with a huge woollen muffler round his throat, was running round and in and out looking for the two missing passengers. Of course there were two missing passengers. No, he could not find them. And at last, when everyone was getting cross, he unearthed them and brought them scuttling to the car.

Now Hannele took her seat, and Hepburn beside her. The driver snapped up the tickets and climbed in past them. With a vindictive screech the car glided away down the ravine. Another beastly trip was over, another infernal joyful holiday done with.

'I think,' said Hepburn, 'I may as well finish what I had to say.'

'What?' cried Hannele, fluttering in the wind of the rushing car.

'I may as well finish what I had to say,' shouted he, his breath blown away.

'Finish then,' she screamed, the ends of her scarf flickering behind her.

'When my wife died,' he said loudly, 'I knew I couldn't love any more.'

'Oh – h!' She screamed ironically.

'In fact,' he shouted, 'I realised that, as far as I was concerned, love was a mistake.'

'*What* was a mistake?' she screamed.

'Love,' he bawled.

'Love!' she screamed. 'A mistake?' Her tone was derisive.

'For me personally,' he said shouting.

'Oh, only for you personally,' she cried with a pouf of laughter.

The car gave a great swerve and she fell on the driver. Then she righted herself. It gave another swerve and she fell on Alexander. She righted herself angrily. And now they ran straight on: and it seemed a little quieter.

'I realised,' he said, 'that I had always made a mistake, undertaking to love.'

'It must have been an undertaking for *you*,' she cried.

'Yes, I'm afraid it was. I never really wanted it. But I thought I did. And that's where I made my mistake.'

'Whom have you ever loved – even as an undertaking?' she asked.

'To begin with, my mother: and that was a mistake. Then my sister: and that was a mistake. Then a girl I had known all my life: and that was a mistake. Then my wife: and that was my most terrible mistake. And then I began the mistake of loving you.'

'Undertaking to love me, you mean,' she said. 'But then you never did properly undertake it. You never really *undertook* to love me.'

'Not quite, did I?' said he.

And she sat feeling angry that he had never made the undertaking.
'No,' he continued. 'Not quite. That is why I came back to you. I don't want to love you. I don't want marriage on a basis of love.'
'On a basis of what, then?'
'I think you know without my putting it into words,' he said.

And we do too. The farce of this scene from 'The Captain's Doll' – funny and absurd and slapstick all at once – does indeed make us 'know' without putting it into words. Words are here the equivalent of bawling and screaming and lurching up against each other – the preaching and assertions and denunciations of Lawrence himself. The humour of the passage is comprehensive, in that it does everything that in other Lawrencian contexts is done by statement or symbol. And the humour has its own kind of subtlety. The little bus driver, whose acid diminutiveness links him with Hepburn as the doll figure the women have made,[1] or with the small Count Psanek in another story, 'The Ladybird', has the same attitude to glorious holidays amid splendid scenery that Captain Hepburn has to 'love'. He is not taken in: he has his own kind of independence. The whole scene, and its actors, has a visual compactness associated more with a film sequence than with prose narrative; and this is emphasized by Lawrence's always masterly handling of pause and spacing. Note the characteristic Lawrencian use of colons both in description ('And now they ran straight on: and it seemed a little quieter') and in speech ('To begin with, my mother: and that was a mistake'). Also the irony, which at the time of the story would have been appreciated only by the author and his friends, that Hepburn, in those few laconic sentences each broken by a caesura, gives a version of Lawrence's own experience with 'love'.

His sense of humour, and his use of it in art, is also his most shameless quality. 'I am a clown in the water,' he writes to a friend from Italy, in a letter full of the time he and Frieda are having by the sea at Lerici. His inability to swim properly, if at all, is converted into a sort of personal asset, like the weasel cynicism of the little driver in 'The Captain's Doll', or the Captain's own ability to detach himself from the sprucely ludicrous image the two aristocratic young German girls have made of him. Lawrence shameless is also Lawrence at his most superior. And this is not necessarily a very attractive characteristic.

But it can also have an attractive side, the childlike gaiety and good humour of the family scenes in *Sons and Lovers*. The pair shouting at each other in that comic sequence in 'The Captain's Doll' are like an archetypal boy and girl: he pompous and self-important, she derisive but *at the same time acknowledging the male force of his personality*. Sheer vividness of observation, and love of what is seen, give the scene the same kind of lyrically humorous irony that occurs in *Sons and Lovers* in moments like that in which Paul Morel's brother hypnotizes his girlfriend like a snake-charmer before kissing her. Or the even more open humour of the passages in *Mr Noon* which glance at the comic mutual vulnerability of Gilbert and Johanna (Lawrence and Frieda) on their hike through the mountains to Italy.

Milan Kundera has remarked on the novel's 'consubstantial irony'. I suspect that the phrase means no more, but also no less, than that all the best novels tend to be funny, deep down inside. Unlike any other literary form the novel must recognize Sancho Panza as well as Don Quixote, the inextinguishably comic and earthy side of human beings as well as their aspirations, their spirit and their dignity. As one might expect, Lawrence has his own way of doing this; and it can be very complex, leaving the reader not quite sure what to make of things. In the above quoted passage, for example, Hepburn's convictions about 'love', and about his attitudes towards it, are Lawrence's own: deeply felt and experienced, and addressed as much to the reader as to Hannele. Yet this does not affect the solemnity, the male pomposity of Hepburn, his self-satisfaction in believing in and presenting himself as he does. And it is this which Hannele sees, as something personal to him, something ludicrous but also impressive, a combination perhaps lovable.

Lawrence often 'consubstantializes' the funny and the serious by filling a stock character or conventional novel situation with his own sort of originality and lambent intelligence. This can work like a sort of reverse parody, a disconcerting takeover of a novel's context of expectation. *The Rainbow*, for example, presents the kind of family and 'generation' pattern so comfortably worked out in many novels of its period, from Galsworthy downwards; but it presents it in an entirely new and unponderous way. *The Plumed Serpent* as a novel, and stories like 'The Horsedealer's Daughter' and 'The Princess', do the same thing to a more sensational or adventure type of tale, exploring the kind of realities which are generally ignored in its fictional context, and bringing out incongruities. Lawrence's most controversial use of such inverted parody here seems to be in *Lady Chatterley's Lover*. The aristocrat's wife and the handsome gamekeeper is a sufficiently well-worn fictional cliché, repeated with numerous variations in novels of the later nineteenth century and of Lawrence's own time. Hardy uses it in his own fashion, particularly in his minor works, and we are familiar with Lawrence's interpretations of Hardy's characters and situations, and his metamorphosis of them in the gestation of his own novels.

Lady Chatterley and Mellors retain, therefore, some features of a parodic setting, and this both enhances the vividness with which they are described, and equivocates any appearance of earnestness or portentousness. We have met such figures before – yes – but here they have an unexpected and individual mode of being. The inherent comicality of sexual passion affects them as stock characters but not as the individuals whom they have become. The play of incongruity makes them memorable, makes them seem uniquely alive.

The process is still more equivocal in the case of *The Plumed Serpent* and 'The Woman Who Rode Away', to which I shall return later. Here it is worth noting that in these works the stock figures of Indians, tall handsome Mexicans, white women going native or spirited away by savages, are perhaps necessarily less individuals than Mellors and Connie and retain much of the wooden quality of their prototypes. This does not matter so much in the case of comparatively short graphic tales like 'The Woman Who Rode Away' and 'The Princess', but where *The Plumed Serpent* is concerned it becomes a serious drawback. Doctrine and daydream take over, and the natural play of incongruity and comedy is in abeyance.

Fundamental to Lawrence's humour is his own unique personality, and the way it relates to his reader, in what I should describe as a perpetual war of superiorities. In spite of his famous but misleading injunction about trusting the tale and not the teller, Lawrence and his 'story' are at their best synonymous; both, as it were, wholly conscious of the play of forces within them. Personality and fable are at one, and the unifying force is Lawrence's own high spirits, and his sense of mastery in any given literary context. Laughter, defined by Hobbes 'as sudden glory in the mind', constitutes his deepest claim to superiority. His detractors, of whom he has always had many, try to feel superior in their turn by calling him humourless, and pointing to what they feel to be the *unintentional* absurdity of some of the sexual charades in *Lady Chatterley* – the flower wreathed penis and all the rest of it. And yet, if we respond at all to Lawrence's personality and style, these things have the overdone, the blissfully exaggerated quality implicit in a joke. In the face of a joke our own form of superiority is to deny that it has come off: something like that is implicit in our war of superiorities with Lawrence. Ideally we may be prepared to laugh with him, to respond to the gleam in his eye; but a kind of lively competitiveness always exists, and should exist, between him and his reader. The recognition of this has always been obscured, in Lawrence criticism, by the critic's need and wish to criticize, to expound and to explain him, whether for purposes of praise or blame. To admire Lawrence, as Leavis does, for his infallible sense of 'where life runs', can be to take him too solemnly; as those critics also have to do when they object – often with cogency and dispassion – to his views on sex.

Like most others, Leavis's study gives no indication of the possibility of his comedy generating a measure of antagonism between Lawrence and his reader: a relation that might almost be likened to certain kinds of comedy confrontation in the world of art itself. Benedick and Beatrice have much in common with Birkin and Ursula, or Hannele and Hepburn; and the reader who gets absorbed slips naturally into a similar relation. My feeling is that the continued appeal of Lawrence's art has less to do with whether he was right or wrong, about sex or power or life in general, than with his unique gifts as a showman in art, continually goading his audience to a comparable liveliness of response.

Undoubtedly Lawrence becomes 'funnier', in the sense I am trying to convey, as he goes on writing. He startles the reader by sudden changes of tone; he suddenly swerves away from one literary context into another, as if deliberately to baffle the reader and rouse him to a new kind of attention. The first novel in which this trait appears is *Women in Love*, but it is a tendency especially marked in the later stories and even in *Lady Chatterley*. A kind of Laurence Sterne increasingly comes out in Lawrence's literary personality. Other writers, professionally sensitive to effects and technique, are probably more aware of this than most readers. Conscious of literary traditions, they look to the way the writing has been done, rather than what it is 'saying' to the reader. This can bring out unexpected aspects of comedy in Lawrence's repertoire. Anthony Powell, the author of the novel sequence *A Dance to the*

Music of Time, is particularly interested in the rather droll resemblance of Lawrence's gamekeeper, Mellors, in *Lady Chatterley*, to other fictional gamekeepers: those that occur for example in the novels of Surtees. He speculates whether Lawrence, whom he rightly calls an omnivorous reader, may not have been remembering these minor characters, whose role is both comic and picturesque. Lawrence appreciated a touch of military swagger, and Mellors, an ex-soldier, touches his hat in a half-military salute, in the same way as the gamekeeper in Surtees. There is a touch of the *miles gloriosus* in the figure, a comedy personality whose tradition dates far back, and who is a lady-killer as well as a boaster with power to charm. It is a type Lawrence is fond of. (Though it may be noted that he was also 'very fond of Jefferies', whose documentary essay on real gamekeepers, *The Gamekeeper At Home*, has surely also left some trace in Lawrence's conceptions. A similar interweaving of traditional convention and factual experience is observable in 'The Ladybird', when Lady Daphne is briefly attracted to a smiling talkative gamekeeper on her parents' estate: the estate itself being accurately modelled on the Morrells' house at Garsington, and Lady Daphne on Lawrence's friend Lady Cynthia Asquith.)

In assessing the literary make-up of Mellors, Powell quotes an old music hall song of Marie Lloyd, with a decided double entendre, and the refrain: 'Everything he does is so artistic'.[2] This is indeed the impression that Mellors makes, and he makes it as if he were a character from literature, whose 'being' has all the qualities of a work of art. (Keeper Annable in *The White Peacock*, a sombre forerunner of Mellors in some respects, also has obvious roots in conventional Victorian fiction.) The narrator of *A Dance to the Music of Time* remarks at one moment that it is almost impossible for a reader of books to imagine the world of a person in whose life they have no place, and this refers implicitly to Powell's own method of character creation, in which an acute sense of actual and observed human beings merges insensibly into a borrowing of literary personnel from other books and novels. This of course is common practice among writers, and Powell is sensitive to its manifestation in the work of Lawrence. He sees that Mellors is at once an observed human being and a Lawrencian day-dream out of books, and this produces a vividly and equivocally humorous figure, in a sense like one of Powell's own characters.

I must return later to the question of Lawrence's use of literary stereotypes, but it is worth noting now how essentially different, none the less, is the process of his comedy from that of Powell, or from that of any other comic writer. The comedy of character is almost always intended to place us on the side of the author and, as it were, against the character, however much we may delight in and feel sympathy with the latter. Superiority is mutual, as between reader and author. Lawrence drastically alters this process, substituting for the agreement between writer and reader a rivalry, the war of superiorities, with comic overtones. The reader is in a sense encouraged to retaliate, to make his own protestation in comic style (as Powell did when he quoted apropos Mellors that 'Everything he does is so artistic'), to defend himself against Lawrence's strokes.

The brilliance of those strokes is not in question; and another writer and novelist, Dan Jacobson, has used the metaphor very felicitously to give an impression of this aspect of Lawrence.

At his best he writes like a supernaturally gifted sportsman making his strokes: there appears to be no gap whatever between eye, brain, and hand; the words just seem to *happen* on the page rather than to have arrived there as a result of any conceivable process of calculation or volition. The sporting analogy I have just drawn is inadequate in at least one important respect: often enough, what this brain and eye were observing, and this hand was transcribing, was not so much external 'events' as internal states and feelings. Yet the effect is the same: the observation and the act of communicating it are perfectly integrated with one another and the writer has total, impersonal confidence in both.[3]

That is an admirable impression, by a writer, of the effect this writing makes. Lawrence's total confidence might also be equated with his shamelessness, for the only aspect of the sporting metaphor that Jacobson's metaphor misses is that such play is highly aggressive, competitive: a war of superiorities with Lawrence is always match play.

Instead of the rather ponderous division into good and bad which critics usually impose on his writing on moral and aesthetic grounds – *Sons and Lovers*, *Women in Love*, good; *The Plumed Serpent* and *Lady Chatterley's Lover*, bad – it might be more illuminating today to see him at his natural best when most playfully antagonistic, irrespective of argument or doctrine. Lawrencian argument and doctrine at their most effective are in any event inseparable from play and display, and from sport's cheerful assumptions of antagonism. Just as most novelists want us on the side of their comedy at the expense of their characters, so they are also careful – and from the same motives – to conceal, or at least to disguise, their private fantasies. Lawrence parades his. He makes them a part of his adversarial humour and his verbal skills.

In his essay on 'Fantasy and ethics'[4] Dan Jacobson has observed that 'the borderline between fantasy and moral consciousness is everywhere and nowhere'. That is probably true of all fiction but it is supremely true of Lawrence. His attitude towards his fantasies, and towards ourselves as recipients of them, is central; and the two are closely interconnected. I have suggested that part of his skill is implicitly to dare us to reject them, and to give the impression of remaining insouciant if we do. Comedy is never far from the process. In 'The Escaped Cock' ('The Man Who Died'), the slightly jaunty note of bible language which Lawrence assumes for the occasion is deliberately dismissed in the last sentence by a cliché from quite a different context: 'Tomorrow is another day'. This not wholly unfamiliar reflection of 'the man who had died' seems not only to cock a snook at the style of the tale but also at the 'wisdom' which Lawrence is consciously putting into it. (And also the continual flicker of shrewdness, as in the picture of Mary Magdalen, whose 'beautiful face' was still dense with excessive need for salvation from the woman she had been'.)

This seems to me the real significance of the last sentence – a paragraph in itself – of 'The Woman Who Rode Away'. It seems an unequivocal statement, the conclusion that Lawrence draws from his story of the wise and secret Indian community, dwelling in the heart of the mountains. Their sacrifice of the woman, and her desire to be sacrificed, exemplify 'The mastery that man must hold, and that passes from race to race'. That sentence, which could have been written in a contemporary European propaganda pamphlet, puts on an air of portentous certainty. But the fantasy that has gone before contradicts it, as Lawrence must have known quite well. He enjoys his fantasy but he knows its limitations, and he won't be caught inside it. It is his heroine, the woman, who is caught. '. . . this peculiar vague enthusiasm for unknown Indians found a full echo in the woman's heart. She was overcome by a foolish romanticism more unreal than a girl's.' Lawrence indulges his own romanticism, but he is not going to let the reader feel superior about it. It was a fashionable craze of the time, and in several stories he plays with it in his own way. Others, like the offhand husband of the woman, may none the less feel 'vulgar excitement at the idea of ancient and mysterious savages'. Lawrence intuits the manner in which art – his own art in particular – works by having things both ways, by engaging in secret comedy concurrently with its own assertiveness.

This is not frivolity. In the war of superiorities Lawrence usually wins easily by forcing his reader to be more serious than he is: more serious, in particular, in criticizing Lawrence's own racial or sexual ideas. But his art understands the invisible and shifting border between fantasy and the moral consciousness, and how deep if equivocal a role the former plays in the latter. The centre of Lawrence's humour lies in his attitude towards his own fantasy inventions. It is because they are so necessary, for art and for the sense of life, that they need not be serious. One of Lawrence's achievements, as can now clearly be seen, is to have assimilated Freudian theory, rather as Shakespeare invisibly assimi-lated Montaigne and Plutarch, and to have given it in his art – particularly in that of his stories – a human face, and a comic face. Our response to Lawrence is only intelligent, and therefore only beneficial, if it is light-hearted: not earnestly and rigidly serious. In his essay 'Up at the ranch', Dan Jacobson gives a gruesome but also rather touching account of a ceremonial at Taos, with 'readings' from the works.[5] Humans need reverence, and a relation like this to gods they temporarily worship; but when the fashion of worship is over, the real meaning of a great writer endures, as in a case like that of Tolstoy; and the real enlargement of human experience that goes with that meaning.

Lawrence would have mocked such worship. And he was well aware of the comedy of his own compensatory fantasies, wish fulfilments, equivocal iden-tifications. His stories especially often give an impression of deliberate indulg-ence, comic relaxation. He identifies with all bright-eyed, watchful, foxy males, even when there is a faint suggestion of parody about them, as with Count Psanek in 'The Ladybird'. He does not mind his identities seeming portentous, for his superiority with words, and therefore in himself, makes him confident he can overcome and evade ever getting trapped in portentousness. He enjoys making use of vapid or cliché characters from popular literary mythology – gypsies, sheiks, haughty maidens, damsels in distress – and giving them his own twist of meaning, wit and penetration. His relation to his own day-dreams, parables and stories of himself, is disarmingly unembarrassed. As a man who cannot swim he saves girls from drowning, as in 'The Horse Dealer's daughter' and 'The Virgin and the Gipsy'; he saves them from their polite English husbands, as in 'The Ladybird'; but he is also the girls themselves – the Princess, the Horse Dealer's Daughter, the Virgin, the Woman Who Rode Away. All this is done transparently, impudently, as if he was daring his reader to shake his head at the spectacle, to say 'dear Lawrence – how much he loves to be one up all the time.'

One-upmanship is inseparable from Lawrence's humour – perhaps from all humour – but Lawrence's cocky attitude to the reader gives it with him, as I have suggested, a special status. In several stories, and some of the best, like 'The Blind Man' and 'Smile', he involves his reader wholeheartedly in the comedy his deft words engender. Of course there is a seeming cruelty in the process: neither J. M. Barrie nor Middleton Murry could have been particularly gratified by their roles in 'The Blind Man' and 'Smile'; and Murry plays a rather more ignoble role as the cold abject lover of 'The Border Line', who is displaced by the warm ghost of the dead Lawrencian husband. Lawrence is a good hater, and can get humour even into his hatred, but I would argue that in these cases humour and art, the impersonal friendliness of high spirits, do cleanse the act of any damaging malice. In claiming superiority Lawrence is never self-protective. In showing up another he always reveals himself.

This can lead to misunderstanding, none the less, as in the case of 'The Woman Who Rode Away', which I would maintain to be as essentially and deliberately funny a tale as 'Smile'. The Blue Sisters in that tale, with their creamy hands demurely wrapped in wide sleeves, or fluttering free of them, are as much an erotic fantasy as the dark powerful Indians and haunted mountains of the Mexican tale. In 'The Woman Who Rode Away' Lawrence fully and openly eroticizes a Rider Haggard type melodrama, and hence gives it his own sort of suggestive intelligence. Individuals do live by erotic myth, however vulgar and incoherent; and Lawrence was not only adding his comment to the cinema and travellers' tale of the time, but showing how our need for such things is compatible with self-examination and civilized intelligence. Something in him, no doubt, swooned at the idea of being sacrificed by dark powerful Indians, just as a young girl might do in the cinema; but his work makes itself, and the reader, free of any self-destructive idolatry in such matters, while playfully licensing the impulse and its indulgence. No close reading of Lawrence can sustain the idea of his total seriousness in such areas.

But it would be misleading to let him have things all his own way. Any careful reader, however engrossed by Lawrence's immediate spell of place and atmosphere, might observe with interest that the Woman Who Rode Away has little if any feeling for her children, the boy and the girl. Lawrence hated Frieda's maternal feelings, and may well be satisfying a hidden urge in himself here, and a lack of sympathy with which he could never consciously come to terms. He is refusing to allow, in such a context, the normal divisions and incoherences of living. Frieda might have been subject to the 'vulgar excitement' and the 'foolish romanticism' which impel the Woman; but she also had common sense and love and solicitude for her children. Lawrence cannot allow such a human mix-up in his stories. Their fantasies of power and wish-fulfilment – the defenestration of Mrs Hepburn in 'The Captain's Doll', the execution by falling tree of Banford in 'The Fox' – have a merry irresponsibility about them, but they are also acts of personal cruelty. Comedy will not take us all the way here, as it does in such a specialist in black comedy as Saki. Indeed the point where it ends, and an intenser sadism begins, gives a unique dramatic tension to the stories. And yet the erotic can itself become wonderfully and also touchingly comic, as in 'The Blind Man', where Maurice, the man blinded in the war, feels all over his friend's Bertie's head.

> Maurice accidentally knocked off Bertie's hat. . . . Then he laid his hand on Bertie Reid's head, closing the dome of the skull in a soft, firm grasp, gathering it, as it were; then, shifting his grasp and softly closing again, with a fine, close pressure, till he had covered the skull and face of the smaller man, tracing the brows and touching the full, closed eyes, touching the small nose and the nostrils, the rough, short moustache, the rather strong chin. The hand of the blind man grasped the shoulder, the arm, the hand of the other man. He seemed to take him, in the soft, travelling grasp.

It is one of the most erotic passages in Lawrence, far more so than the obvious ones, and eroticism is enhanced by the feel of a joke, of something both farcical and tender. The state of blindness seems deliberately created and explored by Lawrence as a state of sexual power. Bertie suffers as 'the blind man stretched out a strong naked hand to him'. The marvellous apt word transposes blindness into nakedness, the state of sexual intercourse. The soft caressive passage, full of the hesitancy of commas, explores the body until the final moment of 'taking', and the strength of the 'soft, travelling grasp'. The joke is not only in the fact that sexual suggestion is all the stronger for being transposed into one of Lawrence's delusive events, but that poor Bertie is completely miserable about it, does not respond at all. He is based on the playwright J. M. Barrie, whom Lawrence had met through Lady Cynthia Asquith, and who was a little man who shrank from any physical touch or intimacy.

A cruel joke? Not entirely. It smiles with and sympathizes with Bertie's 'one desire – to escape from this intimacy, this friendship, which had been thrust upon him'. While enjoying the blind man's bizarre sexual power, Lawrence is equally in tune with the man who shrinks from this grotesque manifestation of it. Because it is so much funnier, the scene is more understandingly, less wilfully erotic than such Lawrencian set pieces as the wrestling match between Birkin and Gerald in *Women in Love*. It has the calm of true humour about it. Indeed in its acceptance of 'the way things are', rather than insistence on scoring a sexual point, the moment has a good deal in common with a scene of true, and indeed beautiful, comedy in *Women in Love* – the attempted destruction by Birkin of the moon's reflection in the water.

'Moony' lays to rest, in a paradoxical way, the war of superiorities: calling a tacit truce between men and women as it does between Lawrence and his reader. But his comedy of artifice none the less depends on keeping up a perpetual banter with the reader, even on the simplistic level of the crossword clue about the Siamese functionary which old Granny tries to solve in 'The Virgin and the Gipsy'. (The reader feels a slightly guilty elation when Old Granny next appears carried off by the river that floods through the house, 'her blind blue eyes bolting, spume hissing from her mouth'). The willed fantasy event still goes with Lawrence's comic style, his swagger, his derisive dominance. And yet he could also be touchingly funny in a quite different, almost naive way, when he wrote something he had no real idea of his readers ever seeing. This occurs frequently in *Mr Noon*, the autobiographical 'novel' he wrote after beginning to live with Frieda, whose second half drops the usual stance of his fiction about himself, and becomes a vivid day-to-day record of the journey they made together from Germany down into Italy.

This is Lawrence with no thought of his Benedick and Beatrice pose with the reader. Instead he himself seems lost in an enchantment of contemplation, awareness of himself and Frieda; and humour seems to bubble from this as naturally as water from a spring. Already the pattern is set, and he seems well aware of it, that they need someone else there beside each other; and they join up with friends, two young men: with one of these Frieda makes love, partly to please herself and to cheer him up, partly out of pique with Lawrence and his tiresome ways.[6] It is out of pique that she at once tells Lawrence what has happened, and he at once becomes immensely forgiving and understanding. This irritates her deeply. The writing records this as childishly almost as it seems to record Lawrence's own small satisfactions and dissatisfaction with different aspects of their sex life.

Contrasting as they do with the glinting comedy of the mature Lawrence, these simple confidences strike a particularly charming note. But they also show how much he depends, comes to depend, on his own superiority in a humorous relation. When he mocks American restlessness, for instance, it is no use our pointing out to him that he himself is the most restless of men: he knows it, and that knowledge is itself for him in his writing a liberating joy. So is his knowledge of his own sexuality, with its dependence on women and its desire for men. And it is this sense of liberation and irresponsibility, rather than any more positive message, which is Lawrence's truest gift to his reader. He wants us to be superior along with him; even to share, with him, the ultimate joke. Which is of course that he knew quite well how absurd he is being about 'the will', when he says of the Woman Who Rode Away that 'she had no will of her own'. Of course she did. She hankered to get away from it all; she hankered for a life that Philip Larkin in one of his poems sardonically calls 'reprehensibly perfect'. So did Lawrence, but in his art he knows he will never get it; and his reader knows it too.

Lawrence's humour tends to desert him most evidently when, as in *The Plumed Serpent*, he seeks to impose fantasy characters of his own upon a realistic local background: that of Mexico and Mexican society in the disturbed and revolutionary atmosphere of the 1920s. It has often been pointed out that he does much the same thing in *Kangaroo*, apparently importing some of the political activity and struggle which had been going on in Italy; but in *Kangaroo* the Australian background is done with such marvellous and casual truth and authority that the superimposition scarcely seems to matter. Lawrence himself is present too, in the character of observer and partaker of the fictional experience, and this is a very important point. As Lovat Somers, Lawrence can be amused by his own pettiness and irritable fastidiousness, as in the delightful scene when he is appalled by the names of the little bungalows, names like 'Wyewurk' and 'Torestin'. Somers even vainly hopes that they might turn out to be Aboriginal names. There is no Somers in *The Plumed Serpent*, and the fantasies of a visionary Mexico full of the old gods can go unchecked. Lawrence abandons himself uncharacteristically to his own fantasies, and abandonment lacks the balance of humour, the equivocation that is so effective in 'The Woman Who Rode Away', as in most of the other stories.

Bad books can have more influence than good books. Lawrence in his apocalyptic vein has, by the same token, more of a following than Lawrence the humorous artist, who restores the human balance between reverence and irreverence, scepticism and belief. Men must believe in something, as Lawrence so insistently tells us, often putting it in his letters and articles with all the crudity of a bible-thumping evangelist. It was this zeal, this fire in the belly, that won him a following, as did his rhetoric of prophecy. But time tends to turn prophets into artists, if they had in the first place the true artistic genius. Clinging today to Lawrence's message, or messages, can result in absurdities of the kind associated with the *Lady Chatterley* trial, solemn comic displays that have no connection with Lawrence's own internal humour. A bench of divines gravely testifying to the sacramental quality of Lawrence's sex passages cannot be taken all that seriously, and to claim that Lawrence's doctrine is similar, where sex is concerned, to that of the contemporary Christian church, was less than convincing.

The trouble here, oddly enough, is trusting the tale and not the teller. *Lady Chatterley*, and even *The Plumed Serpent*, can be interpreted in almost any way, and suited to the tastes and convictions of any age, but at the cost of ignoring Lawrence's own complex and lively personality, that of the teller. It can be argued, for example, that the three versions of *Lady Chatterley* represent an evolution of the tale, from the comparative realism and slightly awkward comedy of the original gamekeeper, Oliver Parkin, to the more Lawrencian figure of Mellors; and that this shows a progress towards a visionary world, a possible Eden struggling to realize itself against the ugly negation of Wragby and Clifford Chatterley. But Lawrence's tales do not lend themselves to interpretation at different levels: the personality behind them is too strong for that, too mercurially complex. Ultimately, the singular lesson of Lawrence's humour, and the way it operates throughout his work, suggests that both for maximum enjoyment and for truest understanding it is he, the teller, whom we should trust, rather than his tale.

Notes

1 And whose colleague in *Sea and Sardinia* (ch. VII) may also be remembered.
2 Anthony Powell, *To Keep the Ball Rolling, A Dance to the Music of Time*, vol. 3 (London, 1983).
3 Dan Jacobson, '*Women in love* & The Death of the Will', *Adult Pleasures* (London, 1988).
4 Dan Jacobson, 'Fantasy and ethics', *Adult Pleasures* (London, 1988).
5 Dan Jacobson 'Up at the ranch', *Adult Pleasures* (London, 1988).
6 *Mr Noon*, ed. Lindeth Vasey (Cambridge, 1984). The young man, called Stanley in the text, was Harold Hobson, a close friend of David Garnett, the other young man with them.

2 Equality puzzle: Lawrence and feminism

Janet Barron

'Those of us who admire the fiction of D. H. Lawrence,' Lydia Blanchard commented in 1975, 'and particularly those of us who are women, are faced with continuing difficulty in our attempts to separate his work from his reputation.'[1] This reputation had become, as Blanchard put it, that of 'the archetypal male chauvinist', to an extent which any reader familiar with a feminist perspective cannot fail to recognize. Many women readers have felt unease with Lawrence's works, and many have admired his achievements. In one sense, there is in Lawrence a potential oppressor of women. To many women of earlier generations, however, this was of less significance than his importance as a liberator: it was easier to close one's eyes to things which were disturbing than to deny his admirable lack of hypocrisy in celebrating sensual fulfilment. Sexuality was an area which many of Lawrence's contemporaries found difficult to discuss. 'It was plain that sex had for him a meaning which it was disquieting to think that we, too, might have to explore,' Virginia Woolf noted anonymously in the *Times Literary Supplement*;[2] and though she was relieved to find that in *The Lost Girl* 'sex, indeed, was the first red herring that crossed our path', she was also disappointed that Lawrence did not make more of it.

'I shall do my work for women,' Lawrence declared, 'better than the suffrage.' An early draft of the *Sisters* describes his theme as 'woman becoming individual, self-responsible, taking her own initiative'; yet what she did become, as Kate Millett pointed out in her best-selling *Sexual Politics* (1970), was:

> only a nonentity, utterly incorporated into Birkin. . . . Sexually, she wants to be the epitome of passivity: 'she wanted to submit, she wanted to know. What would he do to her? . . . She could not be herself. . . . She abandoned herself to him.' Hereafter, marriage represents not only the taming of the woman, but also her extinction.[3]

Millett's analysis, appearing at the height of the Women's Liberation movement of the late 1960s, expressed many of the emotions which women were beginning to articulate. At the beginning of the decade, Penguin Books had successfully made *Lady Chatterley's Lover* the test case of a censorship rooted in laws whose origins lay in the Victorian double standard. In the wryly mocking chronology of Philip Larkin's famous poem, sexual intercourse began with the end of the Chatterley ban: an event further commemorated by the Beatles first LP. 'Whether you were in favour of letting it all hang out, or just some good wholesome fucking,' Sheila Macleod says of her days at Oxford in the 1960s, 'Lawrence was your ally and your advocate. And it was all right to call it fucking, because if the act was not shameful, so neither was the word.'[4]

Lawrence's combination of sexuality with the more conventionally elevated notions of fiction troubled many of his contemporary readers. 'I much prefer a more frankly pornographic book to one like this,' John Galsworthy said of *The Rainbow*. 'That at all events achieves what it sets out to do, and does not leave the painful impression of a man tragically obsessed to the ruin of his gifts.'[5] This was at least a more defensible response than that of the journalist who proclaimed that *Women in Love* was 'dirt . . . in heaps – festering, putrid heaps which smell to high heaven'.[6] In an amusingly self-conscious reaction, the socially distinguished Lady Cynthia Asquith prayed that the volume of poems that Lawrence, with whom her mother believed her to be in love, proposed to dedicate to her was not erotic.

Subsequently, others have felt that the 'tragically' excessive sexual pre-occupation which readers detected in Lawrence was not his own at all, but rather that of the readers themselves. 'Sex is a way of talking about something else,' Mark Kinkead-Weekes argued in 'Eros and Metaphor' (1978), seeking to move the critics' debate on to a more intellectual plane.[7] But the problem with that tactic is that when Lawrence discusses sex, sex is often what he is talking about, however much endowed with mystical significance. If marriage guidance counsellors recommended his works and adolescents perused them under the bedclothes, it was because Lawrence's descriptions of sexuality struck a chord whose resonance was not solely on the level of metaphor.

By the late 1960s Lawrence was once more under attack, his paean to sexual tenderness burned as ritualistically as the bras of women's libbers. 'The celebration of the sexual passion for which the book is renowned,' Kate Millett observed of *Lady Chatterley's Lover*, 'is largely a celebration of the penis of Oliver Mellors, gamekeeper and social prophet.'[8] While radical student protest commanded a nightly space on the news, women were beginning to realize that they were still being kept in their place:

> Men led the marches and made their speeches, and expected their female comrades to lick envelopes and listen. Women who were participating in the struggles to liberate blacks and Vietnamese began to recognise that they themselves needed liberating – and they needed it now, not 'after the revolution'.[9]

The very value which their parents had placed on Lawrence as a 'Priest of Love' now made his message seem like a confidence trick. Lawrence may have championed sexuality; but in what followed from this he was opposed to emancipation. He did not believe in education for women – the right to which women were for the first time beginning to enjoy fully with the expansion of the universities – and claimed that women who worked were pursuing a false goal, enslaving themselves to the industrial machine just as men had mistakenly done. He even hated women cutting their hair, which could otherwise have kept them out of mischief as they combed it 'by the hour in luxurious quiet'.[10] Though he insisted that 'all is not *sex*',[11] there is often little else for his heroines to do but Be, while waiting for the 'Sons of God' to come down to the 'Daughters of Men'. Female friendship is tinged with the 'shame' of lesbianism, motherhood is often a way of not stepping over the threshold into 'selfhood' – even when Alvina in *The Lost Girl* gains strength of personality by her medical training, what she really desires is the awful mystery of Cicio, 'manliness' shining through a cheap suit. A generation of women in rebellion against traditional roles were bound to respond to such notions with outrage: how could their mothers so foolishly have believed that Lawrence was on their side?

Kate Millett's *Sexual Politics* had been preceded by Simone de Beauvoir's *The Second Sex* (1949, English translation 1953), the first systematic attempt this century to challenge men's authority to pronounce on female experience. Of the five male authors whom de Beauvoir analyses, D. H. Lawrence is the only English author discussed – a chance which, coupled with Lawrence's reputation as a 'sexy' writer, gave an especial impetus to further feminist studies of Lawrence. 'Not for him to define the special relations of woman and of man,' de Beauvoir argues, 'but to restore both of them to the verity of Life.' This apparently involves an equal sexual union, in which both partners relinquish individual personality to a greater force, the relationship itself, but because Lawrence identifies sexuality with the phallus, this places the male in the dominant role. 'A social advantage for man is grafted upon this cosmic advantage,' de Beauvoir continues:

> No doubt because the phallic stream is impetuous, aggressive, because it spreads into the future. . . . It is for man to 'carry forward the banner of life'; he is intent upon aims and ends, he incarnates transcendence; woman is absorbed in her sentiment, she is all inwardness; she is dedicated to immanence. Not only does man play the active role in the sexual life, but he is active also in going beyond it; he is rooted in the sexual world, but he makes his escape from it; woman remains shut up in it.[12]

'The very expression "phallic marriage",' she concludes, means that 'Lawrence passionately believes in the supremacy of the male.'

'What is particularly surprising . . . is how very much Lawrentian marriage resembles another sleep, even a death,' Kate Millett comments.[13] This unease over the fate of even the strongest heroines is shared by many women readers. 'Ursula in *The Rainbow* was someone I could admire, someone with whom I could tentatively identify,' Sheila Macleod agrees, until 'her later succumbing to Rupert Birkin filled me with dismay.'[14] Ursula in *Women in Love* ends the novel as a timid voice, trying to persuade Birkin against his deep conviction that he need not look outside their marriage for a 'higher' lover. But her sister Gudrun takes over the stage; and Gudrun has that rare thing in a Lawrencian woman – a talent of her own, as an artist. Her story ends on an altogether more intriguing note, as she departs with her fellow artist Loerke – a man whose sexual presence creates a fascination which the 'priggish' Birkin believes himself to monopolize.

This contrast between the sisters in *Women in Love* embodies a central ambiguity in Lawrence's fiction. His heroines are urged to 'submit' to the phallus and worship it: this passage, from *The Plumed Serpent*, could almost be a pastiche:

> Ah! and what a mystery of prone submission, on her part, this huge erection would imply! Submission absolute, like the earth under the sky. Beneath an over-arching absolute.
>   Ah! What a marriage! How terrible! and how complete! With the finality of death, and yet more than death. The arms of the twilit Pan.[15]

If they do submit, they cease to exist as characters, yet if they fight back they are more convincing: 'You a lord and master!' mocks Harriet in *Kangaroo*; 'Ph! look at it!' Somers makes love to her, casting himself as an other-worldly creature, fresh from the depths of the sea, but Harriet debunks him with frivolity: 'That was *chic*.'[16]

Lawrence's men and women rarely know what their lovers are thinking: even in the companionate marriage in *Mr Noon* there is a tension of miscomprehension, though here it has taken the form of banalities over the tea table. 'She never knew what he saw when he looked at her,' we are told of Hannele in 'The Captain's Doll': what she sees when she looks at him is hairy forearms and well-shaped legs, and 'She was heavy and spellbound, and she loved the spell that bound her. But also she didn't love it.' Sexual attraction thus acts against the characters' sense of self, drawing them into painful conflicts from which they would often prefer to be shielded; yet it is through this battle of the sexes that Lawrence believes we can be 're-born'.

The diagrammatic approaches to Lawrence adopted by de Beauvoir and Millett fail to take account of the complexities of his narratives, drifting instead into generalizations about Lawrence's antipathy to women. Analyzing *Sons and Lovers*, Millett concluded that 'Paul Morel is of course Lawrence himself', an image of the 'male ego rampant' who is 'treated with a self-regarding irony which is often adulation,' while:

> The women in the book exist in Paul's orbit and to cater to his needs; Clara to awaken him sexually, Miriam to worship his talent in the role of disciple and Mrs Morel to provide always that enormous and expansive support.[17]

But recent feminist critics have drawn attention to the limitations of such an approach. In *Feminist Literary Theory* (1986) Alison Light focuses on the misreadings which result from Millett's view:

> Against her insistence on seeing the novel as Lawrence's autobiography, and the arrogant Paul Morel as simply his mouthpiece, I had scrawled exasperated comments in the margin – 'But we see this!' and 'Lawrence shows us!' . . . My objections . . . point to my recognition that if Lawrence *is* Paul, he is also Paul's mother and girlfriends, and if, as Millett does, we take their part, we haven't somehow escaped Lawrence but exposed the way in which novels, as constructs of the imagination, might be attempts at 'ungendering' and, however unsuccessful, at dispersing or even transgressing the gendered experience of an author and its usual restraints.[18]

In *Sons and Lovers* the women are presented through the eyes of the adolescent Paul, whose understanding Lawrence shows us to be incomplete. Frieda had warned him that this resulted in a restrictive presentation of women:

> It does not seem to me the deepest and last thing said, if for instance a man loves in a book the pretty curl in the neck of 'her', if he loves it ever so intensely and beautifully, there is some thing behind that curl, *more* than that curl, there is *she*, the living, striving she.[19]

In Lawrence's subsequent works we see a deliberate attempt to present female consciousness, making women instead of men the centre of many of his narratives. At the same time that he is trying to portray 'the living, striving she', however, Lawrence is also creating his own mythology of the female:

> There is behind every woman who walks, and who eats her meal, a Venus of Melos, still, unseeing, unchanging, and inexhaustible. And there is a glimpse of it everywhere, in somebody, at some moment, a glimpse of the eternal and unchangeable that they are.[20]

This is not the 'angel' of Victorian inconography – in fact Lawrence's peacock, described as 'just like a woman', defecates on a tombstone angel – but rather a vision of 'womanly woman', glorious in her own female nature. It is, though, a very limiting model for a heroine, wrapped up in her own sexuality. For while Lawrence is seeking to develop the 'feminine consciousness', he is looking at this in relation to man – how will his heroines respond to the 'sons of God' whose love will be their ultimate fulfilment?

Tracing the fate of the heroines through the chronology of Lawrence's career, Mark Spilka (1978) argues that we can see a pattern emerging.[21] In the early works, including *Sons and Lovers*, Lawrence is in sympathy with the women whose lives he describes, although Paul is often too obtuse to understand them: this sympathy extends further, to the feeling that men are actually the inferior sex compared with female emotional strength. By mid-career, Spilka suggests, Lawrence is trying to develop a matching strength in his men, creating a precarious balance in 'an emerging and rather shortlived *equivalence* in male strength, an equivalence easily confused with the urge to dominate because that issue is, for the first time, stridently posed' in such works as *Women in Love* and 'The Captain's Doll'. This equivalence, however, then turns into a desperate need to insist on male superiority, which is never fully accepted by the female characters: in the contemporaneous works *The Plumed Serpent* and 'The Woman Who Rode Away', we have a woman making her submission but 'as far as I need, and no further', and a woman actually being sacrificed to the power of the phallus. This sadistic element, Spilka argues, was never entirely absent in the final works, though in *St Mawr* Lawrence presents the male principle as inadequate to the desires of the female.

Over the last two decades, feminist criticism in general has changed in emphasis. Where the original concern was with the role of woman as reader of a predominantly male literary canon, analysing the discrepancies between the 'female' as presented in literature and women's actual experiences in history, we now have the rediscovery of works by women writers, establishing a parallel tradition. In this process of recovering 'lost' women writers, the original distinction between 'male' and 'female' writing has, however, come to seem more complex than it had appeared initially. Women writers often share the 'patriarchal' attitudes of their time quite as much as men: the historical context thus becomes increasingly important. Turning again to the works of male writers as a basis for comparison, therefore, many feminists have come to place a new emphasis on the cultural conditions which influence literature.

In *D. H. Lawrence and Feminism* (1982), Hilary Simpson explores the historical context of Lawrence's works. Kate Millett had suggested that 'It is important to know that he began in the midst of the feminist movement, and that he began on the defensive'; Simpson analyses Lawrence's involvement with the Suffragettes and the reasons for his later disagreement with the women's cause. Many of Lawrence's friends were active in the campaign – Jessie Chambers and Alice Dax in Nottinghamshire, Helen Corke and Louie Burrows in London. The atmosphere in Eastwood at this time is conveyed in a letter by Enid Hopkin Hilton:

> The Pankhursts, Annie Kenny and others . . . came home with us and stayed at our house, and discussions went on and on far into the night, intense, but friendly and a bit gay. . . . Meetings were held in our small town and there was much enthusiasm, many fights and some really productive effort. Keir Hardy stayed with us, Ramsay Macdonald, Philip Snowden, Edward Carpenter, Margaret Bondfield – many others.[22]

In this context, Harry T. Moore argues, Lawrence can be seen as one of the more enlightened men of his generation:

> Like most members of our civilization, D. H. Lawrence was brought up in the tradition of male dominance. Unlike most others, however, he was aware of this situation and, although he often accepted it, if only unconsciously, he often fought against it – something for which he has not usually been credited.[23]

It has also to be remembered that Christabel Pankhurst's slogan 'Votes for Women' carried a second demand: 'Chastity for Men'. Though many women objected to her definition of man as enemy, this provided a strategic platform for the Suffragettes: gaining the vote, they argued, would not result in promiscuity, but would actually serve to improve the morals of the nation. Lawrence regarded this aspect of the women's cause not as an extension of freedom, but of repression, a cruel denial of the needs or realities of human nature, female no less than male. Since most feminists today would share this view, this casts an odd sidelight on the ready identification of him as 'counter-revolutionary'; the histories of revolutions are generally more complicated than revolutionaries remember.

None the less, enough has already been said in this essay to show the point of Millett's celebrated identification of Lawrence as a 'counter-revolutionary sexual politician', and Simpson relates this aspect of his literary stance to the changing social situation for women during the First World War. As women entered the traditionally male trades in increasing numbers, she suggests, many men began to feel that women were taking over the country. Part of 'getting things back to normal' was thus to urge women back into domesticity.

This reading certainly can be made to fit the short story 'The Fox', which appears to offer us a sort of shorthand version of many of Lawrence's theories. Two women, living together in a friendship with lesbian overtones, are about to lose a wartime independence now that the men are back: not that, being Lawrencian women, they have enjoyed their work much anyway. A mysterious, potent male presence, whose appearance is animal-like, breaks into their relationship, gaining control of the farm and of the body of March, contriving to kill the 'grimalkin' Banford and to bring March back from her role as an androgynous farmhand to her 'proper' appearance in skirt and blouse, a role that she was in any case seemingly anxious to reassume. Sexually accessible and vulnerable in clothes that are not too frail for her to venture out of doors without the warmth of a male embrace, she snuggles into his greatcoat with a childlike sense of relief at handing over responsibility for herself to the capable power of a man. . . .

Q.E.D.? Perhaps not quite. 'Many readers object to Henry Grenfel's apparent dominance over March at the end of 'The Fox',' Julian Moynahan noted in an essay ten years ago,

> but I think a more adequate reading would be to see Henry as a piece of embodied Celtic nature, essential to March but not really in control of her as she searches down to the bedrock of her nature, becoming 'deanglicized' and 'empty' in the process.[24]

Moynihan is right that Grenfel is certainly not in real control of March, and his point may be taken further. It is noticeable that Grenfel is mostly described not as 'the man' but as 'the boy', and increasingly so in the final pages where we (and he) might have expected that he would bend her to his will. He has a 'puppyish laugh' and is much younger than March; when he takes her to his hometown while they wait to travel West, she kicks against this. In the conclusion, we have a scene which recalls that between Tom Brangwen and the child Anna in the barn of *The Rainbow*: 'she looked round at him, with the strained strange look of a child that is struggling against sleep'. In true Lawrencian fashion, the hero believes that when they have left, 'she would go to sleep. She would close her eyes at last and give in to him':

> Then he would have all his own life as a young man and a male, and she would have all her own life as a woman and a female. There would be no more of this awful straining. She would not be a man any more, an independent woman with a man's responsibility. Nay, even the responsibility for her own soul she would have to commit to him. He knew it was so, and obstinately held out against her, waiting for the surrender.

But when he tries to reassure her that this will be so, she is still straining against his promise that she will 'feel better':

> 'Yes, I may. I can't tell. I can't tell what it will be like over there.'
> 'If only we could go soon!' he said, with pain in his voice.

As the final line of the narrative, this is hardly 'submission absolute', though Grenfel may be trying hard to reincarnate 'the arms of the twilit Pan'.

These ambiguities, alternating between male and female perspectives and ending in uneasy compromises, are characteristic of Lawrence's fiction, even if in abstract form the divisions appear clear-cut. In Alison Light's phrase, this is an attempt at 'ungendering', and Lawrence did consistently try to develop the female point of view, however provocative the results at times. In the draft of *Le Gai Savaire*, he sets down the problem as he saw it: 'We start from one side or the other, from the female side or the male, but what we want is always the perfect union of the two':

> It needs that a man shall know the natural law of his own being, then that he shall seek out the law of the female, with which to join himself as a complement . . . they are two, but . . . they are two-in-one.[25]

This programme, though conventional, accounts no better than Hilary Simpson's historical-context approach for the vehemence, the *personal* intensity, of many of Lawrence's outbursts against modern women. Sheila Macleod finds an answer in Norman Mailer's comment on Lawrence's slightly uncertain masculinity and consequent insecurity. Lawrence, Mailer had written,

> illumines the passion to be masculine as no other writer, he reminds us of the beauty of desiring to be a man, for he was not much of a man himself, a son despised by his father, beloved of his mother, boy and young man and prematurely aging writer with the soul of a beautiful woman. . . . Dominance over women was not tyranny to him but equality.[26]

Here, thought Mailer, was the root of the huge fascination which Lawrence's writings have had for women:

> Never had a male novelist written more intimately about women – heart, contradiction, and soul; never had a novelist loved them more, been so comfortable in the tides of their sentiment, *and so ready to see them murdered*. (my italics)

For Macleod this squares well with her wish to dismiss what she now sees as her own misguided early fascination with Lawrence's mysticism. The outcome of her 'common-sense' approach is a rejection of Lawrence's presentation of sex, which she thinks has been largely overrated, and a moral condemnation of the actions of his characters. Of the kiss which Mrs Morel gives Paul in *Sons and Lovers*, Macleod remarks: 'as the mother of two grown-up sons *I find her conduct inexcusable*' (my italics).

Such a comment illustrates a central difficulty in feminist criticism of Lawrence. We may well feel that his characters are apt to behave in inexcusable ways; but this was also the line which *John Bull* had taken in calling for Lawrence to be banned as an 'obscene' writer:

> In real life we should not be troubled with Mr. Lawrence's characters – they would be safely under lock and key. For instance, there is the idiot who undresses and wallows in wet grass, delighting to have his back scratched with thistles and his skin lacerated with fir-cones. Doctors have a name for this sort of thing.[27]

'They all seem determined to make a freak of me – to save their own short-failings, and make them "normal",' wrote Lawrence in 1929.[28] Within normal morality, Mrs Morel should not kiss her son as a lover: but we are not always governed by rationality.

In looking at Lawrence's work in the light of feminism today, we need to be wary of letting his more outrageous comments bias us. He can, on occasion, be annoying and even offensive, but his aesthetic achievements are always far more subtle than his polemic. As an example of the way in which emphasis on his misogyny may distort our reading, consider Faith Pullin's essay on *Sons and Lovers* (1978). 'Lawrence is a ruthless user of women,' Pullin believes, who because of his 'basic sickness', his Oedipus complex, 'never emerged from that infantile state in which other people are merely instruments.' Analysing the passage in which Paul 'cremates' Annie's doll, she concludes that:

> What is particularly significant . . . is the language used here to describe Paul's emotional response to the situation, 'wicked satisfaction', the 'stupid' doll, the gratuitous smashing of the already burned arms and legs. And then, so typical of Lawrence, the summing up with the clinching insight, 'he hated the doll so intensely, *because he had broken it*'. (Pullin's italics)[29]

'In just the same way,' Pullin extrapolates, 'Paul hates Miriam because he has broken her.'

A number of preconceptions are evident here. While Paul's emotional response is filled with hatred, this is less straightforward than Pullin would have it in her accusation that 'these men, so passive in their relations with actual women, will revenge themselves on female substitutes when they think they can get away with it.' The doll may indeed be a 'female substitute', but if we turn back a little to the scene in which the doll is broken, we will see that Annie hates the doll too. It is big and ugly, a present admired for its lavish status but rejected as a plaything. In breaking the doll, Paul may actually be carrying out Annie's secret desire, for the doll can be seen as a symbol of her future, a future she resists in her tomboyish actions. If we see the doll as 'child', too, Paul's reactions may be in a sense self-reflexive; what he fears is not Annie's anger but the rage of the mother when she finds out. It is a measure of Lawrence's art that he can hold all of these possibilities within a single incident, itself a vivid embodiment of childhood passion, rebellion and fear of reprisal. And the 'clinching insight' here is a misquotation: it should read, 'He *seemed* [perhaps to Annie] to hate the doll. . . .'

At the time of writing (1989) current feminist attitudes to Lawrence fall chiefly into two main schools of thought. In radical feminist polemic, invisible perhaps to those who do not venture into the stock of women's bookshops, he remains the archetypal male chauvinist. Taking at random a study with the uncompromising title of *Pure Lust* (1984), we find Mary Daly enraged at the report of a conference which she accuses of 'honoring that misogynist':

> Prof. Evelyn Hinz attempted to rescue Lawrence's work from the charge of misogynism that has recently plagued it. Professor Hinz, in a re-visionist paper, asserted that Lawrence did not despise women, but rather vener-ated them. It was agreed by all sides in the discussion that the fact that

Lawrence used to beat his wife, Frieda, had n̶ she was a singularly difficult woman.[30]

Daly's impression derives from de Beauvoir and Mil̶ arguments into blanket condemnation; it would be h̶ attempts to create a new 'woman-made' language with̶ tive comment that 'women, when they speak or write, u̶ word that men have not taught them' – a point often made by ̶

The other school of feminist criticism of Lawrence that has deve̶ present decade has already been illustrated in this essay. Essentia̶ accepts de Beauvoir's and Millett's basic analyses while nevertheless se̶ need to counteract any excessively reductive readings of the works. It is a point that was in fact made by Millett herself: despite the limitations of her literary criticism she does not seek altogether to condemn Lawrence, but to articulate the uneasiness which women readers quite reasonably feel, relating this to a wider cultural context. None the less, recent feminist readings of Lawrence do at their best show a more subtle awareness of the ambiguities of his narratives, as Alison Light illustrates.

But one aspect, or dimension, of Lawrence's writing remains unexplored by feminist critics, and if the present writer is no better qualified than anyone else to mount an expedition into this blank space on the map, it may at least be worth while pointing out what seems to be holding us up. All criticism has its basis in ideology, whether explicit, as in Marxism, or the accepted 'universality' of liberal humanism. The feminist ideology is quite clear: it starts from women's situation in society, defined as 'The Second Sex', and maintained in that status by 'Sexual Politics'. We seek to challenge the assumptions of a culture seen as historically patriarchal, and the challenge remains relevant: men obviously do still exploit women through sex and gender today, aided by manifest economic inequities and powerful social traditions? But in the effort to think accurately about the issues that such injustice raises, feminists of the late 1980s can sometimes be heard thinking thoughts that earlier feminism would find politically unacceptable.

'Sex doesn't work without an element of theatricality and fantasy,' writes one feminist film maker, 'and for a woman that means being dominated by a man.'[31] This may be thought a tendentious and horrifyingly dangerous remark, and indeed in many contexts it would certainly be so. But it is also a reflection of the fact that we simply do not as yet have an adequate vocabulary for comment on female responses to erotica: pornography, for example, is for the most part produced wholly in accordance with male criteria, with women as its material. In many less glaringly obvious ways, too, society is still so unequal in its treatment of men and women that it is remarkably difficult to distinguish between women's actual reactions and the potentially discriminatory consequences. Lawrence's creed of 'phallus worship' is 'counter-revolutionary' in the role he assigns to women; yet we may privately respond to the idea of the male erection *as a symbol* of desire: the problem lies not in the fantasy but in its misogynistic interpretations. Feminist criticism, and criticism generally, has not quite got Lawrence right yet; our analyses still distort as often as they identify.

a Blanchard, 'Love and power: a reconsideration of sexual politics in D. H. Lawrence', *Modern Fiction Studies*, XXI (1975), 431.

2 Virginia Woolf, review of *The Lost Girl*, *Times Literary Supplement*, 2 December 1920.

3 Kate Millett, *Sexual Politics* (London, 1970), 265.

4 Sheila Macleod, *Lawrence's Men and Women* (London, 1985), 10.

5 John Galsworthy, letter to J. B. Pinker, 1915, quoted in *D. H. Lawrence: Penguin Critical Anthologies*, ed. H. Coombes (Harmondsworth, 1973), 102.

6 W. Charles Pilley, review of *Women in Love*, *John Bull*, 17 September 1921, quoted in *Penguin Critical Anthologies*, 144.

7 Mark Kinkead-Weekes, 'Eros and metaphor: sexual relationship in the fiction of Lawrence', in Anne Smith (ed.), *Lawrence and Women* (London, 1978), 102.

8 Millett, *Sexual Politics*, 238.

9 Quoted by Dale Spender, *For the Record* (London, 1985), 20.

10 D. H. Lawrence, 'Energetic women', in *Pansies*, Penguin edition of *The Complete Poems* (Harmondsworth, 1964), 537.

11 D. H. Lawrence, *Fantasia of the Unconscious* (Harmondsworth, 1971), 17.

12 Simone de Beauvoir, *The Second Sex* trans. H. M. Parshley (London, 1953), 245−54.

13 Millett, *Sexual Politics*, 264.

14 Macleod, *Lawrence's Men and Women*, 8.

15 *The Plumed Serpent* (London, 1955), 308. (Camb. edn, 311.)

16 *Kangaroo*, Penguin edition (Harmondsworth, 1954), 164.

17 Millett, *Sexual Politics*, 246.

18 Alison Light, 'Feminism and the literary critic' in Mary Eagleton (ed.), *Feminist Literary Theory* (London, 1986), 176.

19 Quoted by Keith Sagar, *D. H. Lawrence: Life into Art* (Harmondsworth, 1985), 108.

20 ibid., 111.

21 Mark Spilka, 'On Lawrence's hostility to wilful women: the Chatterley solution', in *Smith, Lawrence and Women*, 189−211.

22 Quoted by Harry T. Moore, *The Priest of Love* (London, 1954), 118.

23 Harry T. Moore, 'Bert Lawrence and Lady Jane' in *Smith, Lawrence and Women*, 178.

24 Julian Moynahan, 'Lawrence, woman and the Celtic fringe', in Smith, *Lawrence and Women*, 130.

25 Quoted by Sagar, *Life into Art*, 137.

26 Norman Mailer, *The Prisoner of Sex* (London, 1972).

27 Pilley, review of *Women in Love*.

28 D. H. Lawrence, letter to Lady Ottoline Morrell, 5 February 1929, quoted in *Penguin Critical Anthologies*, 196.

29 Faith Pullin, 'Lawrence's treatment of women in *Sons and Lovers*', in Smith, *Lawrence and Women*, 56.

30 Mary Daly, *Pure Lust* (Boston, MA, 1984), 212−13.

31 Catherine Breillat, quoted in *The Guardian*, 30 November 1988.

3 Welsh Red Indians: Lawrence and *St Mawr*

Keith Brown

In recent years D. H. Lawrence's *St Mawr* has become a very popular syllabus text. Its convenient length, the commendations of Dr Leavis, and perhaps of Professor Kermode, and its inclusion in the *Oxford Anthology of Modern British Literature* have all helped to 'foreground' one of Lawrence's secondary works in a way which he himself could not have foreseen, and would scarcely have thought desirable. For thousands of readers, especially outside Britain itself, *St Mawr* has become the usual introduction to Lawrence's work.

Yet even if *St Mawr* deserves most of the praise it has received, surely it ought at least to be pointed out what an eccentric introduction to Lawrence's work it represents: that it is a freak among his writings, an arcane text. Its sources, its biographical context, its rationale, many details of its working-out, and its underlying design, all, if examined, force one to the same conclusion: that *St Mawr* is an experiment, successful surely, and not discontinuous with ideas and technical interests reflected elsewhere in Lawrence's work; yet of a peculiarly exhaustive kind that he was never again to attempt. To grasp this, is not to reject Dr Leavis's interpretation of the book – indeed in many ways it amounts to an elaboration of his reading – but it does give considerable warrant for the doubt, puzzlement and dissatisfaction often felt by ordinary readers on their first encounter with this novel. For even in a post-structuralist age, our conception of the highest art still tends to be of something 'organic', totally integrated; and arcane texts, cacheing one reference-system inside another, do not meet that condition unless their inner scheme of ideas (as with the veiled Christian reference of some kinds of medieval poetry) is also part of the general cultural background against which they are written: a requirement that Lawrence, obsessed with strange gods, never fulfils in *St Mawr*.

St Mawr was written during Lawrence's time in New Mexico, after a brief return to England (December 1923–March 1924) during which he visited Shropshire to discuss with his friend Frederick Carter the meaning of the Quetzalcoatl myth. Carter has left a short account of their meeting, describing their walk up to the Devil's Chair, Lawrence's interest in his house (which becomes Mrs Witt's in the story) and some of their topics of conversation: including talk of the possibility of a new kind of use of symbolism.[1] One thing that Carter does not say, however, though we know it from other sources, is that Lawrence arrived in Shropshire already aware of the theory that the ancient myths of Mexico, by which he was so fascinated at this time, were Celtic in origin.[2] This must have made his visit to the Marches of Wales particularly stimulating to his imagination.

Lawrence's interest in the world of the Celts is easy to document, though little discussed. He certainly knew enough to use the term 'Celt' in its proper sense, to cover not only Ireland and the surviving British 'Celtic Fringe', but also the vanished world of Gaul and Ancient Briton. Thus Lewis in *St Mawr* has not a Welsh but a *'British* [i.e. Ancient British] stare'; and Gauls are rather dragged into what is repeatedly described as 'the Celtic world' of *The Man Who Loved Islands*. In *Kangaroo*, a novel which he did not complete until he reached New Mexico, Lawrence included two chapters of demonstrably accurate reminiscence of his own Cornish experiences (for 'Celts, Cornish, Irish, they always interest me. . . . They remember older gods, different ideals, different gods') including an account of going out into the *Cornish* night to call on the older gods by *Irish* names. 'Tuatha De Danaan! he would call softly. . . . Be with me! . . . And it was as if he felt them come.'[3] (In the New Mexican night he felt the presence of Indian deities in much the same way.[4]) But in a letter it is the Welsh *Mabinogion* that Lawrence invokes to define the atmosphere of Cornwall; while an Irish correspondent is elsewhere castigated for failing to view Irish traditions within a wider Celtic context.[5] In short, the references to Wales in *St Mawr* are for Lawrence evocations of something very much more than the Principality itself: yet how many commentators point out even the Welsh meaning of the book's name? And the interweaving of Celtic and Indian motifs in the story has been given still less attention; though this too is apparent even in the choice of title.

'St Mawr' looks to be a Welshified spelling of *St Maurus* (St Maur), a name that Lawrence, with his strikingly accurate and retentive verbal memory, could easily have remembered from Chaucer's *Prologue*. But there is no doubt that his stay at Monte Cassino, shortly before leaving Europe – a visit that made an overwhelming impression on his mind[6] – must have fixed the name more firmly in his consciousness. A well-born Roman, Maurus became one of the two principal disciples of St Benedict after the latter, shocked by the decadence of his own times, had withdrawn first to a cave in the foothills of the Abruzzi, and then to the hill-top which was to become the great monastery of Monte Cassino. (It may be noted that the original worship of Pan was also associated with remote caves and high places.) From these holy hills St Maurus brought the Rule of Benedict to France, where the cloister of St Maur was thought of as his monument. Lawrence's 'high-bred' stallion that 'doesn't seem to fancy the mares' and brings the vision that in effect guides Louise Witt, too, to the Convent of St Mawr in the end, is thus deftly named; for Lou is quietly but firmly associated with France: she comes from an old Louisiana family and has a Parisian education – as well as a French given-name, and a mother with a French maiden-name: a Gallic Witt indeed.

Mawr, however, is also the Welsh for 'great'. For though a name borrowed from a Christian saint[7] may serve for the stallion, it clearly won't do for the Hidden God who shines through him. From this point of view, 'St Mawr' means rather *The Great Holy One*: in short, that Great Spirit worshipped by all true Red Indians in the fiction and poetry Lawrence had read[8] and still remembered in New Mexico. It is neatly done, to offer a Celtic name for an Indian concept, as title for a story in which the hills of Wales, glimpsed to the westwards early on, foreshadow the highlands of the American Southwest at the close: criticism of *St Mawr* speaks, perhaps, too readily of 'Pan'.

But of course He is there. *Pan in America* makes it clear that for Lawrence there is really no fundamental difference between the ancient concept of *Pan* and that of the Great Spirit of the Indians. That hidden power whose presence even Mrs Witt, thanks no doubt to her Welsh grandmother, half-senses in the landscape of the Southwest before the novel ends, *is* Pan: 'Unfallen' Pan, *not* – as Cartwright (Lawrence's representation of Frederick Carter) has made clear – the mere Goat-god to which civilization degrades that deity, but the true sacred Life Force, '. . . the mystery, the hidden cause' . . . 'hidden in all things'. And yet, since Lawrence does press at some length this allegedly crucial distinction between Unfallen Pan 'the Great God', and Pan the 'Great Goat', why does he then let his heroine's story end, on a note of triumphant satisfaction, with the purchase of a ranch called Las Chivas – 'the she-goats'? True, the actual herd, stinking, polluting and destructive, has gone before Lou buys Las Chivas, but the name remains: we are left in no doubt that it is to The Place Of The She-Goats that she has come.

Critics seem to see the name as a kind of guarantee that Lou, a non-Christian surprised by a hunger to come into the presence of God, really has found her way to Pan. Yet, when the associations of she-goats are precisely with that Goat-god which the story emphasizes that Lou has left behind her on her way to the True Spirit, would Lawrence really have been so clumsy? Is this narrative really meant to lead up to an image of Lou herself as just one more she-goat, if an unusually high-minded one? That may be how Mrs Witt sees the situation; but then the whole book is in part designed to show up the limitations of Mrs Witt's vision of things, for all her just impatience with the modern world.

Even without the vigorous hint with which the story ends, therefore, it would surely be sensible to look twice at the name of Lou's property. After all, Lawrence did twice rename the real ranch on which Las Chivas is based; and it does not seem to have been noticed that his final choice (Kiowa Ranch), which appears to be no more than an innocent piece of Red Indian romanticism, actually means *The Ranch Of The Principal People*: a name that encapsulates a quite extraordinary tangle of Lawrencian boast, mockery and irony, in view of the circumstances of his life, and the ideas he was canvassing at this time.[9] He would hardly be likely, therefore, to choose the name of Kiowa Ranch's fictional surrogate with less deliberation; and the fact that the book closes with the pointed remark that Lou's ranch was cheap at the price, 'considering all that there is to it, even the name', shows that he did not do so.

A fair number of place-names in the American Southwest, both Spanish and English, echo the sound of a previous Indian name without preserving its meaning. (It is a reasonable assumption that Lawrence would either have known or guessed this; for his own education had had a philological tinge, and in England Saxon place-names can preserve the phonetic ghosts of their Celtic predecessors in just the same way.) So it should be noted that the sound of the name *Las Chivas* offers a strong phonetic analogy to the sound of the name of *that type of American Indian holy-place known as a 'Kiva'*: a fact of the more interest because Lawrence himself was very intrigued by the concept of the Kiva and wrote about it, or refers to it, on several occasions.[10]

As normally defined, a Kiva is a sort of combined male club-house, temple, council-chamber and symbolic womb: a roughly circular structure, usually entered from above, and constructed partly underground, built over a natural fissure theoretically leading to a mythical subterranean chamber (the *sipapu* or 'hole of emission') from which the forebears of the tribe are thought of as having been drawn by the Earth-Mother into the world. The Kiva is essentially taboo to women: though on very rare occasions a woman who is thought to have been singled out by the gods in some way – like Lou Witt herself? – may be granted the right of admission or membership.

Thus for a woman a Kiva represents a double mystery. Below the male Mystery from which mere gender normally excludes her, is a deeper mystery, beyond gender: the mystery of the Life-Principle itself. A more appropriate place for Lou to come at last to wrestle with her Angel, that wild spirit which she feels 'wants her' yet will 'hurt her' too, and 'wear her down', could scarcely be imagined. True to his own thought, Lawrence has kept the Hidden God half-hidden even in this celebration of Him; and once that is realized the point of allowing Lou to end 'among the she-goats' becomes plain. To Lawrence's mind, there would be a bitter, mocking appropriateness in the idea of the Jesus-bringing Spanish colonists and their heirs, emissaries of a civilization that had reduced Great Pan to a lecherous goat-god, and hence to a manifestation of the Devil, besmirching the site of a Kiva, where the True Pan was once to be found, with the goats of the degraded surrogate. And there is the further wry consideration – already made clear in her mother's reaction – that when the secular world sees Lou alone at her ranch with her virile servant, it will regard her as just another she-goat anyway.

The name of Lou Witt's virile servant is Geronimo Trujillo (*dit* Phoenix). Lou herself is Lady Carrington. None of these names is without significance. 'Carrington' need hardly detain us: a savagely apposite glance at Bloomsbury, via the perverted Strachey-Carrington ménage – Carrington being of course actually a painter, and Lytton Strachey himself (*Eminent Victorians*, 1918) a composer of verbal pictures, and a man of minor-upper-class background analogous to Rico's. There is a characteristic Lawrencian bite in the implication that the admired and successful Strachey is no more than a fashionable but second-rate portrait artist; but this vein of quarrelsome Popian satire is not a major element in the book.

'Lou Witt', however, carries very different overtones, being the name (though normally spelt Lu-Wit or Loo-Wit) of the central figure of the best known of the American Indian volcano-myths. This seems doubly note-worthy, since Lawrence's fascination with the image of the volcano is well attested throughout this period;[11] and *St Mawr* itself is full of images of fire. The heroine of the Indian legend was set by the Great Spirit to be the keeper of The Bridge of the Gods (which it seems may once have existed across the Columbia River, as a vast natural rock bridge, linking the areas around the two volcanic peaks of Mt Hood and Mt Adams.) The Bridge lay between the domains of two mighty brothers, who eventually woke into furious anger, hurling fire, so that the bridge was broken and Lu-Wit herself badly hurt. But the Great Spirit took pity on her, and as recompense transformed her into a beautiful young woman, although she remained an ancient being within herself . . . just as Lawrence's heroine looks at once 'so much younger, and so many thousands of years older'.[12]

Given Lawrence's conviction that, while American Indian culture was doomed to progressive collapse, the essential truth of its animistic religion would regain its lost force in the world (a view propounded in several papers in *Phoenix* and *Phoenix II*) the analogies here speak for themselves. Louise Witt, too, has been chosen by the Great Spirit to be a Lu-Wit, a Keeper of that Bridge which shall carry Unfallen Pan across the mere interlude of Christianity and godlessness (and perhaps, in a sense, across the Atlantic: see notes 15 and 19) — and her accompaniment by 'Phoenix' suggests that the divine fire may shine out again sooner than we think. When it does, the Keeper of the Bridge may again be bruised and burnt: but Lou would be prepared for that. Latent within the calmly resolute close of *St Mawr*, barely touched-in through the choice of names, there is, in fact, the germ of a continuation of the narrative, a quite different story, that Lawrence was at this time simultaneously struggling to capture on paper in *The Plumed Serpent* and 'The Woman Who Rode Away'. Many may feel that it might have been better left beneath the quiet surface of *St Mawr*.

Phoenix looks like 'a certain sort of Frenchman' (more specifically, an *apache* — had Lawrence been reading Colette?) and there is the usual double significance, so characteristic of *St Mawr*, behind the choice of soubriquet. Mrs Witt merely thinks it witty to apply it to an Arizonan newly emerged from the fires of war and shell-shock: had she realized that in this Arizonan's veins runs the blood of both of D. H. Lawrence's Chosen People — Navaho (American Indian) and Aztec — she might also have understood its deeper promise.[13] (Neither of Phoenix's real names are without appropriate overtones either: 'Geronimo', for instance, being the famous chief who led the last Indian rebellion in Arizona–New Mexico, and 'Trujillo' the town from which the great conquistador Pizarro came.)[14]

*

St Mawr, Las Chivas, Lou/Louise, Phoenix . . . the principle of double reference running through Lawrence's choice of primary names and locations in *St Mawr* thus seems clear enough. What is its connection with an insistence upon Lawrence's persistent general interest in the Celts?

Consider the sequence of names that has been emerging in the course of this essay: LuWit — Lou — Louise — (Louisiana) — Lewis. Criticism, distracted by more obtrusive analogies between Lewis and Phoenix, has never made very much of the fact that it is *Lewis* who is the lonely celibate servant of Pan in the first half of the narrative, and *Louise* at the end; yet the structural importance of this in Lawrence's own way of viewing his story is proved by this very bracketing of their names ('Lewis' is of course the English form of 'Louis', *fem.* 'Louise'.)[15]

That Lewis, the Celtic servant of the Great Holy One, should be given a name so overtly Anglo-French in form, seems to be a kind of metaphor for his degraded status in the modern world; for modern France is to Lawrence the land of Bad Sex, over-intellectualism, and Gay Paree,[16] overlaying the 'old savage world' of the Gauls precisely as Anglo-Saxon England overlays the lands of the Ancient (Celtic) Britons. The name 'Edwards' – which despite its manifest Anglo-Saxon origin sounds to modern ears as Welsh as 'Lewis' – is similarly used by Lawrence, as an expression of the degradation of the old Celtic Wales under the shadow spreading from England. *Mr Griffith Edwards* is a Welsh gentleman from Shropshire, who loses his son because he has no idea how to treat the Great Holy One. The despised Rico takes them all moonlight bathing – apparently in Wales – at *Sir Edward Edwards'* place; and a blow from St Mawr disfigures *Fred Edwards* for life, clearly quite deservedly in Lawrence's opinion. Unflattering allusions to (Edward) the Prince of Wales and that 'goaty old satyr' *King Edward VII* (who brings us back to Bad Sex and Gay Paree again) extend this chain, which of course also carries with it the thought that it was Edward I who first completed the subjugation of Wales, and that his son born at Caernarvon (another Edward) was the first heir of England to bear the title Prince of Wales.[17]

Caernarvon, however, is the heart of the ancient Welsh principality of *Gwynedd*, centre of resistance to the English. Today the majority of native Welsh-speakers still live within its borders, and the folk-culture of the region preserved the last flickers of belief in the old Celtic myths even into Lawrence's lifetime. Anglesey (*Mona Mam Cymru*, the Mother of Wales, once the strong-hold of Druidism) is part of Gwynedd, too: and it is not I think an accident that St Mawr killed the son of Mr Edwards by dashing him against an oak, the Druids' sacred tree. Nor is it an accident that Lewis comes from Gwynedd: or more precisely, from *Merioneth*, the southern third of Gwynedd, a county which he says to Mrs Witt '*is* Wales' – thereby distinguishing it from luckless Montgomeryshire, burdened with an imposed Norman-French name. And where else but Merioneth indeed could he come from? As a kind of exiled Prince of Welsh Celtdom, he must come from Gwynedd; yet Mona Mam Cymru has become 'Anglesey' (English Isle) and Caernarvonshire is polluted with Edwards and their vast castles. Moreover, what name *could* an exiled Prince of Welsh Celtdom bear but 'Lewis'? For the name is considered to have come into Welsh as an Anglicized substitution for '*Llewelyn*': and it was a Prince of Gwynedd, Llewelyn the Great, who became the first, last, and only native Welsh Prince of Wales.

Yet Llewelyn the Great is neither the only nor even the major figure who stands in the shadows behind Lewis, which is presumably one further reason (apart from the need to make a 'pair' with 'Louise') why Lawrence would not wish to saddle his character with the original Welsh form of the name. A more ancient hero than Llewelyn is associated with Gwynedd: *Llew of the Skilful Hand*, himself a dim memory of *Lugus*, the Shining One, perhaps the greatest deity in the entire Celtic Pantheon. Far more clearly than Llewelyn, who has at most contributed the echo of a name and an apt, if tacit, historical allusion,[18] both these older figures have irradiated Lawrence's conception of his Welsh groom – and indeed of a good deal of his story besides.

The chain that we have been tracing thus turns out to fall, in suitably Welsh fashion, into two mutually balancing triads:

LuWit ← Lou ← Louise – / / – Lewis→ Llew → Lugus.

Whether this scheme really exists 'in' the text of *St Mawr*, or lies 'behind' it, or is just-something-to-do-with-the-genetic-history-of-the-work, are philosophical worries with which there is little need to become embroiled. It is at least a sequence that may be arrived at by detailed attention to what Lawrence has written, and will seem fantastic only to those who have not followed Lawrence's interests in their own reading (for in this period of his life Lawrence's interests often were fantastic, from the point of view of the determinedly plain man). To trace it, clarifies countless details in *St Mawr* that otherwise seem merely arbitrary, or just blurredly 'symbolic', and frequently elucidates the logical links within this seemingly somewhat disjointed work.

*

Llew and Lugus. It is clear that, in the working out of *St Mawr*, the Celtic myths have stimulated Lawrence's creative imagination in a much more detailed way than their American counterparts, no doubt partly because there is so much more to know about the Celtic material anyway. Despite the vast gaps in our information, Celtic heroes and gods come to us loaded with a fascinatingly diverse clutter of attributes, functions, emblems and stories, that it is simply not in the nature of their American equivalents to possess.

Take as example the figure of *Lugus*, the Shining One (a name from the same root as the Latin *lux*). Lugus has associations with solar myth – a fact calculated in itself to catch Lawrence's attention. And like other Celtic solar heroes and gods, he is also associated with ravens (cf. possibly, Lewis's glossy black hair?). He is 'the Gaulish Mercury': like Lewis, a guide or leader on journeys, and perhaps particularly on mounted journeys, since he also has a strong association with horses. Feats of horsemanship are a prominent feature of his festival of the Lugnassad, celebrated annually in the first days of August (i.e., clearly when Lewis guides his employers and their friends to the summit of the Devil's Chair – and it seems to have been a regular feature of the worship of Lugus that his main temples should be set upon high places). He is frequently represented as bearded, and in the company of a female figure representing material wealth (Mrs Witt?). But he can also be presented youthful and beardless, with a caduceus. (The bearded Lewis emerges as surprisingly youthful when his hair is clipped; and the sight of a murdered snake triggers the stallion's explosion on the Devil's Chair hill.) Caduceus apart, the emblems of Lugus are a cock, goat and tortoise. (The cock hardly requires comment; the goat suggests Pan – 'fallen' Pan but then Lewis himself is a prince in much reduced circumstances; and the tortoise makes the perfect badge for a man moving so quietly around 'within his own shell'.)

It will perhaps be allowed that all this is at least suggestive; but it is Lugus's avatar, Llew Llawgyffes – the Bright One of the Skilful Hand – who seems to stand closest to Lewis.[19] The first point here is geographical: Welsh tradition records two 'Cities of Llew', the one on a deserted mound by the coast of Gwynedd, the other on the Wrekin, in Shropshire, only a few miles from Mrs Witt's village. (Llew's personal fiefs lay partly in Caernarvon and partly in Merioneth, and like Lewis he was brought up by an uncle.) The Wrekin, an isolated crest rising dramatically above the pastoral Shropshire landscape, is an extinct volcano, still complete – as guidebooks are at pains to point out – with deposits of lava and volcanic ash. Moreover, from the direction from which Lawrence himself would have seen it, it presents a suitably volcanic-looking silhouette. It is hard not to think of this as balancing those other tacit volcano allusions latent in the name Lou Witt.

Llew, like Lugus's Irish avatar Lugh (the warleader of the Tuatha De Danaan, whom Lawrence had invoked in the Cornish night), shares the God's – and Lewis's – association with horses. While he cannot match Lugh's claim to have brought the art of horsemanship to men, he does have a famous warhorse: *The Steed Of Yellow-White Footsteps*. The stallion St Mawr is seen as 'pale-gold' with 'flashing hoofs' when he disables Fred Edwards and Rico.

This apart, it may be noted (1) that the legend of Llew is a variant of the world-wide Samson and Delilah myth, which Mrs Witt's clipping of Lewis's hair also brings to mind; (2) that the name of Llew's treacherous wife Blodeuedd *is the Welsh for 'Flora'*; (3) that Blodeuedd's punishment for her treachery is the same as Mrs Witt's.

Mrs Witt, trapped within the limitations of Judaeo-Christian culture, fails to realize, however, that the Bible affords no guide to the procedure for felling a Celtic hero. Instead of seeking to dominate her man by clipping his hair as if he were Samson – a ploy which gets her nowhere, as she soon discovers when she tries to move on to his beard – she should doubtless have copied Blodeuedd, and waited to catch him with one foot on the edge of the bath and one on the back of a goat, under the thatched roof of a wall-less room. . . . But had she known so much, she would have known the fate of Blodeuedd too, and desisted from her blasphemous assault on the divine force immanent in Lewis. As it is, unknowing, Lewis's would-be wife follows Llew's spouse down the path to a living death.

Blodeuedd, having exposed her husband to his enemy in the one set of circumstances in which he was vulnerable, was turned into an owl (a bird particularly associated in Welsh folklore with churchyards) condemned to sleep all day and live in deathly isolation from its fellows: just the fate that overtakes the churchyard-haunting Mrs Witt. Once her impious lack of respect has led Lewis to reject her, this energetic and vital woman begins to slide, mysteriously, towards a state of inanition described by her daughter as 'worse than death': staying later and later in bed, shutting herself off in deathlike seclusion, and finally reaching a condition where the only decision she is willing to make, is never again to decide anything: 'not even to decide to die . . . or *not* to die'. Meanwhile her disconcerting binocular stare, however eagle-like it may once have seemed, also takes on a distinctly owl-like (and hence Blodeuedd-like) quality, as Lawrence quietly alternates between describing it as a 'wide' gaze, and as heavy-lidded.

That Mrs Witt comes to woo, and that *tu-wit, to wooo* is a familiar stylization of the cry of an owl is perhaps no more than a piece of Lawrencian luck; yet it does seem clear that while Lou's mother inherits those owlish aspects of Blodeuedd noted above, the latter's name and floral attributes have gone to Flora Manby: a division reasonable enough, since both women would betray in their own way the spark of Pan in man. For the point as regards the name 'Flora' seems to be that Blodeuedd, in the legend of Llew, was not a real but a manufactured woman, fabricated from flowers; just as Flora Manby's attitude to the other sex (glanced at in her surname) means that on Lawrence's terms she is not a 'real' woman either.[20] That she should be called 'Flora' is exactly the sort of blasphemous travesty that we have already seen in the reference to a Kiva as *Las Chivas*: she is a Blodeuedd, a False Flora, not a minor embodiment of the Classical goddess Flora at all. Her floweriness is that of blossoms disposed with studied artiness indoors and fine 'daisy-fresh' muslin dresses 'from Paris' (O word of fear). Of a Flora Manby, so eager to geld St Mawr, and to challenge Pan Himself from the seat of the Devil's Chair, one could expect no more.

Certainly Flora, unlike her creator, could never have been expected to grasp the significance of the Devil's Chair. It will be recalled that Lawrence had himself climbed to its summit, and talked there with Frederick Carter, as they stared into Wales, 'of the great hilltop rocks, with similar names, that are found all over Europe as seats of the changeful gods.' (They looked back at the hills of Shropshire, too, and must have seen the Wrekin, only 16–17 miles away.)[21] He had read quite enough to be aware that the place where they were talking was unmistakably, seen with Celtic eyes, a Gorsedd Hill; and it makes some difference to an understanding of *St Mawr* if one shares that awareness. A Gorsedd Hill is a High Place, in which authority is invested only 'so long as the sun is visible in the heavens' (the sun is still shining, but only just, as False Flora challenges the Old Order from the seat of the Devil's Chair), crowned with a throne, judgement-seat or sacred stone, to which supernatural power was felt to cling long after the coming of Christianity. Thus the Gorsedd of Arberth, which no high-born person could ascend without either suffering blows or seeing a wonder (Lawrence's baronet receives the blow, LuWit sees the wonder), figures prominently in the very beginning of the *Mabinogion*, a work which we know Lawrence had read. And in Ireland the sacred stone on the Gorsedd of Tara screamed aloud under every prince in whom it recognized the true sovereignty, while wonders befell those princes who chanced to ascend it early in the morning: the greatest of such wonders being that experienced by Conn the Hundred-fighter, to whom the God Lugus came riding with a vision of the future. So when Lou, quite needlessly from a strictly practical point of view, gets up at sunrise to be guided by Lewis to the Devil's Chair, on the slopes of which she hears her own scream as if it were something external to herself as the stallion crushes Sir Henry – and thereafter finds that she experiences a sense of revelation and a vision of the future – the roots of Lawrence's inspiration seem clear enough. (All the information about Gorsedds in this paragraph is to be found on a single page of the study of Celtic Heathendom which Lawrence seems likeliest to have read.)[22] Nor, of course, is it likely to be wholly accidental that Sir Henry is punished just after encouraging Flora to repeat her blasphemies from the Judgement Seat (Gorsedd) of the Devil's Chair.

But even if much of *St Mawr* is explicable in terms of the interplay in Lawrence's mind between the general fascination he felt for both the Celtic and the American Indian worlds, one more specific debt seems equally plain, and that is to the *literary* quality of the *Mabinogion*: a work which to Lawrence was clearly something more than just a quarry for Welsh myths. (It may be noted, incidentally, that some of the details of the story of Lewis hint that Lawrence may have known something of other ancient Welsh texts, too.)[23] From Rhys, or some other scholar, Lawrence had gleaned details of factual information about the Celtic world which helped him to build his book, just as he utilized scraps of autobiographical experience and information provided by Taos acquaintances like Tony Luhan and Jaime de Angulo. But from the *Mabinogion* it would seem that his imagination had gained more vital nourishment, not a plot but a conception: a sense of a style, a possible mode of approach to his theme, and a glimpse of a potential technique for carrying that approach through.

The subject of the *Mabinogion* is primarily mythology in decline; the telling tends towards a loose episodic complexity; and there is a constant assumption that every name must have some hidden meaning or explanation behind it. It presents a world of much riding, and a world where beasts are sometimes as important as men, and where the normal discontinuity between the world of men and beasts sometimes breaks down. It tells (admittedly among much other matter) of the Gorsedd of Arberth and the legend of Llew Llawgyffes. With clear simplicity, it presents an often realistic, sharply seen world, that is simultaneously iridescent with the supernatural; and its does so with a sometimes bright heraldic use of colour notably like Lawrence's own. For four colours must glow retrospectively in the memory of any reader of the *Mabinogion*: red and yellow/gold primarily, but also black and green. A reading of *St Mawr*, with its red-gold stallion, leaves a very similar impression, although in the figures of Lewis, Lou, Phoenix and Mrs Witt (of the once golden curls) Lawrence has considerably sophisticated the simpler pleasure of the older work in vivid heads of black and yellow hair. Another kind of sophistication marks his use of green. The Welsh word *glas*, generally translated 'green', can in fact mean grey, blue or green. When a lady of the *Mabinogion* has a robe of that colour, what shade was it really? We cannot know, so Lawrence, playing it safe as he robes his heroine for her mystical ride to the Devil's Chair, arrays her in a green linen riding-skirt, 'with a close bluish [*sic*] smock'. And her husband is dressed for the same expedition with no less care, for his apricot-coloured shirt is clearly heraldic in (Lawrence's) intention. Infant School children used to be taught to think of wool and such fruits as peaches *and apricots* as the principal exports of Australia; and since apricot is not a Mabinogion colour it is appropriate for an alien upon the Gorsedd Hill too. But beyond that, Rico's shirt constitutes, as good heraldry often should, a rebus or canting device. This is brought out by the emphasis given to Mrs Witt's pronunciation of 'apricot' as 'ap-ricot' (think too of the French pronunciation of the word). For *ap* in Welsh means 'son of': Rico is thus Rico-ap-Rico, the son of the cock of the sterile Wasteland (see n. 17).

*

The contrary-minded reader, however, may demand whether an appeal to the biographical facts does not reduce much of the foregoing pages to mere over-ingenuity? Many details from Lawrence's life in New Mexico are certainly woven into the texture of *St Mawr*: where they occur, does one really need an elaborate structure of alternative explanation of these aspects of the book? Mrs Luhan pranced round Lawrence, trimming his beard: her rival Dorothy Brett, in an extraordinary scene, cut into Mrs Luhan's ear while trimming *her* hair: need one turn to Blodeuedd, then, for an 'explanation' of Mrs Witt's scissor-job on Lewis? And need one invoke volcano-spirits and bridges-of-the-gods, when there was a man in Taos actually called Lew Witt?[24]

The short answer is that Lawrence used almost every item of his Taos experience in a different way, or to a different degree, in *St Mawr*. The memoirs of his Taos friends show, for instance, that the name 'Manby' had bizarre Gothic connotations in the Taos area, of which Lawrence's imagination surprisingly seems to have made no use at all: at the other end of the scale, he exploits the real Kiowa ranch to the full. (While the barbershop incidents at Taos, though patently in a sense 'behind' the scene in the book, do not in themselves account for the name 'Flora' or the owlishness of Mrs Witt.) But it must be agreed that it is the existence of a real Lew Witt that offers the crucial test case; and indeed it is worth examining in some detail, for it affords a perfect illustration of the way Lawrence apparently worked when composing *St Mawr*.

In the first place, the very presence of a Lew Witt in their circle – he was married to a friend of Mrs Luhan – would have been likely to put the name of the heroine of the volcano myth into Jaime de Angulo's mind during his discussions with Lawrence; and Lawrence was himself in just the state to be intrigued by the androgynous quality given to the sound by simultaneous mental reference both to the male carpenter and to the female mountain spirit. (And perhaps also, originally, to a figure in the *Mabinogion* sometimes called Llwyt, an enchanter.) But that is mere speculation. What really catches the attention is that the real Lew Witt somehow managed to be a *one-armed* carpenter or sawmillman: a feat that would virtually have compelled Lawrence, arriving in Taos with the Welsh legends already stored in his head, to think of him at times, privately, as Lew-of-the-skilful-hand.

And thereby hangs a last Celtic tale. For there *was* a one-armed deity in the Celtic pantheon, equipped with both an artificial hand or arm, and a soubriquet extremely easy to confuse with that of the Welsh hero Llew (especially if one is working just on one's memories of the *Mabinogion* plus something like Sir John Rhys's Hibbert Lectures). Normally, this deity seems to be referred to as 'Nodens' or 'Nuada'; and incipient confusion is thus blocked. But the parallel form of the name is *Lludd*; and once in the *Mabinogion*, and two or three times in the Hibbert Lectures, one finds references to '*Lludd of the Silver Hand*'. I would suggest – and with the more confidence because I have caught myself in the same error – that this generated an impression in Lawrence's mind that Llew's own soubriquet implied that he was one-armed, too, or had an artificial hand: in short, that Lawrence unknowingly conflated Lludd Silver- and the Llew Skilful-hand. The fact that Lewis in *St Mawr* had lost the little finger on one hand would seem to bear this out. Far from being a merely accidental detail (I do not believe that any detail in St Mawr is merely accidental[25]), it is surely testimony *both* to the link in Lawrence's mind between the real man and the fictional character, *and* to the latter's attenuated descent from that earlier horseman of Merioneth. But whether all this really makes *St Mawr* the right starting-point from which to launch readers new to Lawrence into a wider reading of his work is another matter.

Notes

1 *D. H. Lawrence: A Composite Biography*, ed. E. Nehls (Madison, 1957), II, 313–19. The 'new kind of use of symbolism' they discussed had already been sketched by Lawrence in a letter to Gordon Campbell ten years earlier: 'You should try to grasp the *complete whole* which the Celtic symbolism made in its great time. . . . We see only the symbol as a subjective expression: as an expression of ourselves. . . . The old symbols were each a word in a great attempt at formulating the whole history of the soul of man. They are *unintelligible* except in their whole concept.' *The Collected Letters of D. H. Lawrence*, ed. H. T. Moore (London, 1962), I, 302 (*The Letters of D. H. Lawrence*, Camb. edn, II, 248).

2 M. Ballin, 'Lewis Spence and the myth of Quetzalcoatl in D. H. Lawrence's *The Plumed Serpent*', *D. H. Lawrence Review*, XIII (1980), 63–78. See p. 68.

3 *Kangaroo*, Phoenix edition, Collected Works of D. H. Lawrence (London), 209, 230. See also p. 68 and p. 242, and ch. XII generally. (Unless otherwise stated, all references to Lawrence's writings are to the Phoenix edition.)

4 *Composite Biography*, II, 349.

5 *Collected Letters*, I, 409, 303 (Camb. edn, II, 498). See also p. 581 (Camb. edn, III, 338): *one has read so many fat books on Gaul and what not.*

6 Lawrence stayed three days at Monte Cassino and was shown over the monastery in some detail. The monastery, or rather the hilltop on which it was built – 'one of man's intense sacred places for three thousand years' ('before Christ was born') – moved Lawrence so powerfully that he was 'almost speechless'. The summit, with its 'huge mossy stones in the wintry wood that was once a sacred grove', would clearly have been recognized by him as a 'Gorsedd Hill', like the Devil's Chair (for fuller explication of this see p. 31 above); and must have been in his mind when, only four years later, he stood on the Chair discussing the 'great hill-top rocks . . . that are found all over Europe as seats of the changeful gods'.

Lawrence particularly mentions being taken to see the 'ancient cell away under the monastery, where all the sanctity started' (and where St Maurus attended upon St Benedict). The reader may care to bear this in mind when reading the comments on the name *Las Chivas*, below.

Underlying thoughts of Monte Cassino seem obvious in the first page of Lawrence's description of Taos pueblo. In *Phoenix*, ed. Edward D. McDonald (London, 1936), 100. Cf. also my account of *Kiva*, below.

7 As Lawrence knew Cornwall so much better than Wales, it seems quite possible that 'St Mawr' started life in his mind as Saint Mawes: another missionary to France, but a Welsh one, who chanced to give his name to the Cornish village en route.

8 Lawrence had an early and lasting enthusiasm for *Hiawatha*, still reflected in *The Lost Girl* (1920): Longfellow uses the terms 'Manito' and 'The Great Spirit' quite indifferently. Lawrence's famous essay on Fenimore Cooper was published in its final form in 1923: Cooper's Indians also worship the Great Spirit, of course.

9 (The definition of *Kiowa* is in Webster's Dictionary.) The Lawrences were given the ranch – by Mabel Dodge Luhan, a rich patroness to whom they certainly felt superior – after their six-month absence in England. Lawrence had theories about a Natural Aristocracy (of which he was himself naturally an embodiment) and a wife who was a member of the Master Race, as well as being a baroness. Living with them and subordinate to them was an English 'Hon.', daughter of a viscount and former childhood playmate of the royal children.

10 The word *Kiva* is brought even closer to the name *Las Chivas* if one spells it with an intrusive *h* – 'Khiva' – and Lawrence does use this spelling, when writing

very fully and warmly of the concept of the Kiva, in an article that postdates *St Mawr* and is concerned with ideas very close to some of those in the novel. (Whereas in 1923 he was using the correct spelling, in an article less closely related to the concerns of his story.) See *Phoenix*, 96 and *Phoenix II*, ed. H. T. Moore and Warren Roberts (London, 1968), 551. For a second 'retrospective' use of *Khiva*, see also *Phoenix*, 146.

Mysterious subterranean chambers were also constructed in Iron Age Cornwall – there are two not far from the Lawrences' temporary Cornish home – and have attracted much speculation. The local name for them is *fougous*: their purpose has never been clearly demonstrated. The possible analogy with the Kiva can hardly have escaped Lawrence, alert for Celtic-Amerindian links.

11 *Kangaroo* (167–70) reprints an entire article from the *Sydney Daily Telegraph* on 'Earthquakes and sleeping volcanoes'. See also Witter Bynner, *Journey with Genius* (London, 1953), 42, and *Phoenix*, 111.

12 It seems obvious that Jaime de Angulo would have been the channel through which Lawrence learned of the Lu-Wit legend, for Mrs Luhan brought de Angulo from California to Taos specifically to talk to Lawrence after the latter's return from Europe. Mr de Angulo had himself just returned from studies with Jung, which he hoped would improve his own understanding of Indian traditions; and his subsequent articles on Indian culture cover topics ranging from Oregon to the Southwest. (The legend of Lu-Wit is from the Oregon –Washington border.)

The mother and daughter in *St Mawr* – two generations of Witts – may perhaps have been in part suggested by the two incarnations of Lu-Wit, first as an old, then as a young woman.

13 Phoenix was part Navaho and part Mexican Indian, though with some Spanish (perhaps Conquistador – see n. 14) blood. Cf. Lawrence's confession to E. H. Brewster: 'The Indian, the Aztec . . . all that fascinates me and has for years. . . . The glamour for me is in the West, not in the fulfilled East' (*Collected Letters*, II, 677). See also ch. 26 of *The Plumed Serpent* (1955) 414 (Camb. edn, 416).

14 The given-name of the other groom in the story, Morgan Lewis, is also that of a celebrated rebel; for 'Morgan' corresponds to the Latin name 'Pelagius'. The Pelagian Heresy was a determined attempt to bend Roman Christianity into a form better fitted to traditional Celtic ways of thought. The parallel with Geronimo, fighting to preserve Indian ways of thought, seems clear.

Readers who find it incredible that Lawrence would have selected names with such nicety should bear in mind that Frieda's first husband, Prof. Weekley, published an *Etymological Dictionary of Modern English*, worked for years on a *Dictionary of English Surnames*, and enjoyed a double publishing success (which must have had a wry interest to the impoverished Lawrences) with *The Romance of Names* (London, 1914, much reprinted, 3rd edition 1922) and *Surnames* (London, 1916, second edition within ten months).

15 In one sense Louise and Phoenix really divide between them, at the story's end, the role which Lewis is serving at its outset. It is therefore interesting to find them bracketed by hair references. Phoenix has 'intensely living' black hair that stands up (for he is of the unfulfilled West). Lewis's thick black hair drops on his forehead (for he is of the fulfilled East). *Lou, who 'bridges' the two worlds*, has vital dark hair that neither stands up nor lies down, but curls into grape-like clusters: a rather forced metaphor clearly meant to go with descriptions of her odd squinting smile as like that of the nymphs. See n. 13.

16 Lawrence's impatience with Paris is made explicit in his *Paris Letter* (*Phoenix*, 119–22). Lou received her mistaken education there, made her mistaken decision to marry Rico there, is even mistaken when she buys French shoes,

and calls Paris 'depressing'. Her mother calls it 'unlucky', 'sinister' and 'unclean'.

17 English medieval history is divided between Henrys & Harrys and Edwards: it is not an accident that Rico is addressed as 'Harry' when struck down by St Mawr. (For the name 'Rico' itself, see *The Waste Land*, V. 386–95. So many of the elements of the latter part of *St Mawr* are present, if reshuffled, in these lines that it is reasonable to view Rico as the cock that crows in the sterile dry times, before the rains return.)

18 The name Llewelyn (really *Llywelyn*) derives, either, from a root meaning 'helmsman' or 'leader', or, from a root cognate with *lux* and Lugus. Since the god Lugus is himself a guide or leader on journeys, this would from Lawrence's point of view amount to the same thing.

19 The legend of Llew – like Irish Celtic culture – has latent links with Spain. If Lewis 'is' Llew (it should be noted that Celtic gods or mythical heroes can die and be reborn, with varying degrees of fullness of reincarnation, as the offspring of mortal women), then there is a 'bridge' here that leads from Morgan Lewis to Phoenix Trujillo. See also ch. 26 of *The Plumed Serpent*, 413 (Camb. edn, 415): 'Celtic or Iberian people'.

20 Both Flora and Rico come from Australia (i.e., from the House that's Upside Down); thus, even though his name is not Edwards, her father is a usurper in his role as a Marcher squire.

21 *Composite Biography*, II, 318.

22 See n. 5 above. The most attractively readable 'fat book' on 'Gaul and what not' available to Lawrence would have been Sir John Rhys's superb Hibbert Lectures on *The Origin and Growth of Religion as illustrated by Celtic Heathendom* (London, 1888): a work still cited by Celtic scholars today. See pp. 204–10, and particularly p. 205. (P. 173 may have given the hint which determines the name of Lou's maid Elena, the Welsh 'Elen-of-the-Host' being so called from her host of maidservants.)

23 An obvious possibility, for example, is the *Hanes Taliesin*, where it is natural to think of Lewis's curious conversation with Mrs Witt about trees, when one reads: 'I was in the battle of Goddeu/With Lleu and Gwydion/They transformed the trees of the world . . .' See the introduction to the Everyman edition of *The Mabinogion* (London, 1949).

24 Mabel Dodge Luhan, *Lorenzo in Taos* (London, 1933), 113, 159 and 160.

25 Anyone wishing to explore further in the labyrinth of *St Mawr* might usefully start with Mrs Witt's Christian name, for which there are at least two reasons. . . . Or there are Spenser echoes . . .

It should also be realized that a considerable amount of second-order corroboratory material has perforce been omitted from these pages. Rhys, like other 'fat books on Gaul', states that there was originally a Gaulish temple to Lugus on Montmartre, for instance: i.e., in the middle of just that area of Paris particularly associated with the modern *apaches* to whom Phoenix is compared. Similarly, it is worth noting that the discussion of Indian religion in ch. 22 of Fenimore Cooper's *The Last of the Mohicans* immediately follows talk of 'The Great Spirit' by references *to a sacred tortoise-emblem*: one of the emblems of Lugus, discussed earlier in this essay! Everything he turned to must have seemed to Lawrence to conspire to push his thought along the channels mapped here, in fact; as even his poetry, with its tortoise- and goat- and snake-poems, also confirms.

*

There are some curious parallels between the materials presented above and the case set out in my article 'Mrs Dalloway on Mount Caburn: A Garden Extended', in the January 1982 number of the *Cambridge Review*, 100–5. Virginia Woolf's novel proves to be planned as a modern re-enactment of a Celtic Midsummer (i.e., Beltane) festival, complete with a human sacrifice. Many of the vatic and surrealistic passages in the novel which criticism has passed over in silence can be shown to be direct and sometimes quite detailed allusions to Celtic mythology. (It should be borne in mind that there was a wave of interest in things Celtic throughout Europe in the late nineteenth and early twentieth centuries, due initially, in large measure, to a theory that Celtic was the original Indo-European language.)

*

In slightly different form, this essay first appeared in *Essays in Criticism*, XXXII (1982), 158–79. My thanks are due to Prof. Marjorie Burns for first introducing me to the legend of Lu-Wit.

4 Opening up the text: the case of *Sons and Lovers*

Paul Eggert

Tracking 'Lawrence' over textual boundaries

I am sure that most literary critics and theorists today think of 'Lawrence Studies' as a more or less enclosed specialism, bereft of its polemical sting of the 1950s and 1960s and unlikely to affect any wider current of debate. While Lawrence scholarship and bibliography have grown remarkably in extent and sophistication over the past decade or so, Lawrence criticism has, over a longer period, tended to become 'professional': competent, predictable in methods and terminology, and blinkered in its conceptions. As yet, it is too early to know whether recent scholarship will now stimulate the development of a convincing new picture – or pictures – of D. H. Lawrence, or whether it will merely afford us a tedious *catalogue raisonée* of the old one. A certain scepticism by now invests the image of Lawrence as a martyred Life-hero, articulating a quickening cure to his own diagnosis of cultural-spiritual collapse in the decades around the First World War – a collapse which criticism has been too content, with only rudimentary attention to historical context, to accept as having happened much as Lawrence described it, and as somehow still happening in the 1960s and even 1970s. The message was potent and, for Lawrencians, therefore sufficient: the near-total absence from discussions of Lawrence's work of anything corresponding to the preoccupations of structuralist criticism shows well enough the general lack of curiosity about medium and method. Better, it seemed, to roam through the works finding and paraphrasing metaphysical restatements and symbolical embodiments of his ideas about the sources of creative life in the individual, to trace reverently the interconnecting filaments, to 'discover' in him, by selection and meditation, a plausible consistency – until one was stuck helplessly but satisfyingly on the prophet's web.[1]

The resulting enclosure of terminology and conception has left Lawrence specialists showing little interest in those post-'68 literary theories which discredit the idea of the author as creative artist and present him as culturally transparent, interpreting texts as the *loci* of ideological conflicts or as the expressions of available discourses and sign-systems. Lawrence ought to be a ripely attractive target for such a deconstruction yet, strangely, he has been left alone.[2] The truce, I suggest, is good for neither side; but the other potential source of change, the ever-ramifying scholarly study of his writings, will itself have no effect if its practitioners fail to conceptualize what is implicit in their methods and findings.

However, although post-structuralist medicine would undoubtedly provide a purgative of the old orthodoxies about Lawrence, it needs some testing before swallowing. Has not one reason for the uninterest of Lawrencians in recent theory been, after all, the unignorable presence of their author in his writings – deeply problematic though it is now to say so? I refer not just to the almost chameleon-like DHL/Bert/Lorenzo personality reflected in letters (fond son-in-law or brother, fallible businessman, earnest cultural critic, sacerdotal confidant) and hotly disputed in the posthumous memoirs and biographies – for those competing roles and images just demonstrate textuality in operation, as the text 'Lawrence' is variously constituted and reconstituted. Rather, and more importantly, I refer to that unmistakable presence which inhabits the rhythms of Lawrence's mature prose. Instead of seeking an illusion of impersonality, the presence is time and again intimately enmeshed (like the reader) in the swelling, accumulative gathering of meaning, most noticeably when the subject is a fictional character's intense state of feeling. Such states are experienced by the reader in the production of them, rather than as reflectively distanced *post hoc* description. Although the generating rhetoric has been partly analysed, in terms of Lawrence's parasyntactical methods and co-ordinative grammar,[3] the steely link between writer and writing here remains unbroken. It exists in a great many less strenuous alloys as well: Lawrence's ability, especially in the 1920s, to allow the part-directed, part-serendipitous progression of a mood (sarcastic, sceptical, mocking, earnest) to dictate the movement of idea or attitude, risking the unpredictabilities and self-exposure of such a personally-based form[4] and often bringing it off, is yet to be adequately recognized. But my own principal concern in this first section will be with another 'presence' whose success has so far been known only in its absence: the many-layered compositional history of Lawrence's dealings with his evolving works. In the second section the mixed success of *Sons and Lovers* will provide the instructive counter-example.

*

The new Cambridge University Press edition of the works of D. H. Lawrence is serving to highlight this hitherto unknown 'presence'. Such a profusion of manuscript and secondary materials (letters, publishers' archives, biographical memoirs, etc.) are available that the evolution of most of the works, as they moved through successive versions towards publication, can be reconstructed in surprisingly full detail, sometimes on a day-by-day basis. The introduction in each CUP volume tells this story of compositional development, and the textual apparatus records the changes. After collating the printed versions with earlier states (autograph manuscript, typescripts, proofs), the editor chooses one to serve as the basis of the text (often the manuscript, which contains none of the hundreds, even thousands of errors and changes normally introduced by typists and typesetters). The editor then incorporates into the base-text the changes which Lawrence subsequently made when revising, say, typescript

and proofs. The end result is a reading text which respects Lawrence's intentions – first and in revision, the later replacing the earlier – and excludes as far
as possible readings which reflect the intentions and mistakes of Lawrence's
coadjutors in the production of his writings: his wife, friends and other scribes,
typists, typesetters, publishers and publishers' readers. In other words, the
edition has by implication *taken a position* – one which perhaps may be familiar
but not, in the present intellectual climate, of such transparent validity that it
should be lightly passed over. The CUP edition, that is to say, is primarily
interested in only one category of textual evidence among those which may be
found in the various documents in which the versions of a work are physically
inscribed. Textual authority is not taken to derive from the contractual
agreement between publisher and author, but from the author alone.

In an age when textual meaning is held by some theorists to be plural and
constantly reconstituted, and by others to be radically indeterminate, for
editors to seek to confine textual possibilities to those the author intended may
seem antediluvian. Editors of twentieth-century literature, however, frequently labour under an obligation to account for the existence and demonstrate the provenance of the manuscript, typescript and proof materials from
which the text of the printed editions can be proved to have derived. Recent
literary theorists, by contrast, appear to suffer from a collective amnesia as to
the existence of such documents: textual genesis, for all the thought given to
the matter, is for them, apparently, a species of miraculous birth. Yet, once in
the world, texts are available for analysis into the pre-existing codes of
meaning – to which the author may have only a marginal relevance. This is one
way of opening up the text.

Editors who are trying to explain how the ink markings got on to the page –
who put them there, and in what order – are opening up the text in a different
way. While not denying social and cultural influences, editors implicitly
privilege the agent and the moment of writing, both at the initial stage of
composition and at subsequent stages of revision. In insisting on the personal
agency and chronological dimension involved in the genesis of a text (evidenced by its successive physical inscribings prior to the actual printing), and
by designing editions to illustrate them,[5] editors help to sustain a bedrock
notion of *the author* that, stripped of its Romantic mystique, continues to make
sense: that capacity in the writer which, part-consciously and part-
unconsciously, probes, sorts and reorganizes, thinking through and around,
and then articulating, the swirl of cultural influences he or she is subject to. The
successive physical inscriptions, swarming with evidence of significant changes
of mind, are the documentary witnesses of authorship as a *participatory* rather
than culturally transparent activity. The author's 'speaking' the influences, the
activity of doing so, testifies to a capacity not caught by the modern formulation
that his writings speak him; this is particularly the case with that 'capacity' or
author-function which we call 'Lawrence'.

One contextual factor bearing on this 'capacity' – at least when a writer lives
by his pen – is his need to produce, for businessmen-publishers, writings in
separate marketable units, each complete in itself, finalized into a *single*
sequence of words and punctuation and of acceptable length. This has always
seemed so inevitable a requirement that Lawrence readers (who, understand-

ably, feel most comfortable with what they are most used to) have not generally bothered to question whether their interest in the imaginative activity of Lawrence is best served, or fully represented, by the volumes which a latter-day version of the original commercial context has done little more than reprint.

It is true that Lawrence provided his English and American publishers with copy that was, if never identical, usually quite similar. But the other writings he produced in doing so – those often extensive and richly interesting documentary records of the textual route towards publication which each work took – open up the question of what the author-function consists in, and how it is knowable. Indeed, as the notion of the autonomously creative author, *fons et origo* of all he wrote, is generally resigned, his existence as shaper and subtle re-shaper of his material *needs* to be foregrounded. Teachers wishing to challenge students' ready-made and unreflecting belief in authorship, but not wishing to vaporize it altogether into a shimmer of textuality, will find the Lawrence editions of assistance.

Take *The Boy in the Bush* for instance. Its readers are aware that two novels are melded within its covers: 'The House of Ellis' (no longer extant) which Mollie Skinner sent to Lawrence in August 1923 in the hope that he could find it a publisher, and the version which he wrote using her material (as well as his own). But it is not widely known that Lawrence's (published) version conceals within itself two further distinct sets of intention. Having, as he thought, finished the manuscript in Mexico in November 1923, he returned to an English winter where, rapidly plunged into depression (see his essay 'On coming home'),[6] he waited to correct the typescripts of the novel. As he waited, fresh hope sprang from unexpected quarters: Dorothy Brett promised to join him and Frieda in establishing an ideal community in New Mexico; he received the Christmas 1923 number of a little magazine from Santa Fe, *Laughing Horse*; and he read Conrad's latest novel, *The Rover*, about the taciturn, inscrutable and solitary old sailor, Peyrol. Lawrence set to work and wrote a new last chapter (the present one) for the novel.

Instead of Jack Grant's returning to Perth (Western Australia) with a flea in his ear after Mary's rejection of his bigamous proposal, the novel ends with Jack confirmed in his determination to remain aloof from the entanglements of civilized society in Perth (a determination reinforced by his new, centaur-like bond with his horse, Adam),[7] and assured of a patriarchal future in the virtually unpopulated North-West with his wife Monica and Hilda Blessington (based on Brett). This new ending had centrifugal effects in his correction of the typescripts. They exhibit a great many alterations preparing for the change in emphasis caused by the new last chapter: the formerly mercurial Mr George becomes more fully implicated in a newly darkened portrayal of the cowardice and enclosure of ordinary social living; in her appearances prior to the last chapter, Hilda is newly charged with suggestions of a latent potential and daring; and Jack, particularly in his relations with Monica but also with other men, is portrayed as more self-controlled, self-sufficient and remote, and more deeply sustained by his relationship with his personal God. For the reader wishing to pursue an interest in this novel, to have regard only to the published text[8] (or, indeed, only to the reading text of the CUP edition) is to conflate two sets of authorial intention, and to distance this 'Australian' novel from a major part of its (actual) context within a series of reviews and essays about American life which Lawrence was writing in 1922 and 1923.

His apprehension of a spiritual emptiness in American living ('there's no inside to the life: all outside': 30 December 1922; *Letters of D. H. Lawrence*, ed. W. Roberts and J. T. Boulton, Cambridge, 1987, IV, 365) is itself a development of his response, in mid-1922, to Australian egalitarianism and mateship; it went with a deepening anxiety about the doctrines of democracy and freedom ('Men are only free when they are doing what the deepest self likes': *Studies in Classic American Literature*, November–December 1922).[9] For Lawrence, the doctrines connect with a propensity to idealism and self-consciousness that he found possible to escape only in Mexico: 'The great paleface overlay hasn't gone into the soil half an inch. The Spanish churches and palaces stagger . . . the peon still grins his Indian grin behind the Cross. . . . He knows his gods' (April 1923; 'Au revoir, U.S.A.', *Phoenix*, ed. E. McDonald, London 1936, 105). In May and June 1923, while in Mexico, Lawrence wrote 'Quetzalcoatl', the first version of *The Plumed Serpent*, where he canvasses the notion of a revived relationship of the peons to ancient gods, mediated by a powerful priest-like figure. (*Kangaroo* is also part of the provenance of the idea; and a letter of 4 January 1923 records another step: 'To me, loyalty is far before love. Love seems usually to be just a dirty excuse for disloyalties': *Letters*, IV, 368.)

In his essays the deity idea rapidly generalized: 'the proper study of mankind is man. Agreed entirely! But in the long run, it becomes again as it was before, man in his relation to the deity' (September 1923; 'The proper study', *Phoenix*, 722). By the time Lawrence came to write *The Boy in the Bush* (September–November) it is understandable, then, that he would seize on the opportunity which Mollie Skinner's story offered him to experiment with the idea of a new source of inner power for the young Briton, Jack Grant, forced to deal with the brutality of male competitiveness and the extremities of climate in outback Western Australia. Although Jack's relationship with his Dark God is portrayed as sustaining his courage and justifying his deeds, he is still the prey of others' mocking scepticism and Monica's disgruntled resentment; he does not escape unscathed. After the revisions in London, however, and the new last chapter (early January 1924), the authority of Jack's position is more generally acknowledged and has become nearly impregnable. The notion of a formidable inner strength, powerful and authoritative and wise, is now past the stage of being experimental; stripped of its connection to the divine it undergirds the mysterious, unaccommodating presence of Alan Anstruther in the powerful short story, 'The Border Line', of March 1924.

Bisecting as they do the textual development of *The Boy in the Bush*, these transmutations of only a single thread of ideas illustrate what I believe is a general truth about Lawrence's writings: that beyond the major landmarks there is to be found an elaborate textual filigree of thematic cross-overs, subject to continual adjustment and (often risky) new development. The particular *public* shape taken by this shifting filigree is defined in large part by the boundaries of the published form of each work – from book review for a magazine editor to a novel for publishers.

In treating Lawrence's major writings in their familiar published forms as more or less complete wholes, adequately representing the workings of his imagination, we thus misconstrue how that 'author-function' we call 'Lawrence' actually responded to and processed new stimuli within an existing matrix of ideas, mediated by a professional awareness of publishers' requirements and audience expectations. For it is clear that, intellectually and artistically, Lawrence rarely stood still; he was ceaselessly experimental, and he worked fast. He never 'finished' his works; they were always in a process of becoming or of (only gradual) abandonment – a process which did not respect publication dates, and which we have only begun to understand. With a writer as important as Lawrence, to continue to respect traditional boundaries, dictated as they were and are by the requirements of the publishing industry, seems to me folly. The traditional position (leaving aside the New Critical isolation of text from context) has been to assume that to bring a work to a finalized public form stimulated the development or resolution of authorial ideas and techniques previously perhaps only latent. This assumption, at best a half-truth, has left the familiar packaging of authorial activity unchallenged; and, worse, it has served to deliver up authorship, bound and gagged, to its post-structuralist fate.

Literary experiment and literary fashion in Sons and Lovers

Sons and Lovers is an enigmatic novel, its disproportions of style and presentation have long been the subject of critical speculation. Given the novel's autobiographical basis, its inner tensions have been repeatedly referred, if with varying degrees of unease, to the particulars of the younger Lawrence's love attachments – even though those tensions can be less vulnerably reinterpreted when the novel is more fully opened outwards into its supporting context of far-from-seamless authorial activity. Through the facsimile manuscript of *Sons and Lovers*,[10] which affords access to crucial stages of the novel's textual development, run two important counter-currents crucial to the novel's published form: an ambitious but only half-understood literary experiment on the one hand, and a countervailing, articulate literary fashion on the other.

The Lawrence of 1909, still engaged in the writing of *The White Peacock*, was yet to face this problem. Very much on the lookout for artistic stimulus, he refers admiringly to 'the new young school of realism' that Ford Madox Ford was encouraging in the pages of the *English Review*, and in which, both in its continental and English versions, he himself was reading widely (*Letters of D. H. Lawrence*, ed. J. T. Boulton, Cambridge, 1979, I, 139). 'He had learned a great deal from other writers – mostly French,' Ford later commented, 'but he had a natural sense of form that was very refreshing to come across.'[11]

In 1908 Lawrence had given some advice to a friend on the writing of short stories, advice which was already pointing towards the art of the home-life scenes in *Sons and Lovers*: 'The great thing to do in a short story is to select the salient details – a few striking details to make a sudden swift impression. Try to use words vivid and emotion-quickening; give as little explanation as possible' (ibid., 78). The following year Lawrence submitted the first version of 'Odour of Chrysanthemums' to the *English Review*. Recalling his first impressions of the tale, Ford gives some clues as to what he meant by 'a natural sense of form'. He praises Lawrence's prose for its economy, specificity and disciplined employment of the natural setting with which he creates the scene of the woman in the first paragraph of the story, 'insignificantly trapped between the jolting black wagons and the hedge', who is waiting for the coal trucks to 'thump heavily past'. Once a man can write this, Ford comments, 'you can trust him for the rest'.[12]

However, when Ford was discouraging about the first version of Lawrence's second novel, *The Trespasser*, Lawrence turned to Edward Garnett, to whom Ford had introduced him earlier in 1911. As George Jefferson's biography of Garnett demonstrates, Lawrence became one of a long line of budding major talents to receive Garnett's close criticism of their manuscripts.[13] Garnett's already awesome reputation as a publisher's reader and his utter self-confidence in his judgements no doubt impressed the young Lawrence whose reputation now rested rather gingerly on *The White Peacock*.

On a fragment of *The Trespasser* manuscript in its unrevised state – which Garnett read in December 1911 – there is a critical note in Garnett's hand: 'Something is wanted to carry off this passage with the Stranger, i.e., – you must intersect his talk with little realistic touches to make him very *actual*. He must not spring quite out of the blue & disappear into it again. He's too much a deus ex machina for your purposes. Make some of his talk more ordinary & natural & slip in the pregnant things at moments.'[14] Lawrence was almost certainly predisposed to accept this kind of criticism. In a letter he had already referred disparagingly to this version of *The Trespasser* as 'a decorated idyll running to seed in realism' when announcing his intention to write the 'restrained, somewhat impersonal novel', 'Paul Morel', which would become *Sons and Lovers* (ibid., 184). Lawrence was speaking Garnett's language, so that the student–mentor relationship was quickly established.

However, the seeds of his later break with Garnett were already discernible. Referring to *The Trespasser*, he wrote to Garnett: 'this is a work one can't regard easily – I mean, at one's ease. It is so much oneself, one's naked self. I give myself away so much, and write what is my most palpitant, sensitive self, that I loathe the book, because it will betray me to a parcel of fools. . . . I often think Stendhal must have writhed in torture every time he remembered *Le Rouge et le noir* was public property: and Jefferies at *The Story of My Heart*' (ibid., 353). Lawrence had criticized an earlier version of his novel as being 'too chargé, too emotional', like 'a sponge dipped too full of vinegar' (ibid., 337). Yet, by his own regretful admission and despite Garnett's assistance, it stayed that way. Fairly safe to speculate, then, that frustration and unease strengthened his intention to turn to 'more restrained, somewhat impersonal' writing.

The term 'impersonal' had a particular meaning for Lawrence. He was recognizing the need to re-direct his personal investment – his emotional participation – in the centre of the narrative into a breadth of unbiased sympathetic interest. ('It is obviously best', Ford later wrote, 'if you can contrive to be without views at all: your business with the world is rendering, not alteration.')[15] Lawrence can be seen, in fact, gradually developing such a mode of dramatic realism in a series of short stories, preparing himself for the art of the home-life scenes in *Sons and Lovers*: the 1909 and 1911 versions of

'Odour of Chrysanthemums', 'Two Marriages', 'Strike Pay', 'Her Turn', 'The Miner at Home' and in his play *The Widowing of Mrs Holroyd*. The development is gradually displacing writing overloaded with his own personality and personal preoccupations: *The White Peacock*, with its forced literariness and its wishful fictionalizing of the hero's family circumstances; the heated emotionalism of *The Trespasser*; a number of overcharged short stories of his Croydon period.

It is tempting but it would be simplistic to see the latter group of works simply as manifesting a bad habit he needed to suppress. These works had appeared to offer ways of elevating, intensifying and generalizing his experience, of equipping him (or so it must have seemed to him) to ponder the larger questions his experience seemed to point to. The means, he evidently realized, were bogus: they led him into an extravagance he was soon ashamed of. However, they *had*, I believe, answered a personal need which his developing dramatic art was temporarily to stifle.

Upon the rejection of 'Paul Morel' by Heinemann in July 1912, Garnett evidently sent Lawrence an encouraging letter, offering to read the novel and suggest alterations. Rendering such assistance to young writers was characteristic of Garnett; Lawrence was gratified and heartened. Upon receipt of the notes Lawrence, now abroad, replied: 'I agree with all you say, and will do all I can. . . . The [notes] are awfully nice and detailed. What a Trojan of energy and conscientiousness you are! I'm going to slave like a Turk at the novel – see if I won't do you credit' (ibid., 427).

Although one cannot help taking Lawrence's intention seriously, his other letters to Garnett raise some doubts about its likely execution. The letters are a strange mixture. We find him promising faithfully to trim his sails but, often in the same letter, also indulging in displays of expansive opinionating, invective and soul-baring intimacy as if he were still revelling at long distance in the stimulating intellectual freedom he had found at weekends with the Garnetts in Kent. He seems to be using his letters to Garnett as an arena in which unreservedly to express and extend his feelings and ideas of the moment – to 'find' himself. The recipient of the letters must have shaken his head, wondering whether this man really would turn 'Paul Morel' into a 'restrained, somewhat impersonal novel'.

Although Garnett's notes do not survive,[16] it is possible to make some informed guesses as to their nature. In November 1912, having finished the revisions, Lawrence sent the novel, now entitled *Sons and Lovers*, to Garnett: 'And I want to defend it, quick. I wrote it again, pruning it and shaping it and filling it in. I tell you it has got form – *form*: haven't I made it patiently, out of sweat as well as blood' (ibid., 476). Lawrence is evidently attempting to anticipate and turn Garnett's expected criticism. But when he goes on to describe his novel's 'form', strangely he describes not so much a 'form' – in the sense of a *mode* of writing – as a psychological or thematic rationale:

> It follows this idea: a woman of character and refinement goes into the lower class, and has no satisfaction in her own life. She has had a passion for her husband, so the children are born of passion, and have heaps of vitality. But as her sons grow up she selects them as lovers – first the eldest,

then the second. These sons are *urged* into life by their reciprocal love of their mother – urged on and on. But when they come to manhood, they can't love, because their mother is the strongest power in their lives, and holds them.

(ibid., 476–7)

Garnett's subsequent reply undoubtedly indicated the need for abridgement, possibly because the novel was too long for Duckworth to publish as it stood.[17] But Garnett must also have had strong reservations about the novel, independent of its length. 'I sit in sadness and grief after your letter,' Lawrence replied. 'I daren't say anything. All right, take out what you think necessary . . . but don't scold me too hard, it makes me wither up' (ibid., 481). Evidently Lawrence's defence of the novel had not impressed Garnett: *his* notion of form was not Lawrence's. Garnett in fact went on to abridge the novel, removing about 10 per cent. (The facsimile manuscript contains the deleted passages with Garnett's markings.) Lawrence was soon grateful for Garnett's efforts: 'The thought of you pedgilling away', he wrote a month later, 'frets me. Why can't I do those things? – I can't' (ibid., 501).

Further evidence that Garnett's objections had been not to the thematic organization of the novel but to the mode of writing is provided in the same letter where Lawrence describes a play he had just written and was sending to Garnett. As if he already knew from his recent experience with *Sons and Lovers* what his mentor would think, he writes: 'like most of my stuff, it wants weeding out a bit'; there is 'stuff' there 'for shaping later on, when I'm more of a workman' (ibid.).

The term 'form' seems to have been in Garnett's critical vocabulary,[18] and perhaps in his dealings with Lawrence he used the term as a kind of shorthand, meaning the way of constructing the story, the assured conscious control of the progressive signification. In any case, the changes he made to Chapter III of *Sons and Lovers* strongly suggest that techniques of dramatic realism were the building blocks of that 'way of constructing'. It has often been remarked that Lawrence seems to spend far too little time on William in the novel to justify his case being considered, in the resumé (and in the novel's title), as of nearly equal importance to Paul's. Garnett, it turns out, is the culprit.

The title of Chapter III in the rejected version is 'Aftermath' changed, on second thoughts, to 'Morel Reaps the Whirlwind'. It was originally intended to record the aftermath of Morel's hitting his wife with the corner of the drawer in the scene where the drop of blood falls on the baby Paul's hair. There is almost nothing about William in the chapter. In the final version, however, before Garnett's deletions, there was a good deal – reflected in the chapter's change of title to the Oedipal designation: 'The Casting off of Morel: the Taking on of William'. Garnett was obviously unimpressed, deleting a total of about eight manuscript pages concerned with William. Sizeable cuts indeed, given that the chapter itself was only twenty-seven pages long.

There are a number of scenes in the chapter where Lawrence works hard to suggest that an abnormally close bond exists between William and his mother. On one occasion William, flouting his mother's wishes, dresses as a Highlander for a fancy dress ball:

'Aren't you going to stop and see me, mother?' he asked.

'No; I don't want to see you,' she replied.

She was rather pale, and her face was closed and hard. She was afraid of her son's going the same way as his father. He hesitated a moment, and his heart stood still with anxiety. Then he caught sight of the Highland bonnet with its ribbons. He picked it up gleefully, forgetting her. She went out.

[The published version ends here: Penguin edition, 1948, 71. The manuscript proceeds:]

He never knew how disappointed he was. The excitement of the moment, and of anticipation, was enough to carry him through the present. But all his pride was built on *her* seeing him. And afterwards, it always hurt him to think back on this ball.

However, he went upstairs in great excitement. Paul helped him to dress.

(*Facsimile MS*, 94)

Although his mother's refusal to share his elation hurts William it does not prevent his going out. Yet Lawrence comments, 'But all his pride was built on *her* seeing him.' The conversation between William and Paul, which follows, demonstrates that this just isn't so: William's vanity, it emerges, needs no pricking. It forms, in fact, the somewhat wearisome subject of the following page and a half: 'Now how do my knees look! – all right, don't they? Ripping knees they are – ripping knees – legs altogether!' (ibid., 95). Although the young boy Paul's ingenuous responses provide a welcome deflating note (*he* can't see what all the fuss is about), Garnett probably objected to the unnecessary authorial intrusion ('He never knew how disappointed he was . . .'), and then finding that its judgement was in any case not dramatized, deleted both it and the following conversation between the two brothers. While there is no doubt of William's abounding interest in the opposite sex, his emotional dependence on his mother is not convincingly established here. Whether or not Garnett posed the objection to himself in this way, he was obviously aware of the resultant slack in the novel at this point. His editor's pencil went instinctively to work. Clearly Garnett cut not just to shorten but to improve. His deletions are frequently aimed at tightening scenes of situational drama, eliminating repetitive elements in them, helping them to become more richly suggestive or more sharply visualized. Quite possibly at Garnett's suggestion, Lawrence rewrote the opening pages of the novel.[19] The new version is tighter; the array of historical and then social facts serves to ground the novel, much as the first paragraphs of 'Odour of Chrysanthemums' had done, in a firmly grasped social environment.

Lawrence understood the function of this important ingredient of realism. An objective correlative from the environment had to be found if the emotion or state of mind were to be implied – and *implied* it had, ideally, to be in the dramatic art Garnett was encouraging Lawrence to write. The well-known scene in Chapter I where Mr Morel brings home a coconut for his wife is a good example (Penguin edn, 14). It has no counterpart in the rejected version: Lawrence had added this scene and Garnett evidently approved of it. The outward fact – the rarity of coming by a coconut – is the occasion of the disagreement between husband and wife. Although the scene is, in one sense, transparent – it feels entirely unforced – it calls for a rather complex response. We have to register Morel's tipsy loquacity, his good-naturedness that is, nevertheless, overdone. We see that Mrs Morel's shaking the coconut is a mixture of placation of, and slight insult to, her husband, and we note his good-natured refusal to take offence. So that when Mrs Morel goes to bed, tired and 'sick of his babble' (we have watched her struggling through an arduous day), she does not carry our undivided sympathy with her.

'External' details such as the coconut and the extra sixpence Mrs Morel pays in rent for their end-terrace are rarely beside the point in Part One.[20] They serve to focus pressures and aspirations with a sharpness that Lawrence does not achieve when he is less sure of the social environment: 'The girls [at Jordan's] all liked to hear [Paul] talk. They often gathered in a little circle while he sat on a bench, and held forth to them, laughing. Some of them regarded him as a curious little creature, so serious, yet so bright and jolly, and always so delicate in his way with them. They all liked him, and he adored them' (Penguin edn, 138). The complexity of response of the kind called for by most of the home-life scenes is not solicited here. The self-congratulatory tone is only possible because the scene is not located with the same sureness: at home there would soon be somebody pricking Paul's balloon.

Garnett's influence can also be felt in the general balancing of Mr and Mrs Morel's responsibilities for the failure of their marriage. In the rejected version, Mr Morel has far fewer redeeming characteristics. His preparations for his holiday walk with Jerry Purdy are seen very much from Mrs Morel's censorious point of view:

> When Morel began, on the Monday morning of the holiday, blithely to bestir himself for his outing, Mrs Morel felt that she could not bear herself. A naturally vain man, he had shaved his beard, keeping a heavy black moustache. . . . He was jaunty and cocky as of old. But now it only irritated Mrs Morel past bearing. At nine o'clock he began to get ready. The old 'beau' was to be furbished up. He shaved himself with evident satisfaction; he parted his waving, glossy black hair very scrupulously. When he was dressed there was about him a perkiness which Mrs Morel loathed.
>
> (*Facsimile MS*, fragment 2, 27–8)

In the final version, Morel is allowed an attractiveness and a vitality that Mrs Morel finds difficult to deny. Now Morel is up much earlier than nine o'clock:

> His wife lay listening to him tinkering away in the garden, his whistling ringing out as he sawed and hammered away. It always gave her a sense of warmth and peace to hear him thus as she lay in bed, the children not yet awake, in the bright early morning, happy in his man's fashion.
>
> At nine o'clock, while the children with bare legs and feet were sitting playing on the sofa, and the mother was washing up, he came in from his carpentry, his sleeves rolled up, his waistcoat hanging open. He was still a good-looking man, with black, wavy hair, and a large black moustache. . . .
>
> When he chose he could still make himself again a real gallant. . . . There

seemed so much gusto in the way he puffed and swilled as he washed himself, so much alacrity with which he hurried to the mirror in the kitchen, and, bending because it was too low for him, scrupulously parted his wet black hair, that it irritated Mrs Morel.

(Penguin edn, 28–9)

No longer content with justifying an attitude, Lawrence has committed himself to the dramatizing of a series of glimpsed scenes which, in following the course of Mrs Morel's uncensored responses, challenges the dismissiveness of her conscious judgement. She is not *merely* irritated.

Lawrence had evidently adopted a deliberate policy of introducing such scenes. (Morel's abusing the pit managers in the pub is another example.) That Garnett permitted the introduction or lengthening of scenes favourable to Morel, where elsewhere in Part One he was cutting severely, suggests that he had criticized the rejected version as lacking the impartiality that dramatic realism requires. In Part Two, however, Lawrence seems to renege on the artistic practices Garnett's criticisms had been fostering. There is an insistent drive in both the Miriam and the Clara sections to find an unambiguous clarification of Paul's problems when the art *had* appeared to be better fitted to present conflicting and unreconciled perspectives – which, one felt in Part One, properly reflected the complexity of the emotional issues.

Criticisms of the novel are usually aimed at the unfairness of the presentation of Miriam – and they can be very persuasive. There is, undoubtedly, a great deal of 'first degree' interpretation of Miriam which purports to be neutral observation: 'Often, when wiping the dishes, she would stand in bewilderment and chagrin because she had pulled in two halves a cup or a tumbler. It was as if, in her fear and self-mistrust, she put too much strength into the effort. There was no looseness or abandon about her. Everything was gripped stiff with intensity, and her effort, overcharged, closed in on itself' (Penguin edn, 191). The external event (the cup's breaking) does not in this case initiate a dramatic scene which reveals character. Instead we get a brief meditation on her inadequacy. No independent arbitration of the claim in the last sentence is offered, nor any conflicting view. The claim is part of a theory (it is usually argued) which is consistently imposed on the story. That Miriam cannot give herself to the activity of swinging (as Paul *can*) only prefigures her inadequacy in the love-making scene. Essentially the story is no further developed. Pared down to too few elements, it has simply become clearer through repetition. And *this*, when the art of Part One thrived on dramatic complexity and abundance. So the argument proceeds, picking up alarming momentum the more one considers it. Does not the novel, after all, *invite* the comparison of the rich dramatic non-certainties of Part One with the overcertainty of Part Two?

It does – if one restricts one's attention to the published novel itself. But when considered in the larger context of Ford's and Garnett's effects on Lawrence's practice as a writer of fiction (encouraging, enabling, but also constricting), the problem becomes rather different. The narrator in Part Two is, after all, not simply following the day-to-day events of Paul's growing up as he had been in Part One. The focus is more concentrated; the probing of Paul's experience for its significance is almost continuous. Lawrence wants to deal more directly, intimately, at a greater depth with Paul's changing emotional states, in order to find a representativeness in his dealings with different kinds of destructive women. That representativeness was his intention is confirmed by the letter to Garnett about the novel's 'form'. Paul's story, Lawrence writes, 'is a great tragedy. . . . It's the tragedy of thousands of young men in England' (*Letters*, I, 477).

In Part Two Lawrence has allowed the issues themselves to determine the artistic form – at whatever cost to the disciplines Garnett had advocated. Miriam's urge to possess, her 'tightness' of being, her spirituality, together with Paul's contrasting characteristics, become (with the home-life scenes in mind) larger than life; they, as it were, fill out the narrative 'space'. The contrast with the less claustrophobic art of Part One is disagreeably obvious. But that is because Lawrence is not yet sure of what he is doing, which way his art is going.

Struggling to justify what he perceived to be an inevitable but as yet unclarified direction in his own writing, the only language Lawrence had to hand – and it is quite inappropriate – was Garnett's and Ford's. Ford had told Lawrence that the early version of *The Trespasser* ' "has no construction or form – it is execrably bad art, being all variations on a theme" ' (ibid., 339). Half-recognizing that he had run together two very different approaches to his material in Parts One and Two of *Sons and Lovers*, Lawrence tries to encompass them both (in what I conceive must have been a reflex action) under the one heading, 'form', stretching the term by so doing into meaninglessness.

No wonder that we find him, in letters, reviews and essays, conflating different kinds of artistic form: Garnett's notion of 'visualized' realism, Flaubert's meticulous arrangements and juxtapositions, Arnold Bennett's 'rules of construction' (*Letters*, ed. G. Zytaruk and J. T. Boulton, Cambridge, 1981, II, 479). No wonder we find him growing hostile to the very idea of form, and rejecting the idea that the form of works of art are in any way comparable. ('Each work of art has its own form, which has no relation to any other form': *Phoenix*, 477). No wonder we find him, several years later, making a plea for 'apparent formlessness' even as he is applauding the masterly, and undeniably realist, fiction of Giovanni Verga (ibid., 248–50). A few months after his letter defending *Sons and Lovers* we find Lawrence, in another letter to Garnett, describing the next novel he embarked on (one he put aside, unfinished) as something 'quite different in manner from my other stuff – far less visualised. It is what I *can* write just now, and write with pleasure, so write it I must, however you may grumble' (*Letters*, I, 511). Lawrence was gradually realizing that his attempts to confine the exploration of his interests within a mode of dramatic realism circumscribe them artificially. And he is letting his mentor know that he knows.

Garnett had in fact refashioned Part Two of *Sons and Lovers* relatively little. Probably he did not feel confident that he fully comprehended its direction – whereas he had felt very much at ease with the art of Part One. Although Lawrence began sending early drafts of *The Rainbow* to Garnett for comment, the split between the two men was widening. Lawrence was struggling to create an artistic vehicle to which he could harness his burgeoning powers: his development of an innovative language and idiosyncratic syntax that would plot the deeper movements of the subconscious. 'All the time, underneath, there is something deep evolving itself out in me,' Lawrence wrote, in April 1914, to Garnett who had disliked the direction 'The Wedding Ring' (as *The Rainbow* was then called) had taken (*Letters*, II, 165). Lawrence sensed that Garnett had not the flexibility of mind to appraise the novel rightly: 'it is only that I have a different attitude to my characters, and that necessitates a different attitude in you, which you are not as yet prepared to give' (ibid., 182). The final split with Garnett, only months away, was now inevitable.

Lawrence, after all, was to prove right: he had to guard, with a justified pride, that which was 'evolving out of him' over a period of time (we can now see) before, during and after the composition of *Sons and Lovers*. Traditional study of the internal relationships of the novel's final state cannot tell the full story; only by reference to a wider network of influences, personal and intertextual, and to a greater array of textual traces than are provided by the novel in its published form, can its inner tensions be properly understood. Clearly, for Lawrence the activity of authorship was a continuum: always subject to new stimulus, influence and experiment. His published volumes only partially represent this continuity, their inadequacy accentuated in this case by a publisher's reader's extensive involvement.

Notes

1 Argued in my 'Lawrence criticism: where next?', *Critical Review*, XXI (1979), 72–84; and 'Lawrence and the futurists: the breakthrough in his art', *Meridian*, I (1982), 21–32.
2 Except (principally) by feminism: see pp. 12–22 above. See also Diane S. Bonds, *Language and the Self in D. H. Lawrence* (Ann Arbor, Mich., 1987).
3 Cf. Garrett Stewart, 'Lawrence, "being", and the allotropic style', *Novel*, IX (1976), 217–42; and my 'D. H. Lawrence and the crucifixes', *Bulletin of Research in the Humanities*, LXXXVI (1983), 67–85, especially 74–6.
4 The term's usefulness is argued in my 'D. H. Lawrence and the crucifixes'; for 'strong' and 'weak' subjectivity in *Twilight in Italy* (1916), see my 'Real or imaginary encounters in the travel book: the case of D. H. Lawrence', in Joy Hooton (ed.), *Studies in Prose Literature*. Occasional Paper no. 5, English Dept, Faculty of Military Studies (Duntroon [Canberra], 1985), 20–33.
5 In the CUP editions the textual apparatus is, strictly, a record of emendations of the base-text, but with all variant readings occurring *subsequent* to it noted, whether authorial or not – though not variant readings *pre-dating* it (as when the base-text is a revised typescript and the autograph manuscript is extant). Only some variants of the latter are then recorded in the explanatory notes.
6 *Phoenix II*, ed. Harry T. Moore and Warren Roberts (London, 1968), 250–6.
7 The route to Adam from *Laughing Horse*, which in no. 9 (Christmas 1923) reprinted the Navajo 'Song of the Horse' (a mythical turquoise horse travels with a joyous neigh daily across the sky from east to west), may be traced via Lawrence's 'Dear old horse: a London letter' (written by 9 January 1924; published in no. 10 (May 1924), and reprinted in *The Letters of D. H. Lawrence*, ed. Aldous Huxley (London, 1932), II, 590–3).
8 There is in fact no *one* published text; the English and American first editions differ in hundreds of readings, and subsequent typesetting introduced hundreds more.

9 Approximate dates of composition are provided in the text; for dating of other writings, see Keith Sagar, *D. H. Lawrence: A Calendar of his Works* (Manchester, 1979), and the chronologies in each volume of the Cambridge edition of *The Letters of D. H. Lawrence*, ed. J. T. Boulton *et al.* (1979–   ).

10 *'Sons and Lovers': A Facsimile of the Manuscript*, ed. Mark Schorer (Berkeley, 1977). The forthcoming Cambridge edition (ed. Helen and Carl Baron) will provide a more complete access, including Lawrence's extensive proof emendations (and some further tinkering by Garnett).

11 Memoir by Ford reprinted in *D. H. Lawrence: A Composite Biography*, ed. Edward Nehls (Madison, 1957), I, 121.

12 ibid., 109.

13 George Jefferson, *Edward Garnett: A Life in Literature* (London, 1981).

14 E. W. Tedlock, *The Frieda Lawrence Collection of D. H. Lawrence Manuscripts* (Albuquerque, 1948), illus. p. 8.

15 Ford Madox Ford, *Joseph Conrad: A Personal Remembrance* (London, 1924), 87; reprinted in *Critical Writings of Ford Madox Ford*, ed. Frank MacShane (Lincoln, Neb., 1964).

16 But some of his preliminary jottings do: see Helen Baron, '*Sons and Lovers*: the surviving manuscripts from three drafts dated by paper analysis', *Studies in Bibliography* [hereafter *SB*], XXXVIII (1985), 320–1.

17 'A seven and sixpenny novel usually ran to 120,000 words and *Sons and Lovers* in manuscript made 180,000 words' (Jefferson, *Garnett: A Life*, 150); there is evidence on the manuscript of a word-count.

18 Cf. his 1902 essay on Henry Lawson, *Friday Nights* (London, 1929), 145–6.

19 The earlier version of the opening, in Fragment I in the *Facsimile*, is part of the version of 'Paul Morel' written November 1911–April 1912, then revised May–June 1912 and rejected by Heinemann. Sections of this version (and as revised) are incorporated into the autograph manuscript of the final version of *Sons and Lovers*. The Fragments are parts of the earlier version (and as revised) which were not so incorporated.

   Schorer, in his introduction to the *Facsimile*, mistook these chronological relationships, and Wayne Templeman followed. See 'The *Sons and Lovers* Manuscript', *SB*, XXXVII (1984), 234–43; cf. Helen Baron's clarification, 'The surviving manuscripts', 289–328.

20 The extra sixpence appears, however, in the version prior to the rejected version (autograph manuscript, 'Paul Morel'; Harry Ransom Humanities Research Center, University of Texas at Austin) and therefore in itself predates the time of Garnett's influence. In 'Mrs Morel ironing', *Journal of the D. H. Lawrence Society* (1984), 2–12, Helen Baron compares corresponding passages in this and the final manuscript versions.

*

I would like to thank the University of Kent at Canterbury, where this essay was prepared, for making facilities available to me as Visiting Scholar. The second section of this material first appeared in *The Critical Quarterly*, XX, no. 4.

5 *The Lost Girl*: discourse and focalization

Roger Fowler

Theory

In this essay I wish to utilize concepts from discourse theory to consider whether Lawrence creates a sense of independent consciousness in his central characters, or whether that consciousness is infiltrated by 'authorial' evaluation of the world of the fiction and the experience of the character. 'Discourse theory' here draws from Halliday, Berger & Luckmann, Gramsci, Foucault. In addition I will make use of the specialized concepts of 'polyvocality' (Bakhtin) and of 'focalization' (Genette). Explanations and references for these theoretical ideas will be given in a moment.

But why choose to discuss *The Lost Girl*, when better known Lawrence texts also manifest the problem referred to? Well, it has been roundly dismissed by the critics ('*The Lost Girl* does not demand very prolonged consideration'),[1] and given the choice, a new paper on *The Lost Girl* seems fairer to the Lawrence canon than yet another study of one of the 'big' novels. *The Lost Girl* is also structurally very interesting. Written rapidly in 1920, the book may in part (to what extent we cannot know) be based on material written seven years earlier; an uneasy quilting of diverse styles may reflect different phases of Lawrence's writing career. The stylistic or discoursal difference between the beginning and the end of the book is part of a more complex stylistic intertextuality unusual in Lawrence. There are relations with the earlier novels (in the language used to handle Alvina's perception of sex, for example; see below, on *Women in Love*) and, in the final pages, with Lawrence's Italian writings. There are also links with Arnold Bennett, whose 'social realism' in *Anna of the Five Towns* (1902) Lawrence was apparently trying to emulate when he began the text in 1912 (as what remains as the fragment 'Elsa Culverwell') and again in 1913 (in the lost 'Insurrection of Miss Houghton'). There are also borrowings from Dickens – the grotesque circus people in *Hard Times* and, at first, something of the narrative tone of that book. Finally, *The Lost Girl* is an interesting text for discourse analysis because of its explicit self-consciousness about speech. Almost as a matter of routine, the narrator refers to speech mannerisms when he introduces a character, commenting on or implying their social significance: 'his beautifully modulated voice all but sang . . . his musical voice' (James

Houghton, 18, 19; Camb. edn, 7), 'a parvenu little fellow whose English would not bear analysis' (the first tenant of the shop, 21; Camb. edn, 9), 'It was evident that she was not a lady: her grammar was not without reproach . . . her soft, near, sure voice, which seemed almost like a secret touch upon her hearer' (Miss Pinnegar, 24; Camb. edn, 12), 'her voice had a curious bronze-like resonance that acted straight on the nerves of her hearers: unpleasantly on most English nerves' (Alvina when rebellious, 37, cf. 34, 41, 44, 47, etc.; Camb. edn, 23, cf. 21, 28, 30, 33, etc.). The narrator is always interpreting the meaning of personal forms of speech, the significance for a person's attitudes and social position. The ideological significance of language variation is the fundamental principle of the model of discourse analysis used here.

'Discourse' is speech or writing seen from the point of view of the beliefs, values and categories which it embodies; these beliefs (etc.) constitute a way of looking at the world, an organization or representation of experience – 'ideology' in the neutral, non-pejorative sense. Different modes of discourse encode different representations of experience; and the source of these representations is the communicative context within which discourse is embedded. Contemporary discourse analysts would usually cite Michel Foucault as the authority for such a position,[2] but I prefer a more linguistic formulation. To make the matter concrete, here is a simple example from the novel:

> Now James Houghton, at the age of twenty-eight, inherited a splendid business in Manchester goods, in Woodhouse. He was a tall, thin elegant young man with side-whiskers, genuinely refined, somewhat in the Bulwer style. He had a taste for elegant conversation and elegant literature and elegant Christianity: a tall, thin, brittle young man, rather fluttering in his manner, full of facile ideas, and with a beautiful speaking voice: most beautiful. Withal, of course, a tradesman. (*TLG*, 12; Camb. edn, 2)[3]

Traditional novel criticism would regard this as a 'description' of a 'character'. But it is, rather, a 'descriptive mode of discourse' which articulates a system of categories from polite early twentieth-century representation of society – 'tall', 'thin', 'elegant', etc. – and attaches them to a name. In this quotation the social categories are very overt, because the narrator is being ironic in this representation;[4] elsewhere they might have to be inferred· indirectly on the basis of the reader's knowledge of appropriate discourse and its contexts.

Modes of discourse carrying different sets of beliefs can usually (but not necessarily) be recognized by characteristic structural differences in the language, differences between styles or registers; there are characteristic linguistic forms for gothic, romance, news reporting, travelogue, scientific report, etc., and within these even finer distinctions. All carry their characteristic social and ideological meanings.[5] We would expect the stylistic diversity of *The Lost Girl* to be matched by diversity of point of view.

Values and beliefs are carried by discourse because discourse is an interaction between an addressor and an addressee within a specific socio-cultural context. Thus the passage introducing James Houghton, just quoted, assumes communication between a narrator and an implied reader who share some knowledge about the attributes of male elegance and refinement in the early twentieth century (and, separately, 'conversational' knowledge of the linguistic cues for irony: see note 4). The printed novel text has a more implicit structure of interaction than does face-to-face conversation, but the principle of signification through the implication of shared knowledge is the same. Note that in the 'interaction' model of the text, the reader has a very active, positive role in the construction of the text's meanings. And if a text is preserved for a long time, social and ideological change may mean that later readers cannot occupy the position implied for contemporaneous readers. For example, Lawrence's views on women and on female sexuality have become problematic because of the changes of consciousness produced by the feminist movements in the last three-quarters of a century.[6]

Modern studies of point of view have stressed the 'interactive' nature of communication in fiction, drawing attention to *polyvocal* and *dialogic* aspects of novel texts. The polyvocal model partakes of the poststructuralist democratization of fiction: the author is banished,[7] the reader is ascendant,[8] the characters are respected as (imagined) subjectivities, not objectivized.[9] No longer is the novel a monologic, authoritarian block of language; several voices, or points of view, interact: *the implied author* – the image of the writer constructed by the text, which may itself be complex, as here; *the narrator; the implied reader* or 'viewing position' into which individual reading subjects have to read themselves if they are to make sense of the book; *characters*, usually third person, which are imaginary creations constructed of names, sets of attributes, and a part in the story; and perhaps other third persons *external to* the story and to the author/reader speech event – Fielding's 'judges', 'critics', 'the malicious', 'that higher order of women'; or by intertextuality, other books.

Some of the discourse interactions included in this analysis are literally dialogic, i.e., presentations of speech events among characters. But all discourse is inherently dialogic in the sense that it is oriented to an addressee: we anticipate our hearers' and readers' responses, we make assumptions about what they know and believe. This situation clearly applies to the author/reader relationship, and on reflection it also applies to the narrator/character and reader/character relationships. The narrator/character 'dialogue' has become very important in modern critical analysis: the meanings of this relationship have been interestingly studied with reference to techniques for representing speech and thought.[10]

One more piece of technical apparatus: the notion of *focalizer* and *focalization* introduced by Genette.[11] Genette makes the simple observation that the narrator of a story may or may not be the focalizer of some part of it. That is to say, an event or experience within a narrative may be 'focalized' by – seen through the eyes of, evaluated through the values of – some consciousness which is not that of the narrator: the focalizer could be a character, or, by intertextuality, some addressor external to the text. These possibilities characterize the polyvocal text. Conversely, one can point to texts or parts of a text in which a character's personal experience is not focalized by her/himself, and in which internal perspective is infiltrated by or even subjugated to the narrative discourse. The concept of focalization is of great pertinence to Lawrence, since his characters tend not to be permitted to be focalizers.

Polyvocality

The Lost Girl is a polyvocal text, or to use a sociolinguistic term, *heteroglossic*. A heteroglossic community is one whose speakers have between them a wide and diverse range of linguistic varieties or discrete languages: Belgium, Switzerland, Kenya, Norway. The different varieties usually have distinct, regular, communicative functions.[12] A heteroglossic text contains several or many varieties – styles, dialects, languages – and we may assume that they have their special functions, i.e., they do not occur fortuitously. They embody different representations or evaluations of experience. Clear examples of heteroglossic or polyvocal texts would be *Tristram Shandy*, *Hard Times*,[13] *Ulysses*, Dos Passos's *USA*, Faulkner's *The Sound and the Fury* or *As I Lay Dying*. *The Lost Girl* could be added to this list, *Women in Love* or *Anna of the Five Towns* could not. Limitations of space forbid extensive quotation to display the polyvocality of our text; readers are requested to look up the following passages representing the stylistic range:

1 Take a mining townlet like Woodhouse, with a population of ten thousand people, and three generations behind it. . . . Rule him out. (p. 11; Camb. edn, 1)
2 'Ay, that's the road it goes, Miss Huffen . . . as if th' roof had laid its egg on you . . .' (p. 63; Camb. edn, 47)
3 And then, for Turns, his first item was Miss Poppy Traherne . . . and stood on each other's heads and on their own heads . . . (p. 134; Camb. edn, 107)
4 'There are two kinds of friendships . . . ever can be eternal.' (p. 141; Camb. edn, 113)
5 'Hi Cic—! Cicio!' he yelled. . . .
    'Nay.' Cicio shook his head . . . (pp. 189–90; Camb. edn, 154. The Cambridge spelling is 'Ciccio'.)
6 She gasped . . . this lustrous dark beauty, unbearable. (pp. 243–4; Camb. edn, 202)
7 Alvina looked at the room . . . oak-twigs filling the corner by the hearth. (p. 366; Camb. edn, 310)
8 In February, as the days opened . . . lilac-flamed in the laboratory of the hospital at Islington . . . (p. 392; Camb. edn, 332)

I have not arranged the passages structurally; they are simply in the order found in the book. For the moment I mean them not to have any structural relationship but simply to illustrate stylistic plurality in the most straight-forward way. Passage 1 has the brisk syntax and sardonic tone of the early chapters of *Hard Times*, for instance 'The Key-note' chapter describing Coke-town and its inhabitants: note the involvement of the reader through the imperatives 'Take . . .' and 'Rule him out'; the short sentences and clauses arranged to suggest an emphatic, rhetorical but personal intonation, especially the inversion in the fourth sentence; the density of animating metaphors – 'fled', 'disembowelled', 'clambering', 'kicking'. The tone of the opening chapters does become less Dickensian but remains personal and lively; Kermode puts it very well (though arguably his phrase ignores the self-consciousness, the irony): 'The text has a certain matey discursiveness.'[14] Passage 3 once more recalls *Hard Times*, the treatment of the circus people, e.g., 'Sleary's Horsemanship', page 77, '"Meanwhile, the various members of Sleary's company . . .'. Passage 2 is part of a longer speech in which the dialect of a collier is suggested by a set of very salient, defamiliarizing linguistic techniques. Dialect appears elsewhere in the book in contexts where it has a dramatic purpose: e.g., Chapter 9, where Alvina is confronted by her drunken, black-mailing Yorkshire (this is said) landlady after her first sex with Cicio. Passage 4 is spoken by the theatre manager Mr May, a Dickensian comic grotesque. Lawrence explicitly draws attention to his manner of speech and its significance, and it is clear that he took great care over the technical details of Mr May's mannerisms and intended them to have precise significances. 'Of cauce' and 'yuman' are probably hypercorrections,[15] phonetic signs of social pretension; the vocabulary is also affected ('quite', 'nice', 'decent'), as is the textual structure, a pseudo-intellectual expository scripting ('There are two kinds . . .'). Passage 5 is self-annotating: 'Their conversation . . .' The Natchas speak in broken English sentences larded with exclamations and with fragments of other languages. Their speech signifies alienness from Woodhouse's ideas (indeed they use French to conceal their meanings from Alvina); intimacy with each other ('thee'); brutishness ('noises'). Elsewhere they are made to speak mysticism, liturgy. Passage 6 gives Alvina's response to her first sex with Cicio; she is the focalizer, but the style (metaphors, transitivity) is familiar to readers of Lawrence as characteristic of his way of handling women's perception of male sexuality (dumb admiration of the male, mysticism, the acceptance of force and subjugation). There are about half a dozen passages like this in the latter part of the book. Passage 7 is one of only a few brief passages in the novel to break out into the linguistic conventions of visual realism: discourse analysis would need to focus on locatives, deixis, the lack of action verbs but the textual prominence of the one verb of perception, 'looked'.[16] There is a *tour de force* of this kind of writing in *Anna of the Five Towns*, Chapter 7, the description of the kitchen dresser. Finally, 8 is a romantic engagement with a natural scene, a quite distinct style again and one found elsewhere in Lawrence's novels and travel writings. For intertextuality with the travel writings I could also have quoted passages from the end of the book describing peasants, inns, markets.

Focalization

Critical consensus has it that the beginning and the end of *The Lost Girl* are to be praised. Even Hough grudgingly finds in the opening chapters 'excellent genre-painting', evidence of 'what a competent social realist Lawrence could have been'.[17] As for the final chapters, they are generally admired for the particularity and vividness of the landscapes and of the observations of peasant life. But the critics find it hard to accept the wide difference between the two parts of the book; and specifically they condemn the implausible device of having Alvina join a troupe of vaudeville players, one of whom carries her off to his birthplace in Italy. One can see what Lawrence is saying: bourgeois life in the industrial Midlands is repressive, uninspiring, mechanized; it chokes and

frustrates Alvina. The Natcha-Kee-Tawara, like Sleary's horse-riders, are supposed to 'retain a contact with the instinctual life that the respectable have
lost'.[18] Aligning herself with the Natchas, Alvina affirms freedom, expressivity
and, most of all, passion; and the flight to Italy is an escape to a life of primitive
simplicity and natural instinct. This scheme, we know, conforms to Lawrence's
own experiences and values. However, the objection to the Natchas is not just
that they constitute a 'creaky mechanism', insufficient to bear Alvina away;
more damning is the fact that they are plain ridiculous, and absurdly handled –
distastefully, for some readers, e.g., Katherine Mansfield.[19] In any case, in
relation to the whole sequence of her narrated experiences, Alvina's motivation is not precisely established, and it is not given an adequate autonomy from
the views of the implied author. An analysis of discourse in terms of focalization may help us articulate these latter problems more fully.

In discussing focalizations which are *not* those of characters, it is essential to
make a distinction between *implied author* and *narrator*. The narrator is the
'Dickensian', 'matey', discursive persona that Lawrence has created. The
implied author is signalled by other kinds of discourse, most clearly seen in
passage 6 above: 'Lawrencian' discourse.

Often focalization-by-narrator is dominant; in passage 9 below, such discourse is clearly marked by narrative signposts ('so far, the story . . .'), by the
magisterial 'we', by generalization ('thousands of girls'), by proverbial formulation ('Ordinary people, ordinary fates'), by direct comments on contemporary historical conditions ('The all-to-one-pattern modern system . . .'). This
is palpably the voice of the omniscient narrator of classic 'realist' fiction (Eliot,
Hardy): the authoritative, dramatized narrator as pretend 'author', or the
confident voice of the essayist – a high-profile discursive persona:

9 Now so far, the story of Alvina is commonplace enough. It is more or less the
   story of thousands of girls. They all find work. It is the ordinary solution of
   everything. And if we were dealing with an ordinary girl we should have to
   carry on mildly and dully down the long years of employment; or, at the
   best, marriage with some dull schoolteacher or office-clerk.

   But we protest that Alvina is not ordinary. Ordinary people, ordinary
   fates. But extraordinary people, extraordinary fates. Or else no fate at all.
   The all-to-one-pattern modern system is too much for most extraordinary
   individuals. It just kills them off or throws them disused aside.

                                                          (p. 107; Camb. edn, 83)

Not surprisingly, given the dominance of this kind of intervention, focalization by character is clearly recognizable only very infrequently. Here is Mr
May:

10 Poor Mr May had to gather together his wits and his sprightliness for his
    next meeting. He decided he must make a percentage in other ways. He
    schemed in all known ways. He would accept the ten pounds – but really,
    did ever you hear of anything so ridiculous in your life, *ten pounds!* – dirty
    old screw, dirty, screwing old woman! He would accept the ten pounds; but
    he would get his own back.

                                                          (p. 117; Camb. edn, 92)

And Alvina:

11 Against her usual habit, Alvina joined the plumber and her father in the
scullery. Arthur Witham saluted her with some respect. She liked his blue
eyes and tight figure. He was keen and sly in business, very watchful, and
slow to commit himself. Now he poked and peered and crept under the
sink. Alvina watched him half disappear – she handed him a candle – and
she laughed to herself seeing his tight, well-shaped hindquarters protrud-
ing out from under the sink like the wrong end of a dog from a kennel. He
was keen after money, was Arthur – and bossy, creeping slyly after his own
self-importance and power.

(p. 77; Camb. edn, 58)

Focalization by character is marked by the presence of verbs of perception
('seeing') or mental process ('schemed'); by colloquialism of lexical register
('dirty old screw') coupled with avoidance of words characteristic of a framing
discourse (contrast 'voltaic', pp. 52, 53; Camb. edn, 37, 38); by homely
comparisons ('like the wrong end of a dog') as opposed to literary metaphors;
by speech syntax suggested by short information units, dashes, exclamation
marks; by other syntactic colloquialisms ('. . . was Arthur').

As a matter of fact, I had to search hard for clear examples of focalization by
character, examples in which the style and the values are distinct from those of
the narrative discourse or authorial discourse. In 10, the representation of Mr
May's thoughts is authenticated by the fact that it follows the idiosyncratic
patterns which Lawrence had so carefully constructed for his *speech* style. This
happens with none of the other characters. Although Lawrence consistently
declares the speech mannerisms of the characters, he depicts them only in the
cases of Mr May, the dialect speakers and the Natchas; but the technical
markers of the representation of dialect speech and of Natcha-ese are unsuit-
able for the representation of thought and perception. The fact is that Lawrence
does not, on the whole, employ such markers in his treatment of characters like
James Houghton and Miss Pinnegar, even though both are repeatedly said to
have distinctive voices. Although the technical problems of individualizing the
thoughts of ordinary conventional people (i.e., not grotesques like Mr May)
have frequently and famously been overcome – Mrs Norris, Eveline, Mrs
Dalloway – Lawrence did not go along this road here. Two reasons for his
diffidence may be suggested. First, some characters, notably Cicio, have to
remain inaccessible and mysterious. Second, the minor characters exist largely
as objects for Alvina's attention, or as accidents which propel her in some
direction. In general, Lawrence does not use the minor characters as focalizers,
except sporadically and insignificantly (e.g., Miss Frost, p. 59; Camb. edn, 43,
whose meditations on James Houghton's responsibility for his wife's death are
immediately answered by the narrator with a hectoring diatribe against
women who expect their husbands to make them happy). Alvina is the only
character who is allowed to focalize; the question raised above was the degree
of independence her perceptions have.

Although a recognizable speech idiolect is not necessary to establish a
character as a focalizer, it does help. But Alvina has no distinctive speech style.

She is said to sound a 'bronze-like resonance' (p. 37; Camb. edn, 23), a 'clang' (pp. 41, 44; Camb. edn, 28, 30) in her rebellious moods, but this does not show in the speech assigned to her, nor would it be any use in individuating thought. In fact she speaks very little; briefly, negatively, bluntly. If, in focalization, her discourse is her own, it has to be established independently of her style of speech.

Let us return to passage 11, which appears to be focalized through Alvina. There is a detached, amused eroticism mixed with social distaste, attitudes which are consistent in Alvina's encounters with the Withams and which are important in understanding her relationship with, and flight from, her potential English lovers, and from her social milieu in Woodhouse. But I have cheated with the quotation. If we broaden it somewhat, we will find that it is comprehensively framed by narrative discourse. It is preceded by a short character-focalized paragraph in which Alvina is angered by thoughts of her own spinsterhood and of her father's financial irresponsibility, and which ends:

12 Her old anger against her father arose again.

Arthur Witham, the plumber, came in with James Houghton to examine the house. Arthur Witham was also one of the Chapel men – as had been his *common*, interfering, *uneducated* father before him. The father had left each of his sons a fair little sum of money, which Arthur, the eldest, had already increased ten-fold. He was *sly* and *slow* and *uneducated* also, and spoke with a *broad accent*. But he was not bad-looking, a *tight* fellow with big *blue eyes*, who aspired to keep his '*h*'s' in the right place, and would have been a *gentleman* if he could.

Against her usual habit, Alvina . . . *blue eyes and tight figure . . . keen . . . sly . . . slow . . . crept . . . tight . . . keen . . . creeping slyly . . . power.* He wanted *power* – and he would *creep* quietly after it till he got it: as much as he was capable of. His '*h*'s' were a barbed-wire fence and entanglement, preventing his unlimited *progress*.

(pp. 76–7; Camb. edn, 57–8)

The reasons for perceiving Alvina as focalizer in passage 11 have been given; a similar case could be made for character focalization in the short paragraph ending with the first sentence of 12. But the next paragraph, 'Arthur Witham, the plumber, came in . . .', seems to switch to the narrator's point of view with the shift from the family-relational expression 'her father' to the impersonal designation 'James Houghton', which we find no reason to attribute to Alvina's consciousness. But revisiting passage 11, we now find it lexically cohesive[20] with the preceding narrative matter and with the two sentences at the end of our passage 12: I have picked out the words and phrases concerned in italics. The character focalization apparently illustrated in 11 is now no longer so distinct as first appears: back in context, Alvina's sexual and social perceptions seem one with those of the narrative frame. The word 'tight', for example, no longer signifies Alvina's sexual perception – an area of her consciousness which needs to be made concrete for the reader because of the motivation problem – but is a term from an external ideology of sex used by the narrator and then put into her mouth. John Worthen remarks that Alvina 'does not learn anything from the experience [of the Withams] because she is simply sharing the narrator's stand-point'.[21] Worthen's position (if I may use my technical terms to paraphrase him) is that whatever merit the novel has is due to the persona of a narrator that the discourse of the early part of the novel has created: the 'matey', discursive, ironic, man-to-man, Dickensian discourse. This discourse can handle 'humours' like James Houghton or Mr May, *objectivized* characters as Bakhtin would call them. It cannot allow any sense of subjectivity, individual focalization, to any characters, and specifically not to Alvina: 'Although Alvina is apparently the sympathetic centre of the book, it is not her business either to understand her father or to communicate her understanding to us.'[22]

In passing I would like to mention one aspect of this novel that I have not yet studied thoroughly: the absence of free indirect discourse. There are many passages (for example the moments when first Alvina and then Miss Frost respond mentally to Mrs Houghton's death) where we find instances of a colloquial tone promising internal consciousness, juxtaposed with narrative or literary diction – as in passage 11/12, in fact. But the distinctive deictic markers are absent, the balancing of character's 'now' with narrator's 'then' which yields the delicate dialogue found in Jane Austen and so widespread in the modern novel.

Discourse analysis has so far allowed us to confirm Worthen's insight: passage 9 above illustrates the discursive triumph of the book, the Dickensian narrator of the early chapters;[23] that technical triumph permits comically imagined focalizations like 10, but undermines 11. But surely the problem goes deeper. The discourse of the narrator is the superficial problem; the deeper problem is that this 'matey', discursive *narrator* is not free of the ideology of the *implied author*. Alvina's vision of Witham, even in the humorous passage 11, is framed by Lawrence's stereotypes of women's sexual perceptions of men: woman as *voyeur*, watching him while his head is under the sink, like Ursula and Gudrun watching Gerald Crich swimming (*Women in Love*, Chapter 4); admiring his 'hindquarters' as Ursula feels the 'full, rounded body of [Birkin's] loins' (*WIL*, 353; Camb. edn, 314).[24] This fascination with the common, inarticulate man, whether gamekeeper, plumber, collier, gypsy, is an important part of Alvina's response to Cicio, granted; but it does not individualize her, for it is an inclination which Lawrence attributes to many of his women characters.

It is, I think, very significant that Lawrencian discourse intrudes into character's discourse in a passage like 11/12, for the simple reason that it is not stylistically foregrounded. Just contrast passage 6 above (page 56), allegedly Alvina's focalization of her first sexual encounter with Cicio; it is quite obvious that the discourse partakes of the style of many other Lawrencian set pieces concerning sexual activity and feelings: this could readily be shown by an analysis of the metaphors (darkness, heaviness, mystery), of the negatives (horrible, kill), the hyperbole, the transitivity structures (lover as agent, woman as patient). The point of view of the implied author is not so salient in 11/12, but it is perhaps more subversive for that reason; and the extract is characteristic of much of the text.

One more extended sequence at a point in the story critical for Alvina's psychological history, and for the establishment of her motivation, comes in the chapter 'Two Women Die' (pp. 58–66; Camb. edn, 42–9). The deaths of her mother and of her beloved Miss Frost, and the withdrawal of her father to his crack-brained business fantasies, leave Alvina free to build a new life and relationships. Page 58 (Camb. edn, 42) concerns the last months of Mrs Houghton's life. Alvina (rather than the mother) is the centre of narrative attention here, but she is not the focalizer. We have physical portraits of her sitting in her mother's room, thin, still and pale; she shows no response, and that is clearly part of the point. There are also sections of generalization in the chatty, essayistic discourse of the dramatized narrator: 'To sit still – who knows the long discipline of it, nowadays, as our mothers and grandmothers knew . . .'. Then, on Mrs Houghton's death, there begins a more intimate style: 'Alvina cried also: she did not quite know why or wherefore. Her poor mother!' (pp. 58–9; Camb. edn, 42–3). Judging from the colloquial register and the subject matter, this passage looks set to go into free indirect discourse, but the narrator immediately takes over. He explains that 'Alvina had the old-fashioned wisdom to let be, and not to think'; readers will notice the recurrence of the judgement 'old-fashioned', applied to Alvina by the narrator one page earlier, and here the cue for the re-entry of narrative discourse. The remainder of the long paragraph on page 59 (Camb. edn, 43), and the two short ones following it, explain and comment on Alvina's refusal to reflect on her mother's life, in an aphoristic, repetitive, polysyllabic style uncharacteristic of the taciturn Alvina, but typical of the initial narrative discourse: 'This super-cilious and impertinent exploration of the generation gone by, by the present generation, is nothing to our credit. . . . Wisdom has reference only to the past. The future remains forever an infinite field for mistakes', and so on.

This process of supersession of character's focalization by narrator's commentary is repeated in relation to Miss Frost's reaction to the death:

13 Miss Frost, however, meditated bitterly on the fate of the poor dead woman. Bitterly she brooded on the lot of woman. Here was Clariss Houghton, married, and a mother – and dead. What a life! Who was responsible? James Houghton. What ought James Houghton to have done differently? Everything. In short, he should have been somebody else, and not himself. Which is the *reductio ad absurdum* of idealism.

(p. 59; Camb. edn, 43)

Clearly the narrator speaks the last sentence, breaking in on what had seemed to be a representation of Miss Frost's consciousness. He continues with almost a whole page of energetic retort, a diatribe against the demands on women written in the rhetorical style of a bigot at the Club. The oral style of pages 59–60 (Camb. edn, 43–4) full of exclamations and questions, make this piece of text seem dialogic, but it is not genuinely so: it is quite one-sided; no alternative position is addressed. It is a posture, of course, part of the dramatiz-ation of a certain kind of narrator; we do not need to posit 'sincerity' of these judgements, and take against them. But even if we make that concession, it remains the case that the characters have been given very little space.

The next section of this narrative sequence (bottom paragraph of page 60 to middle of page 63; Camb. edn, middle of page 44 to middle of page 46) has

Alvina sorting out her late mother's things, and settling to running the housekeeping of Manchester House. The rhetoric is quiet, the references domestic. Here, Alvina's situation is at its closest to that of Anna Tellwright; there is even a reference to James Houghton's miserliness (p. 61; Camb. edn, 44–5), recalling Ephraim's. Then, on impulse, she descends her father's coalmine (p. 63; Camb. edn, 46). Structurally, this is not unlike Anna's guided tour of Henry Mynors's works. But where Bennett gives us a documentary of pottery manufacture, Lawrence concentrates on his heroine, and for her the pit and the colliers offer a sexual awakening. The process begins with the speech of the miner who is showing her around (passage 2, page 56 above). As he speaks, the collier stretches 'his bare, grey-black, hairy arm across her vision'; 'his presence edged near her, and seemed to impinge on her'; it is to Alvina a sexual closeness:

14 There was a thickness in the air, a sense of dark, fluid presence in the thick atmosphere, the dark, fluid, viscous voice of the collier making a broad-vowelled, clapping sound in her ear. . . . She felt herself melting out also. . . . Her lungs felt thick and slow, her mind dissolved, she felt she could cling like a bat in the long swoon of the crannied, underworld darkness. Cling like a bat and sway forever swooning in the draughts of the darkness –

(p. 64; Camb. edn, 47)

Coming out of the pit (or out of her 'swoon'), she finds the dismal mining landscape suffused with golden light: 'What a pretty, luminous place it was, carved in substantial luminosity' (p. 64; Camb. edn, 47). Underground, by contrast, is like Hades or like an Egyptian tomb. The miners are 'slaves of the underworld', 'grey from head to foot, distorted in shape, cramped, with curious faces that came out pallid from under their dirt' (p. 65; Camb. edn, 48); they are 'figures of fairy-lore' (p. 66; Camb. edn, 48). Lawrence expresses Alvina's response with the odd word 'nostalgia'; it is instantly replaced by an explicitly (if unconsciously) sexual 'craving':

15 The curious, dark, inexplicable and yet insatiable craving – as if for an earthquake. To feel the earth heave and shudder and shatter the world from beneath. . . .
   . . . the slow, dreadful craving . . . a craving insatiable and inexplicable . . . at this time she did not translate it into a desire, or need, for love. At the back of her mind somewhere was the fixed idea, the fixed intention of finding love, a man.

(p. 66; Camb. edn, 48–9)

The discourse of these pages is quite new to Alvina's consciousness, and it is quite distinct from that of the dramatized narrator. It is 'Lawrencian'. Lawrence uses it to define a craving for a particular kind of sexual object, a common, physical, inarticulate man.

   In using the label 'Lawrencian' without explanation, I am relying on my readers to construe my sense. There is a distinctive style which Lawrence applies to the topic of female desire in other writings. Readers who are familiar with Lawrence will, by intertextuality, construct a point of view for this passage which is external to Alvina's consciousness, indeed external to *The Lost Girl*. As a matter of fact, there is a quite specific link which is likely to be made. Pages 63–6 (Camb. edn, 46–9) of *The Lost Girl* use precisely the same materials as are deployed to characterize an analogous development in Gudrun's sexuality, a development which moves to the same preference although fulfilled in a different sort of man (see *Women in Love*, 128–30 and 11–12; Camb. edn, 115–17 and 11–12). The resemblances are so striking and so detailed that it is unnecessary to go to any length to prove the interdependence. The same gold light bathes the ugly landscape which is parallel even down to the phallic cabbage stumps ('stood shameless', *WIL*, 12; Camb. edn, 11). There is the topos of the underworld with its 'powerful, underworld men who spend most of their time in the darkness' (*WIL*, 128; Camb. edn, 115). There is the same 'broad dialect . . . curiously caressing to the blood. It seemed to envelop Gudrun in a labourer's caress, there was in the whole atmosphere, a resonance of physical men, a glamorous thickness of labour and maleness, surcharged in the air' (ibid.). The words 'nostalgia' and 'crave' occur (p. 129; Camb. edn, 116); 'their voices . . . affected Gudrun almost to swooning. They aroused a strange, nostalgic ache of desire, something almost demoniacal, never to be fulfilled' (130; Camb. edn, 117). There are many other correspondences of phrasing and of situation; and an overall functional parallelism, the two women being shown to develop, in this world of male physical industrial work, the same ambivalent but powerful sexual feelings.

Textually speaking, one of the novels 'borrows' heavily from the other. Lawrence scholars might wonder which way round it is, but the history of the writing of *The Lost Girl* is so obscure that we could never be certain.[25] The 'slaves of the underworld' passage could have been written in 1913 or in 1920, before or after *Women in Love* was written. The question is not really material to the present argument, which concerns discourse rather than text *per se*. In the 'slaves of the underworld' sequence, what is claimed to be a unique and private experience of a character, supposedly focalized by her, is conveyed in a mode of discourse quite external to her, indeed evidenced in other texts by Lawrence.

In a sense I have made a *structural* point about *The Lost Girl*, suggesting that Alvina's consciousness is subordinated to authorial ideology, and supporting this suggestion by citing sections of the novel and referring to other writing by Lawrence. It is not simply a structural point, but a point about the role of the reader in actualizing a text as discourse. Let us think about this from the point of view of readers of the present day in their/our cultural situation. For readers, Lawrence's works have been institutionalized in a very specific, indeed normative, way; the contents page of any introductory survey, or critical overview, will show this. The canon is dominated by the three 'great' or 'major' early novels, which are kept in print, widely discussed by critics, read at school, offered for comment in literature examinations. The 'other writings' are categorized appropriately as 'poems', 'novellas', 'travel writings', 'essays', etc. Any that are problematic are likely to be read against the reader's experience of *Sons and Lovers*, *The Rainbow* and *Women in Love*, which are probably read early and leave a powerful impression. For such a reader, the 'Lawrencian' discourse of passage 6, of 'slaves of the underworld', and other parts of the novel is probably already securely established by the earlier experience of the three big novels. Finding it here, such a reader is unlikely to experience it as just one voice among others in a polyvocal text. It is the dominant, already charged with authorial values which obstruct the individualization of Alvina.

Notes

1 Graham Hough, *The Dark Sun* (New York, 1957), 91.
2 See Michel Foucault, *The Archaeology of Knowledge*, Appendix: The discourse on language (London, 1974). A linguist who bases his notion of discourse explicitly on Foucault is Gunther Kress, *Linguistic Processes in Sociocultural Practice* (Victoria, 1985). For the idea that varieties of language encode representations of the world in terms of categories, see particularly M. A. K. Halliday, *Language as Social Semiotic* (London, 1978); Halliday cites the sociologists of knowledge Peter L. Berger and Thomas Luckmann, *The Social Construction of Reality* (Harmondsworth, 1967), esp. 172ff. in support of the view that language, particularly conversation, is of the greatest importance in maintaining the individual's subjective representation of reality. Antonio Gramsci − *Selections from the Prison Notebooks* (London, 1971), 323, 331 − in a nice phrase speaks of 'spontaneous philosophy' which is 'contained in . . . language itself, which is a totality of determined notions and concepts'.
3 The Penguin text is inferior to the new Cambridge text: *The Lost Girl* [1920], ed. John Worthen (Cambridge, 1981); for instance, it reproduces several bowdlerizations effected by Secker for the first British edition (1981). I have used and quoted the Penguin version because it is the one most likely to be read and owned; the reader's experience of a text is significant in the present approach. [Page references to the Cambridge edition are given after the Penguin edition. *Ed.*]
4 Repetition of the key words relating to 'elegance', amounting to hyperbole, is the cue for an ironic interpretation. In technical terms this is a case of 'flouting the maxim of quantity', i.e., saying more than is justified. See H. P. Grice, 'Logic and conversation', in P. Cole and J. L. Morgan (eds.), *Syntax and Semantics*, vol. 3, *Speech Acts* (New York, 1975), 41−58.
5 M. A. K. Halliday, 'Linguistic function and literary style: an inquiry into the language of William Golding's *The Inheritors*', in S. Chatman (ed.), *Literary Style: A Symposium* (London and New York, 1971), 330−65; Halliday, *Language as Social Semiotic*; Roger Fowler, *Literature as Social Discourse* (London, 1981); Roger Fowler, *Linguistic Criticism* (Oxford, 1986).
6 Lawrence had promised in 1912, 'I shall do a novel about Love Triumphant one day. I shall do my work for women, better than the suffrage' (letter to Sallie Hopkin, quoted by Worthen, *The Lost Girl*, 1981). The library copy of the Cambridge edition which I consulted had a damaged spine and was extensively pencilled with the symbol ♀, signalling a vigorous engagement in feminist debate. For some feminist receptions of Lawrence see Anne Smith (ed.) *Lawrence and Women* (London, 1978) and Janet Barron's essay in this volume.
7 Michel Foucault, 'What is an author?', in Josué V. Harari (ed.), *Textual Strategies* (London, 1979), 141−60.
8 Roland Barthes, *S/Z*, trans. Richard Miller (London, 1975); Roland Barthes, 'From work to text', in Harari, *Textual Strategies*, 73−81.
9 Mikhail Bakhtin, *Problems of Dostoevsky's Poetics*, trans. R. W. Rotsel (Ann Arbor, 1973).
10 Brian McHale, 'Free indirect discourse: a survey of recent accounts', *Poetics and*

the Theory of Literature, 3 (1978), 249–87; Ann Banfield, 'Narrative style and the grammar of direct and indirect speech', *Foundations of Language*, 10 (1973), 1–39.

11 Gérard Genette, *Narrative Discourse*, trans. Jane E. Lewin (Ithaca, N.Y., 1980).

12 Cf. Charles A. Ferguson, 'Diglossia', *Word*, 15 (1959), 325–40.

13 See Roger Fowler, 'Polyphony and problematic in *Hard Times*', in R. Giddings (ed.), *The Changing World of Charles Dickens* (London, 1983), 91–108.

14 Frank Kermode, *Lawrence* (London, 1973), 96.

15 William Labov, *Sociolinguistic Patterns* (Philadelphia, 1972).

16 See Roger Fowler, 'How to see through language: perspective in fiction', *Poetics*, 11 (1982), 213–35; and Fowler, *Linguistic Criticism*, ch. 9.

17 Hough, *The Dark Sun*, 92.

18 Kermode, *Lawrence*, 97. Cf. John Worthen, *D. H. Lawrence and the Idea of the Novel* (London, 1979), 111.

19 Katherine Mansfield, 'Notes on *The Lost Girl*' [1920], in R. P. Draper (ed.), *D. H. Lawrence: The Critical Heritage* (London, 1970), 144–5.

20 M. A. K. Halliday and Ruqaiya Hasan, *Cohesion in English* (London, 1976).

21 Worthen, *Idea of the Novel*, 109–10.

22 ibid., 110.

23 My colleague George Hyde finds the key to the book in the Russian Formalist Eichenbaum's concept of *skaz*, a self-conscious heightening of oral display which would explain the mannerisms of the narrator, Mr May, the Natchas, and so on. This account of the novel will be given in his forthcoming book on Lawrence, to be published by Macmillan in 1990. I think the concept is relevant, particularly in view of the narrator's obviously Dickensian pose, but this account does not for me solve the basic problem of point of view in *The Lost Girl*. I am grateful to Mr Hyde for many illuminating discussions of the novel and for commenting very beneficially on a draft of the present essay.

24 *Women in Love* [1920] (Harmondsworth, 1960) [Cambridge edition, 1987]. And see G. Wilson Knight, '"Through ... degradation to a new health" – a comment on *Women in Love*', in Colin Clarke (ed.), *'The Rainbow' and 'Women in Love': A Casebook* (London, 1969).

25 *The Lost Girl*, Worthen, xix–xl.

6 Lawrence and working-class fiction

Jeremy Hawthorn

D. H. Lawrence was only one of a number of writers of his generation who came from a working-class background; yet although Lawrence's fiction – and particularly his short fiction – has much in common with that of other working-class writers of his age, in many crucial ways it stands apart.

It can be helpful to view working-class fiction as a distinct, but not as a fixed or monolithic genre, nor as one always recognized as such by those who have contributed to it. Some writers indeed testify to a suspicion that the term 'working-class novel' separates off their work from the 'novel proper'.[1] Any attempt to define this genre must go beyond such matters as *the social origin* of authors and the *content* of their works. These issues are certainly important, but only in conjunction with a range of others: the publishing circumstances of the works concerned, the historical situation in which they were written and read, significant formal characteristics and the political-ideological impetus behind and within them.

Many working-class authors writing fiction dealing with their class of origin found (and still find) difficulty in placing their work with established book publishers, and this difficulty typically involved both political and ideological objections to what they had written. Paul Salveson, writing about the Lancashire turn-of-the-century novelist John Tamlyn, has pointed out that his two novels published in *The Northern Weekly* were both rejected because of their political content.[2] Robert Tressell's *The Ragged Trousered Philanthropists*, written a few years later, was published posthumously as a result of the efforts of Tressell's daughter, but only in a highly expurgated version. Tressell's publisher Grant Richards insisted upon significant cuts, and his insistence was clearly connected to his belief that the book was 'damnably subversive'.[3]

Such problems often led working-class authors to less conventional modes of publication, from circulation in manuscript amongst friends and workmates to publication in regional and/or socialist newspapers. And this in turn gave them a far more well-defined and familiar readership, as well as the freedom (even the pressure) to write from an overtly politically committed standpoint. A well-defined and intimately known readership, in turn, could have implications for both form and content, for the writer could now appeal to shared subject matter and story-telling traditions (often oral).

Such publishing circumstances could lead to a unique type of relationship between writer and reader: culturally close, but politically and ideologically distant, as the author imagined being read by people who needed to be converted to his 'subversive' views. We see this in classic form in Robert Tressell's *The Ragged Trousered Philanthropists*, but it recurs in a characteristic blend of celebration and criticism of working-class life and culture in much working-class fiction. Both celebration and criticism can lead into an overtly polemical or propagandist strain, usually socialist in politics.

It is commonly accepted that the novel as literary form has a strong historical connection with the middle class.[4] As a result of this association certain social factors have been recognized as having contributed to the novel's emergence, and perhaps thus incorporated into its maturing identity: individualism, secularism, privacy and the ideology of a market economy. In contrast, it is arguable that the life of the modern industrial working class is characterized more by *collectivism* than by individualism, a collectivism in which *public* rather than private values are dominant; in which the *community* rather than personal relationships are the site of the deepest human experiences, and *work* rather than leisure activities are central to living, thus producing a totally different set of assumptions concerning power, freedom and authority. Moreover, the *family* has a different form and function for working-class people than for the middle class, *parent–child relationships* are of a different sort, *gender roles* are not as they are in the middle class, and the experience of compulsory *education* is of an alien set of values rather than an extension of home values. And, finally, it has been argued that the working class has a fundamentally different relationship to *language*, privileging the spoken over the written and (to use Basil Bernstein's terminology) 'person' over 'status' oriented statements.[5]

In the typical working-class novel the stress is certainly less on individuals, 'inner selves' and personal relationships, and more on the group or community, and this is often connected with a focusing upon the life of a well-defined region: especially if the region includes a workplace such as a pit which is a dominant local employer. Characters are of interest as a result of their representativeness or typicality as much as by reason of their individuality or idiosyncrasy, and indeed an interest in the typical extends beyond the scope of characterization, and is part of a larger commitment to some form of realism.

Both in terms of the speech of its characters and in its own narrative techniques, working-class fiction is likely to betray the influence of oral as well as written narrative traditions, and such things as dialect, anecdote and gossip enter into it in both direct and indirect ways. Conversely, where working-class authors have attempted to make use of previously existing forms of fictional expression, they have often met with problems of 'fit' and familiarity.

What light does all this throw on Lawrence's fiction? Lawrence was not in any conventional sense a socialist, although socialist ideas and concepts won his (often temporary) assent at various stages of his life. And Lawrence certainly *left* the industrial working class through education, through work as a teacher and, eventually, by means of his adoption of the life of a writer and an exile. However, probably no falser comment on Lawrence and his work was made than that in a review of *The White Peacock* by Violet Hunt, in which she claimed that although readers of the novel would 'learn something of the mind of the classes who really returned them to the top of the poll, or turned them down', 'Mr. Lawrence is supremely unconscious of class. His characters simply do not know that class exists.'[6]

Mr Lawrence is, on the contrary, a writer who is supremely conscious of class. Whether we believe that he was a writer of 'working-class fiction' depends upon how we define this term. Moreover, so far as Lawrence's fiction is concerned, only a relatively small part is directly and predominantly concerned with the lives of industrial workers, although if we think more of his treatment of the families of industrial workers the count is higher. And Violet Hunt seems to have had no doubt who was going to read *The White Peacock*; at the time she was writing it is surely correct that few if any members of the industrial working class were going to read Lawrence's novel. For many working-class writers the obtaining of a working-class readership was a *political* imperative: there is no evidence for such an imperative in Lawrence's writing. Indeed, from the evidence of a novel such as *The Trespasser* one can say that, certainly early on in his writing career, Lawrence appeared more clearly concerned to obtain a middle-class audience.

However, Lawrence did come to obtain a significant readership among working-class people, and to exert a very considerable influence upon the development of working-class fiction. In a short but thought-provoking article Andy Croft has pointed out that by the mid-1930s Lawrence 'had somehow come to be seen as the archetypal working-class writer', and that 'for any aspiring working-class writer, particularly a miner, and particularly one from the East Midlands, Lawrence's example was unavoidable.'[7] Croft quotes a passage from Walter Brierley's novel, *Sandwich Man* (1937), in which a young miner from near Eastwood, a man with literary ambitions, looks at his world in terms of Lawrence's biography and Lawrence's novels, and he points out that any new working-class novel in the 1930s was likely to be compared with *Sons and Lovers* by reviewers. He further suggests that Lawrence's influence was responsible for persuading many aspiring working-class novelists to avoid overt political comment or commitment in their work. The point to stress, however, is that the obtaining of a large working-class readership came too late in Lawrence's career significantly to affect his writing.

Sid Chaplin, himself a working-class novelist, gives the following account of his first encounter with Lawrence's work in an interview published in 1984.

I remember, after one meeting, saying to a fellow called Enoch Goynes, who was an engine driver: 'Boy, have you read *The Everlasting Mercy*? Absolutely marvellous'. Masefield, you know. 'Tha come down to our house', he said, 'and ah'll give tha a book that knocks Masefield into a cocked hat'. He took me to his house, and he gave me a paper-covered first edition of *The Widowing of Mrs Olroyd* [sic]. I used to stay with my uncle all day, I had my bike and I can remember setting off about six o'clock and stopping at a street called Cobbler's Hall, and dying to look at this book, you know. I just sat down and read it there, on the dyke side. I'd never come across anything like this before. I knew about Jack Lawson, and I'd read *A Man's Life*. I also knew about Cronin, and had read *The Stars Looked* own in the *Daily Herald*. But all that paled into insignificance as I sat there reading. It was a major event in my life.[8]

This would have been in about 1932–3. Lawrence's work may well have struck home the more deeply so far as working-class readers were concerned precisely because it concentrated more on the felt realities of working-class life than on political preaching. It thus avoided the flatness of propaganda and the simplifications of the melodramatic that were endemic in much working-class writing of the turn of the century.

This is well illustrated by Lawrence's story 'Fanny and Annie'.[9] F. R. Leavis comments of 'Fanny and Annie' that 'though the given class-circumstances and *moeurs* are so essentially of the story, Lawrence's attitude towards his characters is not in any way affected by class-feeling.'[10] Leavis is engaged in refuting the charge of snobbery on Lawrence's behalf, and to this extent his argument is fair enough. But it seems to me that in this comment, and elsewhere in his remarks upon the short story in question, Leavis perhaps underestimates the way in which social class in the story is seen as an integral part of individual personality, and as inseparable from human relations and important life decisions. More than this: both the form and the content of the story (to use a crude distinction) can be understood only in relation to social class. 'Fanny and Annie' is 'working-class' not just because of its 'setting' or subject matter, but because the attempt to portray certain aspects of the life of working-class people *forces* Lawrence to find ways of representing experiences, attitudes, realities which are class-particular.

The problems of human relationships and of individual identity with which this story is concerned are inseparably connected with two rival sets of values: those associated with the middle class such as personal ambition, independence, upward social mobility; and those more public and communal values associated with the working-class. Such a concern is found again and again in working-class fiction, but where many other working-class writers *state* their interest in such a clash of values, Lawrence *enacts* this clash through the language and behaviour of the characters and without overt narrative statement or sermonizing or, most importantly, romanticizing working-class life.

We can note how the story starts by following Fanny's private thoughts; the 'voice' may be third-person omniscient, but the 'perspective' is Fanny's. In the opening stages of the story there is strong reliance on the technique of narrated monologue[11] as a means of displaying Fanny's private thoughts and feelings. However, the story finishes *outside* Fanny's consciousness, with the narrator providing us not with her or anyone else's private thoughts, but with the public statements and behaviour of the different characters. Strikingly, just when one might conventionally expect Fanny's private thoughts and feelings to be of the greatest interest – after the events during the chapel service – Lawrence seems to deny the reader access to them. It is as if Fanny's private thoughts and feelings are relevant only in the context of the aspirations to middle-class norms and values which she brings with her as she steps off the train at the start of the story. That these norms and values involve danger and unpredictability as well as the potentiality for gratification of Fanny's individualistic impulses, is suggested by the narratorial information about the 'brilliant and ambitious cousin, who had jilted her, and who had died'. This, in turn, helps us to understand the security offered by marriage into the working-class community, for here individual betrayal or disappointment can be compensated for by communal solidarity (as she and we are shortly to discover).

Seen in this way, what are otherwise puzzling aspects of the story become comprehensible. Why, for example, should Mrs Nixon's attack on Harry in the chapel seemingly have the effect of strengthening rather than weakening Fanny's resolve to marry Harry? In a middle-class context this would, surely, be the last straw, the final indignity: public humiliation. But Fanny's response is very mild. Surely this is because what Fanny is presented with in the chapel is a powerful, functioning, *public* set of norms: a community that *displays* its solidarity. So that although she witnesses an individual attack on Harry, she also receives a demonstration of the strength of community values and codes of behaviour, for the individual attack is launched within the confines of this larger set of rules. In contrast with this revealed communal strength, the poverty of Fanny's pretensions to gentility stand displayed – to her and the reader.

In common with many other writers with a background in the working class who have attempted to write about this class, Lawrence has recognized the cultural importance of the Sunday meal. Richard Hoggart, in *The Uses of Literacy*, gives a nostalgic description of the meal as he experienced it in his childhood:

> In our house we lived simply for most of the week; breakfast was usually bread and beef-dripping, dinner a good simple stew; something tasty was provided for the workers at tea-time, but nothing costing more than a few coppers. At the weekend we lived largely, like everyone else except the very poor, and Sunday tea was the peak. By six on that evening the middens up the back had a fine topcoat of empty salmon and fruit tins. Pineapple was the most popular because, in that period of what now seems extraordinarily cheap canned fruit, it could be bought for a few pence (there was a recurrent story that it was really flavoured turnip). Peaches and apricots were more expensive, and needed something approaching an occasion – a birthday or a sudden visit by relatives from a few miles away. The salmon was delicious, especially the red middle-cut; I still find it far 'tastier' than fresh salmon.[12]

The Sunday tea in 'Fanny and Annie' is a significant *cultural* event: the meal is the occasion for the family exchange of gossip and information, and the wealth and richness of the food – as Hoggart implies – are indicative of a cultural and human richness. The meal is no place for self-assertion, for personal advancement or private interests; there is no 'awkward silence' during the tea: the 'scandal' is discussed openly, and in the light of an assessment of the worth of the principal protagonists (the parents, interestingly, rather than the pregnant Annie: judgments of people concentrate on their standing within the community). In contrast to the opening of the story, the emphasis is upon the public and communal rather than the private and personal. People are measured not in terms of 'ambition' or 'brilliance', but in terms of their conformity to the norms of the community. And although we know that Lawrence himself frequently felt as much alienated from the working class as from the middle class, in this story there is no doubt that the reader is given a demonstration of the superiority of a certain sort of stable working-class collectivity to the depicted alternative: ambitious middle-class individualism.

Throughout Lawrence's fiction, certain sorts of food, particular eating rituals, serve as tokens of the peculiar collective intimacy of the working-class meal. For both Alvina in *The Lost Girl* and Connie in *The First Lady Chatterley*, grilled bloaters (and their smell) are seductively–repulsively imagined as quintessentially working-class, acting as tokens for a whole way of life. Interestingly, in both of these examples we have a *woman* who is *not of the working class*, responding with a mixture of fascination and repulsion to the food which betokens 'commonness'. When Lawrence sees the working classes, he habitually sees them at least in part as he imagines them to be perceived through middle-class eyes. Some explanation for this may be found in Lawrence's own history and psyche, but it may also stem from his nagging awareness of his potential middle-class readers. The primary meaning of 'commonness' is clearly 'unattractively working-class', but it is hard to avoid the feeling that there is also a partly suppressed recognition of the term's root meaning: 'belonging to a group rather than to an individual; shared'. And although the two examples are complex in their investigation of the inter-relations of sexual and cultural norms, we can note that both Alvina and Connie see a form of cultural liberation and sexual attraction in the common-ness towards which their feelings are so ambivalent.

A comparable mixture of attraction and repulsion can be witnessed in Fanny's attitude towards the community to which she returns. Early on in the story we learn that

> Fanny's aunt kissed her, and it was all Fanny could do to refrain from bursting into tears, she felt so low. Perhaps it was her tea she wanted.

The word 'low' has a social as well as a psychic or physical reverberation here; Fanny feels that her precarious and marginal social superiority is threatened by her aunt's kiss. Ironically, though, her use of the word 'tea' reveals how much she has in common with the culture she perceives as dangerous. (I am assuming that the last quoted sentence above gives us Fanny's consciousness through represented thought.) By the close of 'Fanny and Annie' such human contact is welcomed as an escape from loneliness and sterile isolation. In an odd sort of way, 'Fanny and Annie' gives us a movement in the evaluation of 'polite' and 'common' values that is like *Mansfield Park* turned on its head: is the name 'Fanny' altogether coincidental?

It is entirely appropriate that 'Fanny and Annie' should end with Fanny addressing her prospective mother-in-law as 'mother', almost as if she has decided to marry into the community rather than to ally herself with a particular individual. After Harry and Fanny have returned to the house subsequent to their attendance at chapel, Harry retreats more and more into the background. In the last page-and-a-half of the story he makes just one brief appearance in the text, whereas at the start of the story Fanny's thoughts are focused obsessively upon him. This general movement parallels Fanny's movement away from a concern with individuals and private values towards a perception of the community, its human relationships and its common values. Graham Holderness has argued that

> Whenever [Lawrence's] fiction confronts history with a truly comprehensive vision and unflinchingly faces the inescapably social nature of all human experience and human relations, its form is invariably tragic. Necessarily tragic, because Lawrence's own ideology prevented him from recognising or acknowledging any solution to the conflicts and contradictions of his society except those of personal evasion, transcendence or escape.[13]

It is in the light of such possibilities that, aesthetically, the lack of any imposed solution in 'Fanny and Annie' is something to be thankful for.

Leavis's comment on this story, then, wins only partial assent. Its narrative viewpoint is not affected by class feeling in the crude sense that members of one social class are portrayed as superior to members of another. But the story suggests that personal qualities are inseparable from class characteristics, and that significant moral choices cannot be made independent of considerations involving an awareness of social class. It should be repeated, too, that the formal characteristics of the story are not mere technical matters, but are in part reflective of the differing class cultures dealt with by the story. The shift from a heavy reliance upon narrated monologue to a dominant use of dialogue involves the adaptation of narrative technique to the life and characteristic modes of consciousness of the middle and working classes of Lawrence's time.

The narrative perspective of the story is not, however, wholly neutral. If it responds to the values of the working class, it also enacts those qualities of detachment and unemotional assessment which are more recognizably 'middle-class' than 'working-class'.

> Let us confess it at once. She was a lady's maid, thirty years old, come back to marry her first-love, a foundry worker: after having kept him dangling, off and on, for a dozen years. Why had she come back? Did she love him? No. She didn't pretend to. She had loved her brilliant and ambitious cousin, who had jilted her, and who had died. She had had other affairs which had come to nothing. So here she was, come back suddenly to marry her first-love, who had waited – or remained single – all these years.

The urbane, fleetingly ironic tone is recognizably middle rather than working class, and (as perhaps in *Mr Noon*) distances the narrator from the working-class culture described. If the story suggests no solution to the problems relating to social class that it highlights, it also implies that a middle-class viewpoint at least enables them to be recognized. Norman Page has contrasted Thomas Hardy's and Lawrence's ability to convey the richness of working-class speech in their fiction, focusing in particular on *Jude the Obscure* and *Sons and Lovers*. He suggests that whereas the dialogue of Hardy's novel is stilted and unconvincing, and reflects the great distance which now separated Hardy from the class about which he was writing, in scene after scene of *Sons and Lovers* 'one is filled with admiration for the sureness, the unobtrusive authority, of Lawrence's touch, and this includes a rendering of the social dimensions of speech.'[14] What

one wants to add is that not only can Lawrence reproduce the richness and
vitality of working-class speech in a natural and convincing manner, but that
he can present this through a narrative voice which masters a more urbane and
middle-class register. As Page argues, 'Lawrence's achievement [in *Sons and
Lovers*] was to fuse the novel of ideas with the dramatic rendering of "life
itself".'[15] Lawrence's ability to achieve such a fusion, to master such a range of
linguistic registers, is surely connected to his complex class identity: both 'in'
and 'apart from' the working class.

Typical of many working-class novels is the utilization of an anecdotal voice
in first-person narrative, a technique which brings a richness of oral narrative
traditions into the novel and, simultaneously, 'imports' a sympathetic
'listener/reader' into the text. It is doubtless partly for this reason that autobiography, and the autobiographical novel, have been popular with many
working-class writers. The first few lines of Jack Common's *Kiddar's Luck*
(1951) provide a representative example:

> She was a fool, of course, my mother. Her mother said so: 'Bella is a fool,
> I'm afraid, a weak fool. Here she is marrying a common workman, one
> who drinks and is not a good Christian. She will never know happiness
> now.' You would think the old lady was great shakes herself to hear her.
> And she was in her way.

Lawrence's fiction provides us with nothing quite like this. His first-person
narrators are less informal, less intimate with the reader, less unselfconscious
in their use of common idioms and less at ease in their use of direct address to
the reader.[16] *Kiddar's Luck* presents anyone who has read *Sons and Lovers* with a
familiar opening situation – the 'respectable' woman who falls for and marries
an 'ordinary' workman. And both novelists see this situation from the perspective of a sensitive son, more and more conscious of the mismatch between his
parents as he matures. But the familiar, intimate and colloquial narrative of
Kiddar's Luck forces us to perceive this relationship from within the culture,
whereas *Sons and Lovers* – for all that it is clear that the author is intimately
acquainted with this culture – does not. As readers, we are put into a quite
different relationship to what is narrated.

A similar contrast could be made with the work of Sid Chaplin. The editors of
his posthumous collection, *In Blackberry Time*, note that Chaplin's reverence for
old working-class raconteurs often led him to choose the form of one person
telling a story to another, and Chaplin has himself recounted the good advice a
Scots blacksmith called Alex Wylie gave him: 'Always read what you've
written. Read it aloud – and listen.'[17] Chaplin named Alex Wylie and D. H.
Lawrence as the two major influences on his writing, and it is instructive to
consider why he seems to have felt that Wylie gave him something that
Lawrence – for all that he admired him – did not.

The White Peacock has a first-person narrator, but he is a curiously anonymous
and formal individual, while the direct address to the reader of *Mr Noon* neither
springs from a personified or intra-diegetic narrator,[18] nor imparts a sense of
linguistic ease. And of course the bulk of Lawrence's major fiction is not written
in the first person but in an omniscient or semi-omniscient third person. The
nearest that Lawrence gets to the colloquial ease of Common's narrative, an

ease that draws the reader into a whole culture and its values through its language, is in a number of scenes in which *gossip* provides the narration: conversations in the pub in *The White Peacock*, Mrs Bolton's conversations with Clifford about the local characters in *John Thomas and Lady Jane*, and some of the conversations between ordinary people in short stories such as 'Strike Pay'. In such scenes Lawrence manages to unlock a collective narrative voice that has a substantial basis in social reality, and these passages have many parallels with scenes in novels and short stories by other working-class writers.

It is not difficult to understand why Lawrence found industrial working-class culture constrictive and imprisoning; he could not limit his narrative perspective to its confines but had to provide an external vantage point. For many other working-class writers such a need was a *political* imperative. It is well known that there is much telling in Lawrence's fiction, a telling that at its worst can be hectoring and intrusive. But the imperative for Lawrence is more social-intellectual than political. The industrial working class has traditionally had one vantage point on itself which is, paradoxically, both external and also of itself, internal but critical of the class. And that is the political vantage point – specifically that of socialism. Lawrence's non-acceptance of socialism forced him into a narrative perspective on the industrial working class which was, essentially, outside of the class. If we wish to stress the most important way in which Lawrence's work differs from that of other working-class authors, then perhaps we should draw attention to the way in which his political position – or positions – drove him to adopt a narrative perspective on his class of origin which was external to that class.

To state the obvious, collective manual *work* has been central to the personal and cultural identity of working-class people. Gilbert, in *Mr Noon*, refers directly to the identity that work provides. 'In their concerted activities, soldier or labor, they had all their significance.'[19] The statement mixes admiration with a contempt for the implied limitation, and when Gilbert talks of making his life with Johanna, and with his work, it is to *individual* work he refers. It is well known that Mr Morel appears at his most attractive and positive in *Sons and Lovers* when he is working, or talking about his work. But although we watch Morel mending boots or making fuses, and perceive the collectivity of work in the family co-operation that these tasks engender, Morel's work down the pit is witnessed only through his retrospective stories, never directly. In contrast to many other proletarian mining novels,[20] but in common with Lawrence's other novels and short stories in which mining figures, *Sons and Lovers* does not take us down the pit.[21] The reader shares the narrator's isolation from direct involvement in the collective work experience. The miners' powerful collectivity is witnessed in scenes such as the end-of-week paying of wages, but from the alienated perspective of Paul; and the origins of this collectivity in the work process are invisible in the novel. We witness Paul's work in the factory, but this is work of a different order from Morel's, and what we are most aware of is Paul's *witnessing* of the work of those beneath him.

Paul always enjoyed it when the work got faster, towards post-time, and all the men united in labour. He liked to watch his fellow-clerks at work. The man was the work and the work was the man, one thing, for the time

being. It was different with the girls. The real woman never seemed to be
there at the task, but as if left out, waiting.[22]

With the exception of a few of Lawrence's early fictional works, collective work
is something that is typically *observed* rather than *experienced* by his characters.
Gilbert Noon watches the mowers; unlike Tolstoy's Levin, he does not join
them. The work that is experienced in Lawrence is, normally, individual work.
There are no parallels in Lawrence to the detailed and extended descriptions of
work that we find in such novels as Robert Tressell's *The Ragged Trousered
Philanthropists* or Alan Sillitoe's *Saturday Night and Sunday Morning*, descriptions
that present the reader not just with the concrete actualities of the labour
process and labour relations, but also with the workers' mental responses to
these and to their own situation. It is difficult to imagine Lawrence making the
following statement:

> More than anything else in the world I honour and respect the skill of men
> working together in unison. It was one of the cardinal experiences of my
> boyhood. I reckon it is the highest point of human achievement. Now that
> it is embodied in me, I can never forget who I am or why I am living.[23]

Whenever Lawrence gets near to such sentiments (in *Mr Noon*, for instance) he
soon reacts against them and qualifies them from a far more detached and
individualist perspective.

Even the description of agricultural work at the start of *The Rainbow* is poetic
and mythological rather than realist. We have only to set this passage against
the 'mowing' sequence in *Anna Karenina* to appreciate that whatever its (very
considerable) poetic and evocative strengths, the point of view is not that of a
participant in the work. (The work experience that is dramatized for the reader
in *The Rainbow* is that of teaching, and it is Ursula's sense of *isolation* during her
time as a trainee teacher that is emphasized.)

In Lawrence's fiction we frequently find a detailed perception of the effects
of hard manual work – George's comment about sweat and sore hands in *The
White Peacock*, or Connie's shocked awareness of Parkin's work-damaged hands
in the earlier versions of *Lady Chatterley's Lover* – but Lawrence never gives us
the subjective experience of the collective communality of work. Working-
class communality in Lawrence is typically viewed from outside, rather than
presented as lived experience, and one reason for this is that that most
collective of all working-class experiences – co-operative work – is never
conveyed to the reader as lived experience in the way that the *domestic* culture
of the working class is.

Lawrence's view of the differential culture and ideology of men and women
from the working class obviously reflects a social reality – one especially
marked in areas dominated by the mining industry, for in Lawrence's time
women were debarred by law from work underground. Other working-class
writers have provided similar evidence for such a division to that which can be
found in Lawrence's work. It is, typically, the woman, more isolated at home
than the husband is at work, who is seen to have greater aspirations to
middle-class values, more desire for upward social mobility – especially for her
children by means of education and a middle-class job. Lewis Jones's Welsh

mining novel, *Cwmardy* (1937), shows us a working-class mother's desire that a son shall 'better' himself through education coming into conflict with the father's wish for the son to follow him down the pit. Lawrence's portrayal of Mrs Morel's taking the initiative in encouraging Paul to leave the industrial working class by the route of education seems to have been sociologically accurate, although of course hers is a more middle-class background than her husband's.

In Walter Greenwood's *Love on the Dole* (1933) the main character Harry objects to clerking as not 'men's work': he wishes to wear overalls and work in a factory – which is not what his wife-to-be wants. The narrator of Jack Common's *Kiddar's Luck* makes a similar point: 'Most of us [working-class schoolchildren] didn't want better jobs. We despised people who came home clean from their work and had in consequence a somewhat unreal and unaffirmed look, lacking the used coarseness of full men.'[24] As education is seen as the route out of the working class, then a sense of class solidarity can lead to a sullen male prejudice against doing well at school. Lawrence was aware that class solidarity could dissolve into philistinism and anti-intellectualism. The working-class attitude that combines class solidarity with intellectual openness and a valuing of education is typically a political one. When I worked in Wales I lost count of the number of people who reminded me that the University of Wales had been founded on the pennies of the working class. In Nottingham, as Lawrence sarcastically reminded readers of his poem 'Nottingham's New University', the University was built on the pennies of Sir Jesse Boot and his cash-chemist stores. The difference, and what lies behind it, may well be crucial to an understanding of aspects of Lawrence. Lawrence does not seem to have believed that a commitment to culture and to education could also be a commitment to his class of origin.

Notes

1 In an introduction written for a new edition of *Saturday Night and Sunday Morning*, Alan Sillitoe said of the novel that the 'greatest inaccuracy was ever to call the book a "working-class novel" for it is nothing of the sort. It is simply a novel . . .'. In an interview given shortly before his death, Sid Chaplin was asked if he saw himself from the start as a working-class novelist. He replied, 'Yes, yes, but at the same time with enough dignity and presumption . . . to see myself as a writer without any label.' Both comments can be found in Jeremy Hawthorn (ed.), *The British Working-class Novel in the Twentieth Century* (London, 1984). The first comes in David Craig's article, 'The roots of Sillitoe's fiction', 103, and the second in Michael Pickering and Kevin Robins, 'The making of a working-class writer: an interview with Sid Chaplin', 145.

2 Paul Salveson, 'Allen Clarke and the Lancashire school of working-class novelists', in H. Gustav Klaus (ed.), *The Rise of Socialist Fiction 1880–1914* (Brighton, 1987), 191–2.

3 Quoted by F. C. Ball, *One of the Damned* (London, 1973, reprinted 1979), 167.

4 The classic text here is Ian Watt, *The Rise of the Novel* (London, 1957). There is still some dispute around some of Watt's claims, but the general lines of his argument have been extremely influential.

5 Developments in sociolinguistics over the past two-and-a-half decades have

provided us with a range of new points of entry into the analysis of differences between middle- and working-class speech. To take just one example: the early work of Basil Bernstein offers some potentially fascinating points of entry into the language of Lawrence's characters and narrators. I lack the space to develop such possibilities here, but concepts such as 'the positional family', 'public language/formal language', 'restricted/elaborated code', and 'person/status oriented statement', all seem likely to have fruitful applications to the fiction of Lawrence and others – whatever criticisms Bernstein's work has (rightly or wrongly) been subjected to more recently. See the essays in Basil Bernstein, *Class, Codes and Control* (London, 1971).

6   Quoted in Andrew Robertson's introduction to the Cambridge edition of *The White Peacock* (Cambridge, 1983), xli.
7   Andy Croft, 'Lady Chatterley and D. H. Lawrence', *Artery*, VIII, n.d. (1985?), 50.
8   Pickering and Robins, 'Making of a working-class writer', 145.
9   D. H. Lawrence, 'Fanny and Annie', in *The Complete Short Stories*, (London, 1955, reprinted 1970), II, 458–72.
10 F. R. Leavis, *D. H. Lawrence: Novelist* (New York, 1956), 100.
11 Known as *Erlebte Rede* in German and *style indirecte libre* in French. In English various terms have been used, including 'Free Indirect Speech', which I myself used for many years. Recent developments in narrative theory have made 'narrated monologue' a more common term today, with 'represented speech' and 'represented thought' as additional terms allowing for the making of finer distinctions.
12 Richard Hoggart, *The Uses of Literacy* (London, 1957), 36.
13 Graham Holderness, *D. H. Lawrence: History, Ideology and Fiction* (Dublin, 1982), 19.
14 Norman Page, 'Hardy, Lawrence, and the working-class hero', in F. G. Tortosa and R. L. Ortega (eds), *English Literature and the Working Class* (Seville, 1981), 55.
15 Page, 'Hardy, Lawrence', 57.
16 Consider, for example, the awkward way in which the narrator of *Mr Noon* defends his use of colloquialisms such as 'spooning'.
17 Sid Chaplin, 'Seven years in a smithy', in *In Blackberry Time* (Newcastle, 1987), 90.
18 'Intra-diegetic narrator' – a narrator who lives within, and is a character in, the story told.
19 *Mr Noon*, ed. Lindeth Vasey (Cambridge, 1984), 228.
20 Those of Harold Heslop and Lewis Jones, for example.
21 A rare exception is to be found in 'Daughters of the Vicar' although it is revealing that the pit-work description is iterative rather than dramatic, generalizing rather than focusing upon particulars. And even here the consciousness entered is significantly alienated from those of his fellow workers.
22 *Sons and Lovers* (*Phoenix* edn, 1956), 112. Note again that the description is iterative rather than dramatic.
23 The quotation is from Sid Chaplin's autobiographical note 'Heart case', written in 1976 and published in *In Blackberry Time*, 200.
24 Jack Common, *Kiddar's Luck* (London, 1951, reprinted Glasgow, 1974), 105.

7 Lawrence and Germany: a reluctant guest in the land of 'pure ideas'

William Larrett

'It will adore tendenz, and influences. And for heaven's sake put in plenty of little poems or verses as examples.' This is the advice Lawrence gave his sister-in-law, Else Jaffe, when he suggested that she might like to write an article on modern German poetry for the *English Review*.[1] It is sound, seemingly straightforward advice for anyone about to embark on such a task; but its unmistakably ironic tone betrays a mocking stance directed not at Else or at the subject of modern German poetry, but at the intellectual game of literary criticism in which readers and writers alike collude. To locate Lawrence in any kind of historical framework or tradition, especially when linked with Germany and the history of ideas, is a particularly fraught enterprise because it fundamentally entails writing against the grain of his own temperament. Instead of mapping tendencies and charting influences, we should be 'bolting away to escape any further coil of pure ideas'. But if Germany is regarded by Lawrence as the greatest victim of the serpent of the Ideal, he also sees in Germany the greatest potential for freeing the rest of Europe from its clutches.[2] Let us, then, attempt to unwind some of the beast's coils to reveal something of the fascination, and repulsion, that Lawrence felt for this particular serpent. For in view of the ambiguity and ambivalence of Lawrence's attitude towards the German-speaking world, it is interesting to explore the extent to which this patent rejection of much that is German is offset by his latent espousal of attitudes, opinions, and epistemologies rooted in German rather than English literary and cultural tradition.

The possible influence of, for instance, Schopenhauer, of Nietzsche and of the intellectual circle to which Lawrence was introduced through his German wife, all these are issues which have already been explored.[3] What needs further examination is the longer tradition, the pervasive but masked effect of German culture and the German spirit on Lawrence. It leaves its mark on the young student and it is there in the writer of *Apocalypse*; but a work closer to the mid-point of his creative life, his essay 'The reality of peace' published in 1917, well illuminates the contradiction inherent in Lawrence's stance.

Despite its date and title, the reader who approaches the essay in the hope of finding out what D. H. Lawrence thought of the prospects for peace in 1917 will be disappointed. The peace with which the essay is concerned is 'the state of fulfilling the deepest desire of the soul', the peace that exists in the 'perfect consummation when duality and polarity is transcended into absorption',[4] and the creative dynamism of opposites suspended, briefly, in the flower of fulfilment. Yet whilst the essay makes no reference to Germany or things German, its central concept and image – polarity symbolized in the systole and diastole of the heart – derive from Goethe. Similarly, Lawrence's definition of peace as the deepest desire of the soul fulfilled in the transcendance of polarity seems to echo, in philosophical terms, one of Goethe's most famous poems, known to Lawrence in the early 1900s, his brief but intense 'Der du von dem Himmel bist', in which the yearning for peace emanates from a weariness caused by the ceaseless oscillation between conflicting emotions, both joyous and sad. And yet Goethe was a writer for whom, according to Aldous Huxley, Lawrence always felt the most 'intense repugnance'.[5]

Germany, its language and culture, began to play a part in Lawrence's life from the time he went to grammar school. When he applied for a job with J. H. Haywood Ltd, in September (?) 1901, Lawrence claimed he had received 'two prizes for mathematics, as well as one for French and German' (the latter not confirmed by the school records). It seems unlikely that his German was sound enough in the early 1900s to afford him *easy* access to more of German literature in the original than some of the simpler poems, or at least those which were familiar as *Lieder*. It was still far from expert – as letters of that time humorously report – when he first went to Germany in 1912. In September 1908 he wrote to Louie Burrows: 'My days are spent in uttering that mournful lament "Meine Ruh ist hin, mein Herz ist schwer" – "My peace is gone, my heart is sore" (Do you know "Gretchen at the Spinning Wheel"?)', and something of this is echoed in *The White Peacock*, when Lettie seems to tease and deliberately irritate Leslie by playing Schubert's setting of this song.[6] 'Gretchen am Spinnrade' is a simple, touching and seemingly artless song which Gretchen sings as she sits and spins and longs for Faust, her absent beloved. By playing it, albeit archly rather than artlessly, Lettie reveals the extent to which her own composure has been disturbed by her recent leave-taking of George Saxton. Such poems were used by Lawrence in the German lessons he gave Helen Corke in Croydon in 1909–10 as a means of lessening 'the grind of grammar books'. Again, this is reflected in *The Trespasser*, the novel based on Helen Corke's personal experiences: 'She was very fond of what scraps of German verse she knew. With French verse she had no sympathy; but Goethe and Heine and Uhland seemed to speak her language.'[7] It seems, however, that they never 'spoke' Lawrence's language; writing to A. W. McLeod from Germany in 1913, he says: 'I could send heaps of German books if you could read that floundering language, which is alien to my psychology and my very tissue. I should *never* be able to use German, if I lived here for ever.' And a month later he writes to his former pupil: 'Do you read much German? It is a beastly language, one that doesn't fit the cells of my brain.' Again, as late as 1929, he writes: 'I hate reading German, but will do so if necessary.' Despite these disclaimers, and almost at odds with them, he had written two reviews of German books early in 1912 *before* he had met Frieda, and one in 1913.[8] It is interesting to note that in his review of *The Oxford Book of German Verse* Lawrence suggests in his opening remarks that his own knowledge of German verse is wide ranging and based on fond enjoyment:

> This book seems to me extraordinarily delightful. From Walther von der Vogelweide onwards, there are here all the poems in German which we have cherished since school days. The earlier part of the book seems almost like a breviary. It is remarkable how near the heart many of these old German poems lie; almost like the scriptures. We do not question or examine them. Our education seems built on them. . . . Then again, so many of the poems are known to us as music.

In the course of this brief review, Lawrence chooses to quote in full two poems by contemporary poets: one by Detlev von Liliencron (1844–1909) and one by Richard Dehmel (1863–1920), both highly regarded at the time. His choice, however, seems a little arbitrary in that he quotes the *first* of those poems selected by Fiedler to represent Liliencron and the *last* of those by Dehmel. Furthermore, his singling out of these particular poets and his comments on them suggest that he has been influenced by what he has read in the introduction to Jethro Bithell's own anthology of contemporary German verse in translation, published in 1909, an anthology Bithell had even dedicated to Dehmel.[9] Nevertheless, Lawrence cannot have derived a very clear sense of the style, tone and manner of these or other German poets from Bithell alone, since this anthology does not include the German originals and Bithell's own versions adopt outmoded, stilted poetic devices so that the modern voice of these poets is lost in an almost weary English gentility.

Between 1901 and 1912, Germany for Lawrence is a source of ideas, music and literary impulses, the land of 'poets and thinkers'. Before March 1912 his experience of 'living' German derived largely from one of its generally acknowledged strengths, its lyric poetry. Perhaps, grown tired of England, love of German poetry predisposed him to consider applying for a post at a German university as *Lektor.* That he had a German uncle who, as a professor, must have seemed to Lawrence's young imagination the very antithesis of his uncultured coalminer father, may have also encouraged this choice (Fritz Krenkow had married Ada Rose Beardsall, the sister of Lawrence's mother).

However, German and Germany acquired a more intimate dimension in March 1912, when he met Frieda Weekley (1879–1956), German wife of Ernest Weekley, a professor at Nottingham University, whom Lawrence visited in connection with his plan to seek work in Germany. Frieda was the daughter of Friedrich, Baron von Richthofen, and thus belonged to a Prussian aristocratic family, perhaps better known on account of Frieda's distant cousin Manfred von Richthofen, the 'Red Baron', the legendary First World War fighter ace. Within a few weeks of meeting, Lawrence and Frieda eloped to Germany at the beginning of May 1912 and thereafter lived most of their life together abroad, with the exception of the war years 1914 to 1919, spent in England. Theirs was a globally nomadic existence; but they spent at least a few weeks of most years in Germany visiting Frieda's mother in Baden-Baden, and other members of her family, with whom Lawrence established a warm relationship, as his letters and fictional allusions reveal. Through Frieda, and especially her elder sister, Else, wife of Edgar Jaffe (professor of political economy in Heidelberg), Lawrence came into direct or indirect contact with several prominent Germans, including Otto Gross, a highly controversial psychiatrist, and the eminent sociologists, Max and Alfred Weber.[10]

Nevertheless, first-hand experience of Germany seems to have dulled the charm of German as a language, and it may be that he felt he had found a conformity and formalism that stifled life and its vital expression. Certainly, this is the main burden of his criticism of Thomas Mann's work, especially *Der Tod in Venedig* (1912) which Lawrence finds characterized by a very fine style wedded to a stale banality, having 'none of the rhythms of a living thing, the rise of a poppy'. It has lost its life-bestowing, life-affirming, Phoenix-like quality ('the rise of a poppy'). That in *Death in Venice* – as in other works of his – Thomas Mann may be calling into question the very validity of the nature and function of all art by spelling out its insidious threat is hardly an undertaking that Lawrence could endorse.

An awareness that the finest art depends on the delicate balance and interplay between form and feeling is to be found in Lawrence's early essay 'Art and the Individual', delivered as a paper at a meeting of the Eastwood Debating Society on 19 March 1908. This is an ambitious essay for a twenty-two year old student, impressive in the scope of its references and allusions, and one that testifies to a knowledge, however mediated, of some important German sources: Lessing, Schiller and Goethe. Lessing is merely alluded to – if, that is, the reference to the Laocoon group derives at all from Lessing's famous treatise on the subject. Schiller is referred to directly; and even if this knowledge is filtered mainly through Tolstoy, there is something about Lawrence's style and manner which suggests a better than second-hand acquaintance with Schiller's writing: in the sentence towards the end of the essay ('So we condemn one artist because, although he has a sumptuous manner, his feeling is shallow and unprofitable, and another because in the violence of his feeling he outrages art and offends us')[11] the balance of structure and rhythms and the measured authority of tone are remarkably reminiscent of Schiller's antithetical style and categories. (See – a work central to Lawrence's theme – Schiller's *On the Aesthetic Education of Man*,[12] particularly Letter XIII.) Finally, there is the reference to Goethe, of which Carlyle is the immediate source. As the relevant note in the Cambridge edition points out, Lawrence wrongly equates here the 'weaving for God the garment we see him by' (an important metaphor from Goethe's *Faust*) with the 'making of beautiful things', but it is possible that he has perceived intuitively that such a pantheistic vision – nature as the living garment of God – is embodied in and conveyed through a special use of language and that the lasting force of a metaphor such as the roaring 'Loom of Time' owes more to aesthetics than any kind of theology.

Lawrence's choice of the Laocoon as one of his significant examples of art in this essay must reflect the demonstrably strong impression made on him by this work, which he may well have first encountered as a photograph in Volume IX of *The International Library of Famous Literature*, illustrating the extract from Lessing's *The Limitations of Pictorial Art*.[13] His fascination with the work was enough to prompt him to send two postcards depicting it to Arthur McLeod and

Alice Dax on 26 August 1909, and he cites it again in an important letter to Henry Savage in 1914 (19 January):

> It [*The Rainbow*] is very different from *Sons and Lovers*. The Laocoon writhing and shrieking have gone from my new work, and I think there is a bit of stillness, like the wide, still, unseeing eyes of a Venus of Melos. I am still fascinated by the Greek – more perhaps by the Greek sculpture than the plays, even though I love the plays. There is something in the Greek sculpture that my soul is hungry for – something of the eternal stillness that lies beneath all movement, and under all life, like a source, incorruptible and inexhaustible. It is deeper than change, and struggling. So long I have acknowledged only the struggle, the stream, the change. And now I begin to feel something of the source, the great impersonal which never changes and out of which all change comes.

Behind these comments lies one of the best-known characterizations of Greek art ever formulated in German, Winckelmann's assertion that 'the universal and predominant characteristic of Greek masterpieces is noble simplicity and quiet greatness' (these last five words in German 'edle Einfalt und stille Grösse' have become almost proverbial).[14] Wincklemann continues:

> Just as the depths of the sea always remain calm, however the surface may rage, so does the expression of Greek figures, however strong their passions, reveal a great and dignified soul. Such a soul is depicted in the face of Laocoon, and not only in the face, despite his most violent torments. The pain which is evident in every muscle and sinew . . . nevertheless causes no violent distortion either to the face or to his general posture. He raises no dreadful cry [kein schreckliches Geschrei], as in Virgil's account.

The parallels between Lawrence's letter and the above quotation are clear enough, and the echoes become even stronger if instead of 'no dreadful cry' one substitutes 'no hideous shriek' as a translation of 'kein schreckliches Geshcrei', a substitution which may provide us with a pointer to the source of Lawrence's apparent familiarity with the Winckelmann passage. Where he did *not* find it is in the extract from Lessing's Laocoon essay contained in Garnett's *International Library of Famous Literature*, for although Lessing does quote the entire Winckelmann passage at the beginning of Part I of his own essay, the Garnett extract, being but a translation of Part IV only, does not include this passage. The possible alternative source, at once more likely and surprising, is De Quincey, for it is he who translated 'kein schreckliches Geschrei' with 'no hideous shriek',[15] and Lawrence's letter also seems closer to De Quincey's rendering: 'even so the expression in the figures of the Greeks, under the uttermost tumult of passion, indicates a profound tranquillity of soul'.

Of course we cannot know for certain whether Lawrence knew De Quincey's translation or not. Obviously, Frieda or any other member of her circle in Germany might have introduced Lawrence to the Winckelmann essay, but we do know that Lawrence was an admirer of De Quincey, that he was quoting from De Quincey as early as 1905 and, more importantly, that he possessed De Quincey's collected works in an edition so much used and so well thumbed that it needed rebinding.[16] Before pursuing this thread further, however, there is the question as to what Lawrence's letter, with its allusion to Laocoon and the temper of Greek sculpture, tells us about *The Rainbow* and, for that matter, about *Sons and Lovers*.

Lawrence recognized a considerable difference between the two novels: to Edward Garnett (11 March 1913), 'It is all analytical – quite unlike *Sons and Lovers*, not a bit visualised'; and again to Edward Garnett much later in the year (30 December 1913), 'It is very different from *Sons and Lovers*: written in another language almost. I shall be sorry if you don't like it, but am prepared. I shan't write in the same manner as *Sons and Lovers* again, I think – in that hard, violent style full of sensation and presentation.'[17] Are the 'Laocoon writhing and shrieking', the 'visualisation' (cf. 'the still, unseeing eyes of a Venus of Melos'), the 'hard violent style full of sensation and presentation' now regarded by Lawrence merely as a weakness: too physical, too intimate and personal an expression of his own 'struggle and change'? Or was the writhing and shrieking of a Virgil's Laocoon a stage which had to be passed to reach a style more closely akin to that of the sculptor of Laocoon, able to evince 'eternal stillness' in such essentially optimistic and confident visions as that with which *The Rainbow* ends:

> And the Rainbow stood on the earth. She [Ursula Brangwen] knew that the sordid people who crept hard-scaled and separate on the face of the world's corruption were living still, that the rainbow was arched in their blood and would quiver to life in their spirit, that they would cast off their horny covering of disintegration, that new, clean, naked bodies would issue to a new germination, to a new growth, rising to the light and the wind and the clean rain of heaven. She saw in the rainbow the earth's new architecture, the old, brittle corruption of houses and factories swept away, the world built up in a living fabric of Truth, fitting to the over-arching heaven.

If one compares this with the last lines of *Sons and Lovers*, the stylistic difference between the two novels immediately becomes clear, as does the note of transition:

> 'Mother!' he whispered – 'mother!' She was the only thing that held him up, himself, amid all this. And she was gone, intermingled herself. He wanted her to touch him, have him alongside with her.
>
> But no, he would not give in. Turning sharply, he walked towards the city's gold phosphorescence. His fists were shut, his mouth set fast. He would not take that direction, to the darkness, to follow her. He walked towards the faintly humming, glowing town, quickly.

Here the sentences are short, almost staccato. Attention remains concentrated on Paul right up to the end of the novel, whereas at the end of *The Rainbow* the personality of the observer (Ursula) is subordinated to the importance and meaning of her vision, expressed in expansive prose that embodies the sweep of the rainbow, the words carefully balanced: *hard-scaled, horny/clean, naked; corruption, disintegration/germination, growth; sweep away/build up;* culminating in the final polarity of *brittle corruption of houses and factories* and *living fabric of Truth*. It is a passage which recalls the beginnings of Goethe's *Faust* Part II, where Faust reflects upon the constant regeneration of nature and perceives in the rainbow an apt symbol of human endeavour;[18] it also anticipates – just – the language and style of some of the most famous examples of German Expressionist literature, notably the closing vision of 'the new man' ('der neue Mensch') of Kaiser's play, *Die Bürger von Calais*, of 1913.

Common to the endings of both novels is a new beginning, universal in the former and personal in the latter. Paul's turning towards the 'faintly humming, glowing town' is an affirmation of life; he does not follow his mother into darkness in the way that Aschenbach, at the end of Mann's *Der Tod in Venedig*, follows Tadzio's beckoning into death. Intimated, too, in the determination of 'His fists were shut, his mouth set fast' is the end of the writhing and shrieking. In *Sons and Lovers* Lawrence has 'shed his own sickness and become master of his emotions' (20 October 1913).

In his autobiography Goethe wrote in similar terms, when he recalled the writing and reception of his first novel, *Die Leiden des jungen Werther*, which De Quincey thought 'for mere power was the paramount work of Goethe'[19] – a phrase which is about the sum total of De Quincey's praise of Goethe! More typical is De Quincey's view of another novel, *Wilhelm Meister*:

> We do not wish to offend the admirers of Goethe; but the simplicity of truth will not allow us to conceal that in various points of description or illustration, and sometimes in the very outline of the story, the *Wilhelm Meister* is at open war, not with decorum and good taste merely, but with moral purity and the dignity of human nature.

And even this is mild compared with what he wrote in 1824 in a review for the *London Magazine*.[20] He accuses Goethe of 'always travelling into the byways of unnatural or unhallowed interest', and continues: 'Suicide, adultery, incest, monstrous situations, or manifestations of supernatural power, are the stimulants to which [Goethe] constantly resorts in order to rouse his own feelings, originally feeble . . .'. The review continuing in the same vein, concludes with a 'History of Mr Meister's "Affairs of the Heart"', leading to the final judgement that: 'Thus we have made Mr von Goethe's novel speak for itself. And whatever impression it may leave on the reader's mind, let it be charged upon the composer. If that impression is one of entire disgust, let it not be forgotten that it belongs exclusively to Mr Goethe.'

I have quoted De Quincey on Goethe at some length in order to suggest that Lawrence's sweeping and persistent rejection of Goethe derives in no small part from De Quincey, whose work he enjoyed so much: '[De Quincey] is a *very* nice man – I can go on reading and reading him. I laughed over "Goethe" yesterday. I like him, De Quincey, because he also dislikes such people as Plato and Goethe whom I dislike' (23 October 1919). When Lawrence expands upon his own dislike of Goethe, it is very much in terms that echo De Quincey. None the less his words do of course imply that he had himself read some of Goethe's works. For instance, when he dismisses Goethe's poem 'Das Tagebuch' ('The Diary'),[21] he denies it any claim to 'purity'. Writing to Aldous Huxley on 27 March 1928, he includes Goethe in a list of 'grand perverts' who tried to 'kick off, or to intellectualise and so utterly falsify the phallic consciousness', and describes *Wilhelm Meister* as:

> amazing as a book of peculiar immorality, the perversity of intellectual sex, and the utter incapacity for any *development* of contact with any other human being, which is peculiarly bourgeois and Goethean. Goethe *began* millions of intimacies, and never got beyond the how-do-you-do stage, then fell off into his own boundless ego. He perverted himself into perfection and Godlikeness.

In attacking Goethe's understanding and portrayal of the workings of human sexuality, Lawrence seems to be trying to impose upon life an essentially reductive and simplistic pattern of behaviour, and is himself open to the charge of intellectualizing and curtailing the phallic consciousness. In similar vein he condemns one of Heine's simplest, shortest and, on the face of it, most innocent poems 'Du bist wie eine Blume', comparing it unfavourably with Burns's 'My Love is like a red, red rose'.[22] In Heine's poem he sees the sentimentality of the 'elderly gentleman' which is 'the sure sign of pornography'. In Burns's poem there is, by implication, and to quote from his remarks about Goethe's 'Das Tagebuch', the 'purity of pure fulfilment'.

The popular view of Goethe the Olympian, the 'Godlike', was probably enough in itself to arouse the iconoclast in Lawrence. His prejudice against Goethe might have been fuelled early by an illustration, itself a prize example of that almost swooning admiration, depicting Goethe skating on the ice in Frankfurt, basking in the rapturous gaze of female relatives. The artist, in this 'kitschig' picture, has taken his cue from Goethe's mother who describes her son on the ice, decked out in her own shawl, as 'a young god'.[23] This picture is to be found in Volume X of Garnett's *International Library*, within the section devoted to a translation of most of Book One and a short extract from Book Three of Goethe's *Wilhelm Meister*.

Mr Noon provides another instance of the same dislike: a passage that rails at Goethe for 'godlifying' and 'olympizing' himself, and reproaches Napoleon for not giving Goethe a kick in the rump instead of pronouncing 'Voilà un homme'.[24] This view of Goethe's encounter with Napoleon contrasts ironically with Nietzsche's sexist and/or racist interpretation of the same episode, in which he suggests that Napoleon's 'Voilà un homme' was as much as to say: 'But there is a *man*! And I only expected to see a German.'[25] 'Man' is emphasized here as opposed to 'woman', implying that Napoleon regarded Goethe as the exception in a race that had lost its virility.

Whilst it seems very unlikely that Lawrence would have accepted this estimation of Goethe – indeed he was either unaware of or quite unmoved by Nietzsche's high regard for Goethe – Nietzsche's concern for national virility provides an interesting gloss on Lawrence's own experience and perception of Germany in the 1920s. In a letter from Baden-Baden in 1924, he writes: 'Germany is queer – seems to be turning as if she would make a great change, and become manly again, and a bit dangerous in a manly way. I hope so . . . there is a certain healthiness, more than in France, far more than in England, the old fierceness is coming back' (9 February). Four years later, the 'I hope so' has become 'I'm afraid', as Lawrence now registers the development that has taken place, presciently noting the drift into nationalism and materialism: 'The German youth is almost ready to fuse into a new sort of fighting unity, it seems to me: us against the world. But the English are older, and weary even of victory' (7 January 1928). The threat of such a development is increased for Lawrence because it, too, can be regarded as a manipulated mental construct,[26] something implanted from without, and therefore – as the product of cerebration and suggestion – not susceptible to the restraint of genuine human feelings from within. As Lawrence writes on 22 July 1929, reiterating his abiding stricture of the Germans: 'They make up their feelings in their heads, while their real feelings go all wrong. That is why Germans come out with such startling and silly bursts of hatred.'

Without entering upon the rights or wrongs of such an analysis, one must note that Lawrence presents it here as if there were in Germany no cultural tradition concerned with the quest for wholeness of character and the achievement of the right creative balance between the head and the heart, and yet such a concern was of paramount importance to German Enlightenment and Sensibility in the late eighteenth century.

Of course, to recall the eighteenth century in Germany is to conjure up the spirit of idealism which in turn, for Lawrence, inevitably implies renunciation, antagonist of the 'life-passion' itself. It is the clash of 'Du bist wie eine Blume' versus 'My love is like a red, red rose'. However, Goethe, author of 'Das Tagebuch', can embrace both poles, recognizing the indispensability in human affairs of both renunciation and the Phoenix. Lawrence's 'Ah, how many times have I, myself, been shattered and born again, still while I live'[27] has its counterpart in Goethe's 'Die and become! Until you possess this truth, you are but a dismal guest upon the dark earth.'[28] The passion that is all-consuming yet vouchsafes new growth denotes for both Lawrence and Goethe a courageous openness to life. This is the systole and diastole of life.

The beating of the heart is the most fundamental instance of all the double rhythms, oscillations and alternating sequences, of all antitheses, separations and couplings, attractions and repulsions, that together go to make up life. It is the notion that lies at the heart of 'The reality of peace', and it is a notion that occurs over and over again in manifold guises in the writings of Goethe. Compare Lawrence's: 'Perhaps the decay of autumn purely balances the putting forth of spring. Certainly the two are necessary each to the other; these are the systole–diastole of the physical universe' with Goethe's: 'Thus does every breathing-in presuppose a breathing-out and vice versa, and thus does every systole anticipate its diastole. It is the eternal formula of life that is here made manifest.'[29]

The note in the Cambridge Edition of 'Study of Thomas Hardy' referring to this image, which Lawrence also employs at the beginning of that essay, cites Emerson's 'Compensation' (1841) as the probable source of Lawrence's examples of polarity, especially as this essay was also to be found in *The International Library of Famous Literature* (Vol. XV). But Emerson was himself strongly influenced by Goethe from the time of Carlyle's translation of *Wilhelm Meister* in 1824. Ten years later, he bought Goethe's *Collected Works* and without previous knowledge of German set out to read all fifty-five volumes in the original, a task he had more or less completed by 1840! Part of the precipitate of that endeavour is to be found in 'Compensation', where passages alluding to Goethe's scientific studies borrow from Goethe almost verbatim.

The rhythm of relationships, the swing between love and hate, between withdrawal and reconciliation, between secure togetherness and isolation, are all instances of the polarity that Lawrence explores in his work. The consummation devoutly to be wished is the achievement of peace that results – in the terms of *Women in Love* – from 'a conjunction, where man had being and woman had being, two pure beings, each constituting the freedom of the other, balancing each other like two poles of one force'. This same sense is conveyed elsewhere in *Women in Love*, and in *The Rainbow* particularly, through the image of the arch, which stands secure as a result of the equipoise of forces pushing down upon it.

In *Aaron's Rod* husband and wife are unable to resolve their struggle and achieve any kind of harmony. Theirs is a battle of unyielding wills expressed in an image that recalls the Laocoon: 'But when he *had* to come home, there was her terrible will, like a flat cold snake coiled round his soul and squeezing him to death.' What peace Aaron finds, once separated from his wife and family, is that of a 'defined situation'; but it remains 'a situation without a solution'. What Aaron does achieve is greater self-knowledge and a clearer sense of his own identity. This he is able to do because he has dropped the mask, 'his conscious mask', which hitherto had had to do 'all the duty of the man himself'. Aaron's awareness of what has happened and his insights into its significance and implications for him and his future behaviour are contained in Chapter XIII, a pivotal chapter coming at the midway point in the novel and bearing the enigmatic title 'Wie es Ihnen gefällt'.

Why should Lawrence have chosen a German title for this chapter? He was careful in his choice of chapter headings, so it seems unlikely that he simply stuck his thumb into his pie of possible titles and pulled out this particular plum. What is there about Chapter XIII that warrants a German title? The fact that the chapter begins on Aaron's first morning at the house of Sir William Franks in Italy makes its title at first seem all the more out of place. It may be that the philosophic issues raised in the course of the chapter, the blend of insight and reflection within the mind of the hero, to which only the author and reader are privy, simply seemed to Lawrence to fall more readily under a Geman label that points to the homeland of *Geist*.

But of that homeland the praise of Lessing, Herder, Goethe and Schiller made Shakespeare an adopted son. When faced with the phrase 'Wie es Ihnen gefällt', it is impossible for anyone with some knowledge of Germany's culture not to hear it as a near echo of *Wie es euch gefällt*, which is Schlegel's translation of *As You Like It*. ('Ihnen' is the polite form of 'you', either singular or plural – here in the dative as the verb requires – and 'euch' is the familiar form of 'you' plural.) Lawrence's oblique allusion to this famous comedy of masks[30] provides Aaron's musings on the nature of his own true self with an older frame of reference. Within the freedom of his self-imposed 'exile', it is easier for him to drop the mask. Jacques's observation (in *As You Like It*, Act 2) that 'all the world's a stage, and all the men and women merely players' is reiterated and confirmed in Aaron's perception that his hosts and the other guests 'talked and manoeuvred with their visible personalities, manipulating the masks of themselves'. Aaron himself, however, having dropped his conscious mask and with it the need to apprehend the world through language, can continue in a state of 'wordless comprehension'; leaving the fine complexities of discursive understanding to the gentle, 'German' (*Wie es Ihnen gefällt*) reader. It may be added that the heading of the novel's last chapter is 'Words', which, despite the weightiness of the issues it contains, must have the sense of 'mere words', thereby undermining their validity.

The dilemma faced by Lawrence when beset by the contradictory needs of both exorcizing and conveying the intrusive, distorting nature of language is not unique to him. Nor is it a theme peculiar only to German thought, though it does inevitably loom large in a literature with strong roots in mysticism and pietism, a literature in which the dominant concern is with the articulation of inner states, truths and feelings. It is the perceived primacy of this that both attracts and repels Lawrence so strongly. A moment experienced by Will Brangwen, looking at some pictures of the statues which are the main glory of Bamberg Cathedral, puts it in a nutshell:

> He lingered over the lovely statues of women. A marvellous, finely-wrought universe crystallised out around him as he looked again, at the crown, the twining hair, the woman-faces. He liked all the better the unintelligible text of the German. He preferred things he could not understand with his mind. He loved the undiscovered and the undiscoverable.
>
> (*The Rainbow*, Ch. 6)

Will is enthralled by something German but *Gothic*, a product of the Middle Ages and hence, in a Ruskinite, pre-Raphaelite sense, artlessly expressive. The thrilling expressiveness of the statues is, however, further enhanced for Will precisely because the German text is unintelligible to him and consequently cannot get in the way of, or contaminate, his instinctive pleasure and comprehension with 'word-ideas'. Will's preference for the 'things he could not understand with his mind' anticipates Aaron's realization, at the end of *Aaron's Rod*, that 'he understood oh, so much more deeply than if he had listened with his head'. Yet the text also reveals the subtle irony of the linguistic imprint of the German on the narrator, in the very un-English but decidedly German form 'woman-faces' (cf. *Frauengesichter*) and in the pairing of two adjectival nouns to express the mystery not to be clothed in the garment of words.

In many respects, in view of the circumstances of Lawrence's life, it is surprising that so much of what can be said about his relationship to the German cultural tradition must remain tentative. Specific references are relatively few, and there is little to suggest a systematic or thorough reading of any German authors, perhaps because the language remained 'alien to his very tissue'. There is no sustained critical commentary, as there is of English and American authors, none of the marvellously perceptive insights such as those, for example, that Hardy and Melville inspire. And yet so often one is aware of an undercurrent of categories and distinctions which are German in origin, categories which are clearly not alien to Lawrence's psychology, ones which accord with his own intuitive wisdom, or ones by which his own intuitive wisdom is informed. Sometimes the masking of German sources seems to be deliberate, at other times one cannot be sure. When Lawrence has Lilly, at the end of *Aaron's Rod*, reject Nietzsche's form of the will-to-power as too intellec-tual in order to define his own version as 'dark, living, fructifying power' – which is, in fact, much more Nietzschean – he seems to be distorting Nietzsche to disguise his espousal of him. And when towards the end of his last work, *Apocalypse*, Lawrence dwells on the distinction between allegory and symbol, he does so in words which are so close to Goethe's own definition of the two that the congruence can hardly be fortuitous.

Goethe has been cited often in this article because Lawrence's attitude towards the German tradition is most strikingly exemplified by his dismissive opinion of Goethe. Any evaluation of the German tradition has to come to terms with Goethe, and this Lawrence does, as we have seen, in a peremptory manner which seems to invest Goethe with a certain emblematic function. Often the vigour of Lawrence's pronouncements stems from an aphoristic and partial – in all senses of the word – comprehension on his part. With a quick, eclectic mind and imagination such as Lawrence's, a word, a name, will suffice to trigger further elaboration. All is grist to the mill of his fertile brain, all a part of the process of creative assimilation and transformation succinctly expressed by Schiller in his maxim: 'Selbst Gebildetes ist Stoff nur dem bildenden Geist' (Even what has already been given shape is but raw material to the shaping spirit).

Notes

1 In a letter to Else Jaffe of 10 February 1913.
2 [Germans and English], *Phoenix II*, ed. Harry T. Moore and Warren Roberts (London, 1968), 247.
3 See especially: Emile Delavenay in *D. H. Lawrence, A Composite Biography*, ed. Edward Nehls (Madison, 1957), I, 66–70; the chapter on *Women in Love* in Ronald Gray, *The German Tradition in Literature 1871–1945* (Cambridge, 1965); Martin Green, *The Richthofen Sisters* (New York, 1974); Kingsley Widmer, 'Lawrence and the Nietzschean matrix', in Jeffrey Meyers (ed.), *D. H. Lawrence and Tradition* (London, 1985), 115–31; Colin Milton, *Lawrence and Nietzsche* (Aberdeen, 1987); H. M. Robinson, 'Nietzsche, Lawrence and the somatic conception of the good life', *New Comparison*, 5 (1988), 40–56.
4 *Phoenix*, ed. Edward D. McDonald (London, 1936), 693.
5 *The Letters of D. H. Lawrence*, ed. Aldous Huxley (London, 1932), xvi.
6 *The White Peacock*, ed. Andrew Robertson (Cambridge, 1983), 167f.
7 *The Trespasser*, ed. Elizabeth Mansfield (Cambridge, 1981), 101.
8 'A review of *The Oxford Book of German Verse*, ed. H. G. Fielder' and 'A review of *The Minnesingers*, ed. Jethro Bithell', both in *English Review*, January 1912; re-printed in *Phoenix II*, 269–72. 'German books: Thomas Mann', *Blue Review*, July 1913; reprinted in *Phoenix*, 308–13. Certainly, the Mann review suggests a con-siderable command of German, but this may reflect Frieda's influence and help.
9 For the 'Bithell' connection I am indebted to an unpublished D.Phil. thesis by Peter Fjågesund, 'Apocalyptic and Millennial Ideas in D. H. Lawrence: A Contextual Exploration' (Oxford [Bodleian Library], 1988), 155f.
10 For further details see Green, *The Richthofen Sisters*, and Robert Lucas, *Frieda Lawrence, The Story of Frieda von Richthofen and D. H. Lawrence* (London, 1973).
11 'Art and the Individual', *Study of Thomas Hardy and other Essays*, ed. Bruce Steele (Cambridge, 1985), 142.

12 Friedrich Schiller (1759–1805); his treatise *On the Aesthetic Education of Man* (1795) is available in English, edited and translated by Elizabeth M. Wilkinson and L. A. Willoughby (Oxford, 1967).

13 Gottfried Ephraim Lessing (1729–81); his *Laocoon* was first published in 1766. *The International Library*, ed. Richard Garnett (London, 1899), 20 vols., was, according to Jessie Chambers, 'one of the most treasured possessions of the Lawrence household'.

14 Johann Joachim Winckelmann (1717–68); *Thoughts on the Imitation of the Painting and Sculpture of the Greeks*, 1755. (Both the Lessing and the Winckelmann essays are available in English in *German Aesthetic and Literary Criticism: Winckelmann, Lessing, Hamann, Herder, Schiller, Goethe*, edited and introduced by H. B. Nisbet (Cambridge, 1985).)

15 *De Quincey's Collected Writings*, ed. David Masson (London, 1897), XI, 166.

16 See Catherine Carswell, *The Savage Pilgrimage, A Narrative of D. H. Lawrence* (London, 1932, reprinted London, 1951), 119: 'On this occasion he gave us his tattered but complete set of De Quincey's works, with the hope that we might be rich enough to have them rebound.'

17 *Letters*, I, 511.

18 *Faust*, Part II, Act 1, ll. 4725–7.

19 *De Quincey*, IV, 417.

20 This and the following quotations taken from *De Quincey*, XI, 247 and 256. (The essay on *Wilhelm Meister* is immediately preceded by De Quincey's translation of *Laocoon*.)

21 'Das Tagebuch', an erotic poem by Goethe, first published in 1910. Lawrence's view expressed on a postcard to Sir Thomas Dacre Dunlop, 22 January 1916. For a fuller account of the contrasting attitudes of Goethe and Lawrence, see Elizabeth M. Wilkinson, 'Sexual attitudes in Goethe's life and works', in *Goethe Revisited* edited by Elizabeth M. Wilkinson (London, 1984).

22 'Pornography and obscenity', *Phoenix*, 180f.

23 Incident reported by Bettina von Arnim in her *Goethe's Correspondence with a Child*, part of which was also included in Garnett's *International Library*, XI.

24 *Mr Noon*, ed. Lindeth Vasey (Cambridge, 1984), 184. The meeting between Napoleon and Goethe took place in Erfurt on 2 October 1808.

25 F. Nietzsche, *Beyond Good and Evil, Complete Works*, ed. Oscar Levy (London, 1907), XII, 149.

26 Cf. *Phoenix*, 131, where Lawrence talks of the mass-consciousness of the Germans which does not derive from the individual as it does with other races: 'In short, the Teutonic mind, young, powerful, active is always thinking in terms of somebody else's experience, and almost never in terms of its own experience.'

27 *Mr Noon*, 227.

28 Last lines of Goethe's 'Selige Sehnsucht'; 'become' here has the sense of 'be transformed'.

29 *Phoenix*, 678; Goethe, *Theory of Colours*, Part III.

30 The possibility of a Shakespeare allusion here is strengthened by the fact that a later chapter is entitled 'Cleopatra, but not Anthony'. Also, *As You Like It* was one of Lawrence's favourite works, cf. *Phoenix II*, 597.

*

I should like to acknowledge my wife's many helpful suggestions during the preparation of this essay.

8 Lawrence, Dostoevsky, Bakhtin: Lawrence and dialogic fiction

David Lodge

Is there a life after deconstruction? Literary critics of a theoretical bent who would answer the question affirmatively these days are likely to place their faith in the work of the Russian 'postformalist' theoretician, Mikhail Bakhtin. He is, of course, himself dead (b.1895, d.1975), but the fact that much of his work has only recently become available, not only in English but also in Russian, makes it appear excitingly contemporary.

Bakhtin's appeal is very easy to understand. He combines a magisterial grasp of European literary history from classical Greece to modern times with an original and liberating theory of language and an illuminating typology of literary discourse. He is also an analytical critic of great perception and power. Marxists, humanists and formalists can all learn from him. But perhaps what makes Bakhtin's literary theory particularly valuable (certainly to the present writer) is that it is centred on prose fiction and comedy rather than on the genres of tragedy, epic and lyric privileged by traditional poetics. Bakhtin explains why the modern era has been dominated by the novel as a literary form, and at the same time offers a new and illuminating description of its formal character – a poetics of the novel, or a novelized poetics.

The object of this essay is to bring Bakhtin's theory and practice to bear on the fiction of D. H. Lawrence – primarily in the hope of enhancing our knowledge and understanding of the kind of literary discourse Lawrence produced, but also to test the usefulness of Bakhtin's concepts and analytical tools. I have tried to show elsewhere the relevance of Bakhtin to the work of James Joyce.[1] If Bakhtin's poetics of fiction proves relevant to another major modern novelist, generally considered antithetical to Joyce in his literary aims and techniques, it would be impressive testimony to the theory's explanatory power. I begin with a brief summary of Bakhtin's key ideas, drawn from the following sources, referred to subsequently by the abbreviations indicated: *Problems of Dostoevsky's Poetics [PDP]* (1963), a revised and much expanded version of a book called *Problems of Dostoevsky's Art* first published in 1929; *Marxism and the Philosophy of Language [MPL]* (1929), published under the name of Valentin Volosinov, but now thought to be largely the work of Bakhtin; *Rabelais and His World [R]* (1965); and four long essays recently published in English under the title *The Dialogic Imagination [DI]* (1981).[2]

Bakhtin, it might be said, rewrote the history of Western literature by developing a new typology of literary discourse, which is itself based on a new, post-Saussurean theory of language. Ferdinand de Saussure made modern linguistics possible by his distinction between *langue* (the abstract rules and constraints which allow language to function) and *parole* (the actual utterances which language-users produce). Saussurean linguistics is oriented to *langue*, as is transformational grammar and speech act theory. Recently linguists have become interested in the linguistics of *parole*, or 'discourse' as it is more commonly called, and in this respect they were anticipated by Bakhtin. According to Bakhtin, language is essentially social or *dialogic*. The words we use come to us already imprinted with meanings, intentions and accents of others, and any utterance we make is directed towards some real or hypothetical Other. 'The word in living conversation is directly, blatantly oriented towards a future answer word. It provokes an answer, anticipates it and structures itself in the answer's direction' (*DI*, 280).

This insight has several interesting entailments. To begin with, it gets us off the hook of deconstructionist scepticism about the possibility of meaning: instead of having desperately to defend the possibility of a fixed or stable meaning in isolated utterances, we can cheerfully accept that meaning exists in the process of intersubjective communication, since no utterance ever is truly isolated. Methodologically, it means that we cannot explain *parole* simply by reference to *langue*: an utterance can only be understood in context, a context that is partly non-verbal and involves the status of and relations between speaker, addressee and the object of reference. Literature provides illuminating representation of how this works in practice – especially prose fiction. For the 'canonized' genres – epic, tragedy and lyric – are what Bakhtin calls 'monologic': they seek to establish a single style, a single voice, with which to express a single world view. Even if individual characters express distinct and opposing views in such a text, nevertheless an all-pervasive poetic decorum, or the regularities of rhythm and metre, ensure that the total effect is one of stylistic (and ideological) consistency and homogeneity. Prose literature, in contrast, is dialogic or, in an alternative formulation, 'polyphonic' – an orchestration of diverse discourses culled both from writing and oral speech. 'The possibility of employing on the plane of a single work discourse of various types, with all their expressive capacities intact, without reducing them to a common denominator – this is one of the most fundamental characteristic features of prose' (*PDP*, 200). The dominance of the novel in the modern era is therefore explained and justified by its capacity to match the rich variety of human speech and to respect the ideological freedom that variety embodies. 'The one grand literary form that is for Bakhtin capable of a kind of justice to the inherent polyphonies of life is "the novel",' says Wayne Booth in his enthusiastic introduction to the latest translation of *Problems in Dostoevsky's Poetics* (*PDP*, xxii), echoing Lawrence's famous description of the novel as 'the one bright book of life'.

There are, however, in Bakhtin's writings two slightly different accounts of how the novel came to fulfil this grand cultural mission. In the first account, Dostoevsky played a crucial role: he *invented* the polyphonic novel, and thus decisively changed the possibilities of the form. Before Dostoevsky, the novel itself was monologic, inasmuch as a dominant authorial discourse – Tolstoy's, for example – controlled and judged the discourses of the characters, predetermining the resolution of the issues raised by the novel in the interests of some ideological *parti pris*. This is an argument that runs parallel at many points to the distinction between the classic realist text and the modern text put forward by some poststructuralist critics.[3] In Dostoevsky, in contrast, the authorial voice is never dominant, the characters are free to 'answer back', and the reader is confronted with the challenging, disconcerting, ultimately unresolved interaction of diverse discourses representing diverse attitudes and values, sometimes within the same speaking or thinking subject.

Later, it would seem, Bakhtin came to see the pre-Dostoevskian novel as already a dialogic type of literary discourse, and to trace its roots back to the 'serio-comic' genres of classical literature – Menippean satire, the Socratic dialogue and the satyr play. In feudal times this tradition of parodic, travestying, multivocal discourse was perpetuated in the unofficial culture of carnival. At the Renaissance its energies were released into the mainstream of literature by, pre-eminently, Rabelais and Cervantes, and in this fashion the novel was born, and flourished in all its variety – the picaresque, the confessional, the epistolary, the sentimental, the Shandean, the Gothic, the historical and so on. In the nineteenth century the novel achieved a kind of stability, a formal synthesis, and established its dominance over all other literary forms through the unparalleled richness and subtlety of its discursive texture, in which the interplay of narrator's speech and characters' speech, made possible by development of free indirect style, was particularly important. (The voice of the narrator in Chapter I of *Middlemarch*, for instance, ironically, teasingly, affectionately playing off the language of Dorothea's naive idealism against the language of the philistine community and both against the values of the implied author, is already dialogic in Bakhtin's terms.) What Dostoevsky did was to loosen the grip of the authorial discourse and allow the other discourses in the text to interact in more dramatic and complicated ways than the classic nineteenth-century novel allowed. He was an important but by no means unique innovator in this respect.

Bakhtin perhaps never quite managed to reconcile these two accounts of the evolution of the dialogic or polyphonic novel. There are obvious reasons for preferring the later, more gradualist version, since a scheme of European literary history which depends crucially on the work of a single author in a single literary tradition would seem to be inherently vulnerable. But of all Bakhtin's works it is his study of Dostoevsky that is most illuminating in connection with D. H. Lawrence. Before we proceed to the main topic of this essay, however, one more word of explanation is necessary, regarding Bakhtin's typology of fictional discourse.

There are three principal categories:

1 *The direct speech of the author*. This means, of course, the author as encoded in the text, in an 'objective', reliable, narrative voice.
2 *The represented speech of the characters*. This may be represented by direct speech ('dialogue' in the non-Bakhtinian sense); or by the convention of soliloquy or interior monologue; or in those elements of reported speech

which belong to the language of the character rather than the narrator in free indirect style.

3 *Doubly-oriented or doubly-voiced speech*. This category was Bakhtin's most original and valuable contribution to stylistic analysis. It includes all speech which not only refers to something in the world but also refers to another speech act by another addresser. It is divided into several sub-categories, of which the most important are stylization, *skaz*, parody and hidden polemic. *Stylization* occurs when the writer borrows another's discourse and uses it for his own purposes – with the same general intention as the original, but in the process casting 'a slight shadow of objectification over it' (*PDP*, 189). This objectification may be used to establish a distance between the narrator and the implied author, especially when the narrator is an individualized character, perhaps narrating his own story. When such narration has the characteristics of oral discourse it is designated *skaz* in the Russian critical tradition, though Bakhtin argues that the 'oral' quality is less important than the adoption of another's discourse for one's own aesthetic and expressive purposes. Stylization is to be distinguished from *parody*, when another's discourse is borrowed but turned to a purpose opposite to or incongruous with the intention of the original. In both stylization and parody, the original discourse is lexically or grammatically evoked in the text. But there is another kind of doubly-oriented discourse which refers to, answers or otherwise takes into account another speech act never articulated in the text: *hidden polemic* is Bakhtin's suggestive name for one of the most common forms.

Monologic literature is, of course, characterized by the dominance of category 1 in Bakhtin's typology of discourse. In most prenovelistic narrative (e.g., chivalric romance, moral fable) the authorial narrator does not merely impose his own interpretative frame on the tale, but makes the characters speak the same kind of language as himself. The eighteenth- and nineteenth-century novel allowed the individuality of characters' voices to be heard through such devices as the epistolary novel or free indirect style, and even admitted doubly-oriented speech to a limited degree (Bakhtin himself gives some good examples from *Little Dorrit* (*DI*, 303–7)). But clearly the fully dialogic novel is a comparatively modern phenomenon, marked by the attenuation of the first of Bakhtin's discourse categories and an increasingly subtle and complex deployment of types 2 and 3. Dostoevsky's *Notes from Underground*, for instance, one of his most original and distinctively 'modern' texts, is something of a virtuoso performance in the deployment of doubly-oriented speech, as Bakhtin ably demonstrates (*PDP*, 227–34).

There is nothing like *Notes from Underground* to be found in Lawrence's *oeuvre*. For one thing, he very rarely employed the technique Bakhtin calls *Ich-Erzählung*, narration by an 'I' figure. (The only texts of this kind I can think of are *The White Peacock* and the late story, 'None of That', not one of his best, which has two such narrators, one framed within the other.) Lawrence's fiction is remarkably consistent and homogenous in narrative method, invariably using an authorial narrator to frame and mediate the scenic or interiorized presentation of the action to the reader. This narrative voice is generally thought to be the dominant discourse in his fiction, and a formal characteristic that sets him somewhat apart from the modernist movement. I have myself written on another occasion:

> [Lawrence's] narrative voice, however much it varies in tone, from the shrewdly down-to-earth to the lyrically rhapsodic, and whatever character's consciousness it is rendering, is always basically the same, unmistakably Lawrentian. Not for him the mimicry, the pastiche, the rapid shifts of voice and linguistic register, that we encounter in Joyce or [T.S.] Eliot.[4]

This, it must be admitted, sounds more like a description of monologic than of dialogic discourse, and not an encouraging basis for a Bakhtinian reading of Lawrence. However, I think I exaggerated the homogeneity of Lawrence's narrative style, and in any case a variety of linguistic styles and registers is not in itself either a necessary or a sufficient criterion for the polyphonic novel. Bakhtin himself observes that in Dostoevsky's novels there is considerably less 'language differentiation, that is, fewer language styles, territorial and social dialects, professional jargons and so forth,' than in, for example, the work of the more monologic Tolstoy; that Dostoevsky has been accused by many critics (including Tolstoy himself) of a 'monotony of language': but that what makes a novel polyphonic is not the mere presence of different styles and dialects, but 'the dialogic angle at which these styles are juxtaposed and counterposed in the work' (*PDP*, 182). In other words, whereas in Tolstoy the variety of characters' speech is always contained and controlled by the author's speech, in Dostoevsky the characters' speech, though formally less differentiated and individualized, is freer in the way it generates and sustains a continuous struggle between competing interests and ideas. I should like to suggest that the same is true of Lawrence's most impressive mature fiction, and especially *Women in Love*. His development from *Sons and Lovers*, through *The Rainbow*, to *Women in Love*, was in fact a steady progression towards a kind of fiction which Bakhtin had already described in his study of Dostoevsky. There is irony in such an assertion, since Lawrence's recorded remarks about Dostoevsky are generally derogatory, and he expressed a strong preference for Tolstoy[5] but there may have been some 'anxiety of influence' behind those comments. Consider how exactly Bakhtin's description of *Crime and Punishment* applies to *Women in Love*:

> Everything in this novel – the fates of people, their experience and ideas – is pushed to its boundaries, everything is prepared, as it were, to pass over into its opposite . . . everything is taken to extremes, to its uttermost limit. There is nothing in the novel that could become stabilised, nothing that could relax within itself, enter the ordinary flow of biographical time and develop in it. . . . everything requires change and rebirth. Everything is shown in a moment of unfinalised transition.
>
> (*PDP*, 167)

Behind this observation there is another seminal distinction drawn by Bakhtin between the adventure novel and the social-psychological novel of everyday life. In the latter, the plot is articulated through family and class relationships, unfolded in historical or biographical time (such is the classic nineteenth-century novel of, say, Tolstoy or George Eliot) – there is, says

Bakhtin, 'no place for contingency here'. The plot of the adventure novel, in contrast, 'does not rely on already available and stable positions – family, social, biographical: it develops in spite of them. . . . All social and cultural institutions, establishments, social states of classes, family relationships, are no more than positions in which a person can be eternally equal to himself' (*PDP* 103–4). What Dostoevsky did, according to Bakhtin, was to put the adventure plot 'at the service of the idea' – in other words, to make it the vehicle for exploring profound spiritual and metaphysical problems, crossing it with apparently incongruous genres like the confession and the saint's life. *Women in Love*, too, is a kind of philosophical adventure story whose chief characters are questing, with religious fervour, for some new, ultimately satisfying way of life, at a moment of crisis for civilization. One of the most striking and 'experimental' features of this novel is its foregrounding of debates, arguments and moments of spiritual or erotic crisis and illumination, by relegating or deleting the kind of detail that we expect from the 'social-psychological novel of everyday life'.

This tendency is already observable in the later stages of *The Rainbow*, but in *Women in Love* it is taken much further, to a degree that breaks the mould of the traditional novel. The fine, tough mesh of social and kinship relationships and economic factors which conditions the actions of the protagonists in *The Rainbow* (and still more in *Sons and Lovers*) seems to melt away in *Women in Love*. Ursula's and Gudrun's parents, for instance, Will and Anna Brangwen, such powerful presences in *The Rainbow*, are diminished figures in the sequel, who scarcely impinge on the lives or consciousness of their daughters, even though the latter are still living at home. Little attention is given to the practical problems of life in *Women in Love*. The plot is arranged so as to leave the protagonists free to choose their fates – a small private income allows Birkin to give up his job, and his offer of marriage allows Ursula to give up hers. Gudrun agrees to become governess to Winifred Crich not out of economic necessity or self-interest, but as a stage in her relationship with Gerald: 'Gudrun knew it was a critical thing for her to go to Shortlands. She knew it was equivalent to accepting Gerald Crich as a lover' (*WL*, Penguin edn, 1960; Camb. edn, 234).

'Plot in Dostoevsky', says Bakhtin, 'is absolutely devoid of any sort of finalising foundations. Its goal is to place a person in various situations that expose and provoke him, to bring people together and make them collide and conflict – in such a way, however, that they do not remain within this area of plot-related contact but exceed its bounds' (*PDP*, 276–7). Just so in *Women in Love*: the exiguous plot – essentially a double love story – exists merely to bring the protagonists into contact and conflict, and the issues thus raised are neither resolved nor contained within the history of their relationships.

We can appreciate the point more clearly by invoking Frank Kermode's useful comparison between *Women in Love* and that classic nineteenth-century novel of two interlinked couples, *Middlemarch*.[6] The fortunes of the Victorian quartet are traced, in a scrupulously recreated historical context, through 'biographical time', determined at every point by social, familial and economic factors. There is no place for contingency here. *Women in Love*, in contrast, is set in a deliberately ambiguous period which has elements of both pre-war and post-war England, and the reader has little sense of the precise duration of the story. The most memorable events of this story are, precisely, contingent: the drowning of Diana Crich at the water party, for instance, Gerald's brutal control of his terrified horse at the level crossing, the release of the rabbit from his hutch, or Birkin throwing stones at the reflection of the moon. These events do not seem to belong to any pattern of cause and effect – they simply happen, arbitrarily, randomly or spontaneously, and are invested with meaning by the reactions of those who are involved as actors or as spectators. Even when the action does seem to be conventionally motivated, the enactment is usually highly unconventional. Hermione, for instance, strikes Birkin with the paper-weight out of anger, frustration and jealousy, but her murderous attack seems in excess of the provocation, just as Birkin's reaction seems remarkably free from the sense of outrage that would be 'normal' after such an experience.

This is not the place to attempt to say what *Women in Love* 'means'. There have been enough attempts already, and there is some danger that, in the process of trying to extract a coherent body of thought from the novel, one will 'monologize' it, as Bakhtin accuses some of Dostoevsky's critics of doing to the Russian novelist's work. 'The catharsis that finalises Dostoevsky's novels might be . . . expressed in this way,' says Bakhtin: '*nothing* conclusive has yet taken place in the world, the ultimate word of the world and about the world has not yet been spoken, the world is open and free, everything is still in the future and will always be in the future' (*PDP*, 166). This describes very well the ending of *Women in Love*:

> 'You can't have two kinds of love. Why should you!'
> 'It seems as if I can't', he said. 'Yet I wanted it.'
> 'You can't have it, because it's false, impossible,' she said.
> 'I don't believe that,' he answered.

Thus the novel literally ends, the dialogue between the hero and heroine still continuing. It began with a dialogue, between Ursula and Gudrun, about the pros and cons of marriage. In between there are scores of similar scenes, where couples, threes, quartets and larger groups of people conduct debates on issues that are general and abstract and yet of vital importance to the chief characters. Although Rupert Birkin is the principal spokesman for Lawrence's own ideas in the novel, and a kind of self-portrait, he is not allowed to win these arguments. There are no winners. *Women in Love* is not a *roman à thèse*. It has not got a single *thèse*, but several, of which Lawrence's treatment is remarkably even-handed.

We may take as representative of the novel in this respect, Chapter 3, 'Class-room', in which first Birkin, and then Hermione, visit Ursula's school where she is conducting a botany lesson. It is typical of this novel that there is no attempt to evoke the physical specificity of the classroom, or the individual or collective character of the children; they are the thinnest pretext for mounting the debate, and are soon dismissed. Hermione questions the value of education – 'When we have knowledge, don't we lose everything but knowledge?' Birkin questions her good faith – 'You have no sensuality. You have only your will and your conceit of consciousness, and your lust for power, to *know*.' And Ursula questions the value of Birkin's 'sensuality, the great dark knowledge you can't have in your head' (pp. 45–7; Camb. edn, 41–3). We know from other, nonfictional texts, that Lawrence himself believed in the value of such dark knowledge, but Birkin is not allowed to triumph in this scene – indeed, he is often made to look slightly ridiculous (e.g., 'There was silence in the room. Both women were hostile and resentful. He sounded as if he were addressing a meeting,' p. 48; Camb. edn, 44). The advantage is constantly circulating between the three participants in the debate, partly because the latter has a subtext of emotional relationships. Hermione is trying to ingratiate herself with Birkin and to 'upstage' Ursula, whom she recognizes as a potential rival: but Hermione's sentiments strike Birkin as a kind of caricature of his own. Exasperated by this, and driven by a desire to break away from Hermione's influence, he attacks her with brutal scorn. Ursula, for her part, is puzzled and disturbed by Birkin's behaviour and opinions, and yet irresistibly, almost unconsciously attracted by him. When both the others have gone, she weeps, 'but whether for misery, or joy, she never knew' (p. 49; Camb. edn, 45).

What makes this scene dialogic in the ideological as well as the purely formal or compositional sense (i.e., containing a lot of direct speech) is that the narrator never delivers a finalizing judgemental word on the debate or its protagonists. The narrator also 'circulates' between them. The narrator seldom speaks in a clearly distinct voice of his own, from a plane of knowledge above the characters: rather, he rapidly shifts his perspective on their level, and shows us now what Ursula is thinking of Birkin, now what Birkin is thinking of Ursula, now what Hermione is thinking of both of them, and they of her. This fluid, flexible handling of 'point-of-view' was always characteristic of Lawrence's writing, but it was not always so impartial. In the first part of *Sons and Lovers*, for instance, Walter Morel is represented much more objectively, externally, than Mrs Morel. He is evoked for us by description of his dress, behaviour, etc., often in summary fashion. We seldom get the actual movement of his thought represented in free indirect style. He is allowed to speak only in direct speech that is rendered alien and uncouth-seeming by its dialect features. The consciousness of Mrs Morel, on the other hand, like that of her son Paul, is often represented in free indirect speech that borrows its eloquence and well-formed grammar in part from the authorial narrator. Thus, although the narrator *tells* us that Mr Morel was as much a victim of the tensions within the family as any of the other members, we do not as readers *feel* this on our pulses. Mr Morel is made to seem the villain, the Other, by the mobilization of the most powerful discourses in the text against him.

At the other end of his career, Lawrence was apt to forsake the dialogic principle in a more blatant way. In the 'leadership' novels, and to some extent in *Lady Chatterley's Lover*, we do feel that Lawrence is writing the *roman à thèse*, that he has predetermined the outcome of the struggle he has set in motion, fixed the game and rigged the pack. In *Women in Love*, in contrast, the reader is bounced, bewilderingly, exhilaratingly, from one subject position to another, and made to feel the force of each. Of course, the relationship between Ursula and Birkin is meant to seem more positive and hopeful than the doomed, mutually destructive passion of Gudrun and Gerald; but the latter pair have their own nobility and eloquence, and the quality of their carnal knowledge does not seem so very different from some of the 'darker' passages of love-making between Birkin and Ursula. As Frank Kermode has observed, 'in this version of Lawrence's apocalypse, it is necessary for those on the side of life to comply with dissolution in such a way that it is hard to distinguish them from the party of death.'[7] Or, in Bakhtin's words, quoted earlier, about *Crime and Punishment*, 'everything is prepared, as it were, to pass over into its opposite.'

Ursula says to Hermione, of Birkin, 'He says he wants me to accept him non-emotionally, and finally – I really don't know *what* he means. He says he wants the demon part of himself to be mated – physically – not the human being. You see, he says one thing one day, and another the next – and he always contradicts himself –' (p. 330; Camb. edn, 294). Here the contradictions and instability of Birkin's (and Lawrence's) views are brought out by the quintessentially dialogic method of having them quoted by the baffled Ursula to an interested third party. The effect is ironic, almost comic. And, as we have seen, Ursula is left free to defend her own idea of love at the end of the novel. But in *The Plumed Serpent* or 'The Woman Who Rode Away', or *Lady Chatterley's Lover*, there is one privileged ideological position for the heroine to occupy, and towards which a dominant authorial discourse inexorably guides her.

So far, I have been describing the dialogic quality of Lawrence's fiction mainly in terms of the relationship between categories 1 and 2 of Bakhtin's typology of literary discourse – essentially, the dominance of the second type over the first, allowing a variety of subject positions to be articulated in the text without any obvious determination in favour of any one of them. But what about Bakhtin's third category, doubly-voiced or doubly-oriented discourse? It seems to me that we might usefully categorize some of the more heightened and rhapsodic passages describing erotic experience in *Women in Love* as 'stylization' in Bakhtin's terms. Consider, for example, this passage:

'You are mine, my love, aren't you?' she cried, straining him close.
'Yes,' he said softly.
His voice was so soft and final, she went very still, as if under a fate which had taken her. Yes, she acquiesced – but it was accomplished without her acquiescence. He was kissing her quietly, repeatedly, with a soft, still happiness that almost made her heart stop beating. 'My love' she cried, lifting her face and looking with the frightened gentle wonder of bliss. Was it all real? But his eyes were beautiful and soft and immune from stress or excitement, beautiful and smiling lightly to her, smiling with her. She hid her face on his shoulder, hiding before him, because he could see her so completely. She knew he loved her, and she was afraid, she was in a strange element, a new heaven round about her.

(p. 350; Camb. edn, 310–11)

This passage represents Ursula's sensations by borrowing words and phrases, syntax and rhythms, characteristic of the genre known today (somewhat anomalously) as 'romance' – i.e., the heroine-centred love story. I believe many readers, confronted with the passage out of context, would attribute it to a Mills and Boon author, or an earlier exponent of the same genre. It is not, admittedly, stylized or objectified to the extent of, say, the Nausicaa episode of *Ulysses*, but it is certainly comparable to the consciously Decadent prose in which Stephen Daedelus's sexual initiation is described in *A Portrait of the Artist as a Young Man*:

> It was too much for him. He closed his eyes, surrendering himself to her, body and mind, conscious of nothing in the world but the dark pressure of her softly parting lips. They pressed upon his brain as upon his lips as though they were the vehicle of a vague speech: and between them he felt an unknown and timid pressure, darker than the swoon of sin, softer than sound or odour.[8]

In each case, the echo of another discourse, a somewhat suspect written discourse, puts the reader on his guard against identifying to readily and deeply with the emotion of the character that is being described, against confusing sincerity with truth. Ursula's 'bliss' is genuine, and the moment is an authentic threshold to a new and more meaningful relationship with Birkin, but it is only a beginning. She still perceives this relationship in the unregenerate terms of sentimental 'love', and the language warns us of this. For her full initiation into the dark knowledge and power that Birkin offers her, Lawrence turns to a different kind of stylized discourse, borrowed from religious and quasi-religious sources – Biblical, gnostic, occult:

> He stood before her, glimmering, so awfully real, that her heart almost stopped beating. He stood there in his strange, whole body that had its marvellous fountains, like the bodies of the sons of God who were in the beginning. There were strange fountains of his body, more mysterious and potent than any she had imagined or known, more satisfying, ah, finally, mystically-physically satisfying. She had thought there was no source deeper than the phallic source. And now, behold, from the smitten rock of the man's body, from the strange marvellous flanks and thighs, deeper, further in mystery than the phallic source, came the floods of ineffable darkness and ineffable riches.
>
> (p. 354; Camb. edn, 186)

Such passages are often deplored and ridiculed by readers hostile to Lawrence, and treated with embarrassed shiftiness by his admirers. Obviously it is a very risky technique, and there will always be disagreement as to how successful it is in gesturing towards a reality on the other side of language ('she knew, as well as he knew, that words themselves do not convey meaning, that they are a gesture we make, a dumb show like any other –', p. 209: Camb. edn p. 186). But it would be absurd to suppose that Lawrence did not know what risks he was taking – that he was trying to write in a monologically referential style, and somehow failed to observe the normative stylistic criteria of elegance, precision and good taste. As Bakhtin says, 'If we . . . perceive stylisation or parody in the same way ordinary speech is perceived, that is as speech directed only at its referential object, then we will not grasp these phenomena in their essence: stylisation will be taken for style, parody simply for a poor work of art' (*PDP*, 185).

A story which illustrates this point very clearly is the late story by Lawrence called 'Things', a cruel but amusing portrait of his friends, Earl and Achsah Brewster.[9] Technically it is a very interesting piece, being in Bakhtin's terms a kind of stylized *skaz*. It begins:

They were true idealists, from New England. But that is some time ago: before the war. Several years before the war, they met and married: he a tall, keen-eyed young man from Connecticut, she a smallish, demure, Puritan-looking young woman from Massachusetts. They both had a little money. Not much, however. Even added together, it didn't make three thousand dollars a year. Still – they were free. Free!

Ah! Freedom! To be free to live one's own life! To be twenty-five and twenty-seven, a pair of true idealists with a mutual love of beauty, and an inclination towards 'Indian thought' – meaning, alas, Mrs. Besant – and an income a little under three thousand dollars a year! But what is money? All one wishes to do is to live a full and beautiful life. In Europe, of course, right at the fountain-head of tradition. It might possibly be done in America: in New England, for example. But at a forfeiture of a certain amount of 'beauty'. True beauty takes a long time to mature.

(*The Princess and Other Stories* [Penguin edn, 1971] 208)

The rhythm and syntax of this prose – its short, staccato sentences, moodless exclamations ('Ah! Freedom!'), its frequent qualifications and reservations, signalled by the words, *but, however, still* – all create the impression of an oral narrator, of someone speaking his thoughts as they come to him, without the logical ordering, sifting and polishing one expects from writing. More interesting still is the way that the diction seems to be borrowed from the character to whom it refers. It is not only the words 'Indian thought' and 'beauty' that are quoted from the speech of Valerie and Erasmus, though they alone are enclosed in inverted commas. *But what is money? All one wishes to do is to live a full and beautiful life. In Europe, of course, right at the fountain-head of tradition.* This is also a kind of quotation: it articulates the motivation of the couple in their own slightly precious language of idealistic connoisseurship. The implied author lets us hear his own accent and his own opinion in the parenthesis, 'meaning, alas, Mrs. Besant'; but for most of the story he reveals the superficiality of the couple's pursuit of the good, the true and the beautiful by describing it in their own kind of language. The style of the story is a kind of condensation of thousands of remarks, rhetorical questions, and reflections the characters might be imagined as having uttered or formulated mentally to themselves during the years covered by the story. And this discourse is *itself* a kind of doubly-oriented discourse, since it always seems to be anxiously aware of some other discourse – pragmatic, rational, sceptical – against which it is defending itself.

They explored Paris *thoroughly*. And they learned French till they almost felt like French people, they could speak it so glibly.

Still, you know, you never talk French with your *soul*. It can't be done. And though it's very thrilling, at first, talking French to clever Frenchmen – they seem *so* much cleverer than oneself, still, in the long run, it is not satisfying. The endlessly clever *materialism* of the French leaves you cold, in the end, gives a sense of barrenness and incompatibility with true New England depths. So our two idealists felt.

(p. 210)

Here Lawrence tells us how his two characters 'felt', in the kind of language they would have used, perhaps actually did use, to explain and justify to themselves, to each other, and to an Other, their decision to leave France. In the next few lines the Other (an anonymous spokesman for common sense) is allowed to speak directly in the text, and dialogic discourse becomes overt dialogue:

> They turned away from France – but ever so gently. France had disappointed them. 'We've loved it, and we've got a great deal out of it. But after a while, after a considerable while, several years, in fact, Paris leaves one feeling disappointed. It hasn't quite got what one wants.' 'But Paris isn't France.' 'No, perhaps not. France is quite different from Paris. And France is lovely – quite lovely. But *to us*, though we love it, it doesn't say a great deal.'
> So when the war came, the idealists moved to Italy.
>
> (p. 210)

But Italy also disappoints them, and this disappointment is again represented in a tissue of putative quotation from the speech and thought of Erasmus and Valerie, in free indirect style:

> And though they had had a very wonderful time in Europe, and though they still loved Italy – dear Italy – yet: they were disappointed. They had got a lot out of it: oh, a very great deal indeed! Still, it hadn't given them quite, not *quite*, what they had expected. Europe was lovely, but it was dead. Living in Europe, you were living on the past. And Europeans, with their superficial charm, were not *really* charming. They were materialistic, they had no *real* soul.
>
> (p. 212)

'Things' is an ironic quest-story. Disillusioned with Europe, the couple return to America, only to find that they cannot afford a house big enough to accommodate the beautiful 'things' they have acquired in exile. They put the 'things' in store, and experiment with the simple life in a log-cabin in the West, but that is a disaster. They return to Europe, but that is 'a complete failure'.

> [Erasmus] found he couldn't stand Europe. It irritated every nerve in his body. He hated America too. But America at least was a darn sight better than this miserable, dirt-eating continent: which was by no means cheap any more, either.
>
> (pp. 218–19)

We catch here a significant, new linguistic register in the discourse – homely, sardonic, distinctively American – which signals the couple's reluctant coming-to-terms with their real problem: the fact, intimated in the first paragraph of the story, but never faced by them till now, that their income is insufficient to support their ideals. (The economic dependence of ideals upon money is of course an ironic comment on the former.) They are compelled to the conclusion that Erasmus must work for a living, as a teacher at a Midwestern university. This decision is in some sense a defeat, especially for Erasmus, yet it is also a relief. ('He was a changed man, quieter, much less irritable. A load off him. He was inside the cage.') The couple's acceptance of a way of life antithetical to everything they had previously aspired to is represented by the change in their speech, from the refined, cultured, 'European' cadences and constructions of the earlier part of the story, to a native American idiom characterized by a kind of crass, cracker-barrel folk-wisdom. The story ends like this:

> 'Europe's the mayonnaise all right, but America supplies the good old lobster – what?' 'Every time!' she said, with satisfaction. And he peered at her. He was in the cage: but it was safe inside. And she, evidently, was her real self at last. She had got the goods. Yet round his nose was a queer, evil, scholastic look, of pure scepticism. But he liked lobster.

> (p. 220)

In 'Things' Lawrence puts his characters in a double bind, allowing them a choice only between equally inauthentic ways of life, and mocking them with the inauthenticity of the language in which they articulate and defend these choices. The frequency with which the words *but* or *yet* or *still* occur in the text epitomizes the hopelessness of the couple's quest, their restless oscillation between alternatives doomed to be unsatisfying. Thus, in spite of its elaborate use of doubly-voiced discourse, the story is hardly 'polyphonic' in Bakhtin's sense. Though the characters are allowed to 'answer back', their self-defence is undermined by the inherent contradictions of their quest. The story is, however, in its cruel way, comic.

This brings me, finally, to the question of whether it makes any sense to place D. H. Lawrence in the tradition of the serio-comic or carnivalesque writing which Bakhtin came to see as crucial to the evolution of the novel as a literary form. At first sight it seems an unpromising speculation, for though there is incidental comedy in much of Lawrence's fiction, it is generally very much dominated by a basically 'serious' tone and pushed to the margins of narratives that are essentially tragic or romantic in structure, leading to climaxes of death and/or rebirth. Bakhtin himself faced much the same problem in relation to Dostoevsky, who was central to the original formation of the 'polyphonic' novel, but who, at first sight, seems to have little in common with the ribald comedy of the carnivalesque tradition. Bakhtin met this difficulty with the concept of 'reduced laughter', the idea that the carnivalesque subversion of orthodox hierarchies can be achieved without overt comedy:

> Under certain conditions and in certain genres . . . laughter can be reduced. It continues to determine the structure of the image, but it itself is muffled down to the minimum: we see, as it were, the track left by laughter in the structure of represented reality, but the laughter itself we do not hear. . . . In Dostoevsky's great novels, laughter is reduced almost to the minimum (especially in *Crime and Punishment*). In all his novels, however, we find a trace of that ambivalent laughter, absorbed by Dostoevsky together with the generic carnivalisation, performing its work of artistically organizing and illuminating the world. . . . the more im-portant – one could say, the decisive – expression of reduced laughter is to be found in the ultimate position of the author. . . . this position excludes all one-sided or dogmatic seriousness and does not permit any single point of view, any single polar extreme of life or thought, to be absolutized. . . . We speak here of Dostoevsky the artist. Dostoevsky the journalist was by

no means a stranger to cramped and one-sided seriousness, to dogmatism, even to eschatalogy. But these ideas of the journalist, once introduced into the novel, become then merely one of the embodied voices of an unfinalised and open dialogue. . . . Reduced laughter in carnivalised literature by no means excludes the possibility of somber colours within a work. For this reason the somber coloration of Dostoevsky's works should not confuse us: it is not their final word.

(PDP, 164–6)

I have quoted this passage at length because of its suggestive relevance to D. H. Lawrence – in particular, the distinction between the artist and the journalist, which one might usefully apply to the relationship between the ideas expounded by Lawrence in non-fictional texts like *The Crown*, and their appearance in fictional texts like *Women in Love* or *England, My England*. If a suspicion remains that the concept of 'reduced laughter' is a rather convenient 'loophole' (to use another of Bakhtin's own terms) through which writers not obviously recognizable as carnivalesque, such as Dostoevsky and Lawrence, can nevertheless be accommodated with that tradition, it is worth noting that a work has recently been added to the Lawrence canon which may be called carnivalesque without apology or qualification – that indeed can hardly be read without some such generic frame of reference. I refer, of course, to *Mr Noon*.

Mr Noon is an unfinished but substantial novel, written by Lawrence in 1920–1, of which only the first part (included in *A Modern Lover*, 1934, and *Phoenix II*, 1968) was known until the manuscript of the second, longer part came to light quite recently. The whole of the extant work was published in the Cambridge edition of Lawrence's works in 1984.[10] The first part is about a schoolteacher, Gilbert Noon (closely based on a Nottinghamshire friend of Lawrence's, George Henry Neville), who gets into a sexual scrape with another young schoolteacher, and is forced to resign his job in consequence. The second part is set in Germany, where Gilbert (now much more like Lawrence himself) meets and falls in love with Johanna Keighley, the sister of his German professor, married to an Englishman (and a transparent portrait of Frieda Weekley). The remainder of the novel chronicles Johanna's desertion of her husband for Gilbert and their symbolic journey across the Alps on foot, a story based closely on the elopement of Frieda with Lawrence, and its immediate sequel.

As it stands, the two parts of *Mr Noon* do not cohere on the level of either character or narrative, and this was probably one reason why Lawrence abandoned it. The two parts are, however, linked thematically, and there is a character called Patty Goddard, an unfulfilled married friend of Gilbert's, a 'soft full, strange, unmated Aphrodite of forty', in Part I, who was evidently designed to provide the hero with a truly rewarding sexual relationship – a role that, in the event, Lawrence transferred on to the more glamorous, exotic and fact-based character of Johanna. In short, *Mr Noon* deals with a theme (the sexual relationship) and draws on experience (Lawrence's own relationship with Frieda) that were crucially important to him, and which he had written about many times before. But what was unusual about this book was that Lawrence conceived it from the beginning as a comedy, and started it because he was blocked on the rather tiresomely 'monologic' *Aaron's Rod*. 'I . . . can't end it,' he wrote to a correspondent at the time, 'so I began a comedy.'[11] The comedy in *Mr Noon* is generated partly by situation (there are, for instance, several amusing scenes in which the lovers are surprised *in flagrante delicto*, or in post-coital *déshabillé*) and partly by the narrator's voice, which is intrusive but not monologic – on the contrary, it is very varied in tone: teasing, hectoring, facetious, ironic, rhapsodic and prophetic by turns. The two sources of comedy are piquantly combined in Chapter 15, when the authorial narrator prevents the reader, as it were, from disturbing the lovers' privacy. The scene occurs early in the relationship between Gilbert and Johanna, and describes their second sexual encounter, snatched in a brief interlude before dinner is served in the flat of Johanna's brother-in-law. It begins with a powerfully erotic image and a hymn to sexual desire:

> Johanna was hovering in the doorway of her room as he went down the passage. A bright, roused look was on her face. She lifted her eyelids with a strange flare of invitation, like a bird lifting its wings. And for the first time the passion broke like lightning out of Gilbert's blood: for the first time in his life. He went into her room with her and shut the door. The sultriness and lethargy of his soul had broken into a storm of desire for her, a storm which shook and swept him at varying intervals all his life.
>
> Oh wonderful desire: violent, genuine desire! Oh magnificence of stormy elemental desire, which is at once so elemental and so intensely individual! Oh storms of acute sex passion, which shatter the soul, and re-make it, as summer is made up out of the debacle of thunder! . . . The cyclone of actual desire – not mere titillation and functional gratification – or any other-ation – broke now for the first time upon Gilbert, and flung him down the wind. Not, dear moralist, to break against the buttresses of some christian cathedral which rose in his path. Not at all. It flung him smack through the cathedrals like a long-shotted shell. Heaven knows where it did not fling him. I'll tell you later on.
>
> But for the moment, I insist on apostrophising desire, intense individual desire, in order to give my hero time. O thunder-god, who sends the white passion of pure, sensual desire upon us, breaking through the sultry rottenness of our old blood like jagged lightning, and switching us into a new, dynamic reaction, hail!
>
> (pp. 136–7)

Here Lawrence apostrophizes desire in a kind of portentous language akin to the more rhapsodic erotic passages of *The Rainbow* and *Women in Love*, but pretends to be doing so only to give his lovers time to consummate their passion. This Shandean joke is saucily entertaining in its own right and also protects the paean to desire from any ironic scepticism on the reader's part. The reader indeed, soon finds himself on the sharp end of the narrator's irony:

> Oh thunder-god, god of the dangerous bolts – ! – No, gentle reader, please don't interrupt, I am *not* going to open the door of Johanna's room, not until Mr. Noon opens it himself. I've been caught that way before. I have opened the door for you, and the moment you gave your first squeal in rushed the private detective you had kept in the background. Thank you,

gentle reader, you can open your own doors. I am busy apostrophising
Jupiter Tonans, Zeus of the Thunder-bolt, the almighty Father of passion
and sheer desire. I'm not talking about *your* messy little feelings and
licentiousness, either. I'm talking about desire. So don't interrupt. Am *I*
writing this book or are you?

(p. 137)

The narrator of *Mr Noon* frequently addresses the reader directly in this way,
drawing attention to the fictionality of the text by reference to its conventions,
and to the 'real author' behind it (a D. H. Lawrence persecuted by censors and
hostile critics). This metafictional strain in the text, which the Russian Formalists called 'baring the device' and Erving Goffman 'breaking frame', is characteristic of Bakhtin's serio-comic, carnivalesque literary tradition, as are other
features of *Mr Noon*: passages of parodic, travestying, tongue-in-cheek writing,
earthy humour centring on backsides and excretion, farcical incidents in which
the pretensions of polite society are subverted or overturned. Cumulatively,
these features have a very positive effect on Lawrence's treatment of the
relationship between Gilbert and Johanna. Without in any way undermining
the authenticity and credibility of their passion for each other, or diminishing
the joy it brings them, Lawrence also avoids sentimentalizing or idealizing the
lovers, and achieves a remarkable balance and objectivity in dealing with
extremely intimate personal experience. Although its narrative structure is
irreparably broken-backed, and the jocularity of the narrative voice is overdone at times, one cannot but regret that Lawrence abandoned *Mr Noon*, and
never resumed the experiment of writing in an overtly carnivalesque mode.

For the only novel in his *oeuvre* which at all resembles *Mr Noon* is *The Lost Girl*
(1920), which Lawrence wrote not long before, and which he described, while
it was in progress, as 'a rather comic novel' (*The Lost Girl*, ed. John Worthen,
Cambridge, 1981, xxix). Both novels begin in a similar vein, treating thinly
disguised Eastwood personages with high-spirited humour, and have an
elopement to Italy as their narrative climax. There are a few mildly metafictional asides by the authorial narrator of *The Lost Girl* (e.g., 'Surely enough
books have been written about heroines in similar circumstances. There is no
need to go into the details of Alvina's six months in Islington', p. 32), though
nothing like the radically disruptive apostrophizing of the reader in *Mr Noon*.
Nor is there much explicit ribaldry in *The Lost Girl*, since, as John Worthen
shows in his introduction, Lawrence was consciously trying to write a book
that would not be 'at all improper: quite fit for Mudie's' (p. xxx). However, in
Alvina's sudden, spontaneous choice of midwifery as a profession, which so
shocks her bourgeois family (because of its association with what Bakhtin
terms 'the lower body') and for which she trains in an atmosphere of bawdy
humour and sexual harassment (see pp. 32–9), and in the spectacularly
physical Red Indian act of the Natcha-Kee-Tawara troupe, through whom
Alvina ultimately finds sexual and personal liberation, we may see displaced
manifestations of carnivalesque behaviour.

If the Rabelaisian vein of *Mr Noon* was rather regrettably attenuated in
Lawrence's subsequent novels, the best of them nevertheless respond well to a
Bahktinian critical approach, as I have tried to suggest in commenting on

108   *David Lodge*

Women in Love. The compatibility is more than merely formal: there is obviously an interesting parallel to be drawn between the socio-political implications of Bakhtin's theories and D. H. Lawrence's 'metaphysic' – between
Bakhtin's view that carnival behaviour was progressively suppressed, out-
lawed and marginalized in the era of bourgeois capitalism,[12] and Lawrence's
view that man's (and woman's) instinctual life had been denied and repressed
by the same social forces. But to pursue that parallel further is beyond the scope
of this essay.

Notes

1 David Lodge, 'Joyce and Bakhtin: *Ulysses* and the typology of literary discourse',
   Journal of English Language and Literature (Korea) XXIX (1983), 319–33. Re-
   printed in *James Joyce Broadsheet*, no. 11, June 1983, 1–2.
2 The following English language editions have been used: M. Bakhtin, *Problems
   of Dostoevsky's Poetics*, ed. and trans. Caryl Emerson, intro. Wayne Booth
   (Manchester, 1984).
   V. N. Volosinov, *Marxism and the Philosophy of Language*, trans. L. Matejka and
   I. R. Titunik (London, 1973).
   M. Bakhtin, *Rabelais and His World*, trans. Helene Iswolsky (London, 1968).
   M. Bakhtin, *The Dialogic Imagination: Four Essays*, ed. Michael Holquist (London,
   1981).
3 See, for example, Roland Barthes, *S/Z* (London, 1975) and Colin MacCabe,
   James Joyce and the Revolution of the World (London, 1979).
4 David Lodge, *The Modes of Modern Writing* (London, 1977), 161.
5 E.g., '[J. M. Robertson]'s an arrant ass to declare *Crime and Punishment* the
   greatest book – it's a tract, a treatise, a pamphlet compared with Tolstoi's *Anna
   Karenina* or *War and Peace'*, *The Letters of D. H. Lawrence*, ed. James T. Boulton
   (Cambridge, 1979), I, 126–7. The remarks about Dostoevsky, and Lawrence's
   preface to *The Grand Inquisitor*, collected together in *Selected Literary Criticism*, ed.
   Anthony Beal (London, 1961), 229–41, though largely hostile, show how well
   acquainted he was with the Russian novelist's work.
6 Frank Kermode, 'D. H. Lawrence and the apocalyptic types,' in *Continuities*
   (London, 1968).
7 Frank Kermode, *Lawrence* (London, 1973), 74.
8 James Joyce, *A Portrait of the Artist as a Young Man* (London, 1942), 115.
9 'Things' was first published in *The Bookman* (New York), August 1928. Page
   references are to D. H. Lawrence, *The Princess and Other Stories*, ed. Keith Sagar
   (Harmondsworth, 1971). My attention was first drawn to this story by Professor
   John Preston, who discusses its 'dialogic' structure, with a reference to Volosinov (though not Bakhtin), in 'Narrative procedure and structure in a short
   story by D. H. Lawrence', *Journal of English Language and Literature* (Korea),
   XXIX (1983), 251–6.
10 *Mr Noon*, ed. Lindeth Vasey (Cambridge, 1984).
11 ibid., xxii.
12 For a valuable exploration of this aspect of Bakhtin's work, see Peter Stallybrass
   and Allon White, *The Politics and Poetics of Transgression* (Ithaca, NY, 1986).

*

This essay (though its closing paragraphs have been slightly rewritten) first
appeared in *Renaissance and Modern Studies: Lawrence Centenary Issue* (1985), 16–32.

9 Lawrence and Bakhtin: where pluralism ends and dialogism begins

Avrom Fleishman

For many a reader today, the complaints of yesterday's New Critical formalists against Lawrence's fiction may seem outmoded, but equally so the humanistic defence mounted by F. R. Leavis and his followers. In our culture of accelerating change, where conceptual paradigm shifts occur almost daily, a writer of Lawrence's stature must inevitably be exposed to new modes of discourse. Less inevitably but with some regularity, the chosen mode will be language- and discourse-oriented, and in Lawrence's case the terms of discussion are proving, often enough, to be Bakhtinian terms. We are increasingly being asked to see the novelist not as the single-minded 'monological' spokesman for a home-brewed ideology – whether approved or disdained, as by the older critical schools – but as offering the rhetoric, ideas and other inputs of a whole range of characters, representatively modern men and women. There is much to recommend such a treatment, but some dangers loom as well. The present essay means to speak from within the dialogical discourse on Lawrence, yet to stand at a critical remove so as to test its interpretive impulses.[1]

One objection to dialogical approaches to Lawrence is that they tend to be overly defensive, explicitly reacting to charges (some already passé) rather than exploring untapped resources in the novelist by means of Bakhtin's genuinely new insights. There is a suspicion of a 'loophole' defence when Lawrence is found not to be speaking authorially in passages where his characters are propounding ideas or experiencing sexual exaltation – or even in non-character passages of sweeping indignation or mystical reverie. A sign of the times is Wayne Booth's appropriation of Bakhtin for this very purpose: in his introduction to a new translation of *Problems of Dostoevsky's Poetics*[2] Booth makes dialogism a bulwark of his ecumenical brand of critical pluralism. In a more recent centenary address, Booth confessed to past distaste for Lawrence and announced that he has seen the light – all those strident assertions of ideas are made by characters and are therefore no longer chargeable to the author. We are to recover Lawrence as a sociable citizen and aesthetically conscientious story-teller – something closer to the norms and values of his enlightened critics rather than a dinosaur of modernist excess.

The increasing use of Bakhtin in Lawrence criticism – and for other major figures – merits close attention, not so that we may trump the cards drawn from the pluralist hand but rather the better to honour the novelist's unique achievements. If the dialogical is taken with Bakhtin's full meaning, Lawrence is not merely relieved of his stylistic embarrassments but shown in all his strength as a master of language. For in his novels, the language of fiction is deployed to foreground and to criticize the human uses of language, particularly those of modern Western culture.

David Lodge, in the ground-breaking article reprinted in this volume, gives a summary of Bakhtin's categories of fictional discourse that marks a good place at which to begin a careful fine-tuning. First comes 'the direct speech of the author' (p. 94 in the present volume), and Lodge proceeds to defend Lawrence as an authorial narrator, citing his own previous denigration of the novelist's lack not merely of character-narrators but of narratorial variety – '[Lawrence's] narrative voice . . . is always basically the same.' He engagingly apologizes for past error by a would-be Bakhtinian move:

> I think I exaggerated the homogeneity of Lawrence's narrative style, and in any case a variety of linguistic styles and registers is not in itself either a necessary or a sufficient criterion for the polyphonic novel. . . . what makes a novel polyphonic is not the mere presence of different styles and dialects, but 'the dialogic angle at which these styles are juxtaposed and counterposed in the work'. . . . In other words, whereas in Tolstoy the variety of characters' speech is always contained and controlled by the author's speech, in Dostoevsky the characters' speech, though formally less differentiated and individualized, is freer in the way it generates and sustains a continuous struggle between competing interests and ideas. I should like to suggest that the same is true of Lawrence's most impressive mature fiction, and especially *Women in Love*.
>
> (p. 96)

While this testifies to an expanded view of the expression of ideas in fiction, it does not go much beyond the Jamesian norm of the non-intrusive author in practical criticism. When examining one such struggle of ideas in *Women in Love*, Lodge adopts a similarly negative norm: 'What makes this scene dialogic in the ideological as well as the purely formal or compositional sense (i.e., containing a lot of direct speech) is that the narrator never delivers a finalizing judgemental word on the debate or its protagonists' (p. 99). Lawrence's is not, then, the intrusive, Tolstoyan way – where 'the variety of characters' speech is always contained and controlled by the author's speech' (p. 96) – but it has not yet been established as the Dostoevskian way, revealing the 'dialogic angle at which . . . styles are juxtaposed and counterposed in the work'.

Bakhtin's second broad category is 'the represented speech of the characters', and here Lodge makes some keen observations on Lawrence's mastery of personal idiom (or idiolect) as a means not merely of characterization but of dialectical opposition. Granting the dearth of individuating character speech at both ends of Lawrence's career, Lodge urges that 'In *Women in Love*, in contrast, the reader is bounced, bewilderingly, exhilaratingly, from one subject position to another, and made to feel the force of each' (p. 99). Here, too, a liberal taste for a variety of personal styles is in evidence.

A more distinctive kind of character speech in Lawrence – as in Bakhtin's Dostoevsky – is remarked in discussing a passage where Ursula quotes Birkin's windy rhetoric. To quote Lodge again: 'the contradictions and instability of Birkin's (and Lawrence's) views are brought out by the quintessentially dialogic method of having them quoted by the baffled Ursula to an interested third party. The effect is ironic, almost comic' (p. 100). This analysis reflects an awareness that the dialogical is not mere opposition among a variety of speakers but a linguistic relationship that invades each speech act – that it makes not only for many voices but for doubled voices, even within this second realm of character speech.

In developing the third of the discourse categories, that of 'doubly-oriented or doubly-voiced speech', Lodge fully recognizes that this was 'Bakhtin's most original and valuable contribution to stylistic analysis' (p. 95). Though he lists a few of its modes, Lodge seems, however, somewhat reserved as to its applicability to Lawrence. He makes two acute accounts of 'stylization' in *Women in Love*: in the recycling of romance rhetoric when describing Ursula's sexuality and in the allusive use of religious sources when characterizing Birkin's prophetic transfiguration (pp. 100, 101).[3] But both these accounts are defensive gestures, designed to ward off the usual abuse of Lawrence's purple prose, which do not adequately deal with the functioning of double-voiced discourses as both language critique and culture critique.

To return to the 'quintessentially dialogic method' and Lodge's comment that 'a variety of linguistic styles and registers is not in itself either a necessary or a sufficient criterion for the polyphonic novel' (p. 96). In local force, Lodge's negation is right: variety of styles is not what is dialogical; but neither is variety of competing ideas, character idioms or anything else. Here is one of Bakhtin's vigorous formulations:

> all relationships among external and internal parts and elements of [Dostoevsky's] novel are dialogic in character, and he structured the novel as a whole as a *'great dialogue.'* Within this 'great dialogue' could be heard, illuminating it and thickening its texture, the compositionally expressed dialogues of the heroes; ultimately, dialogue penetrates within, into every word of the novel, making it double-voiced . . . ; this is already the *'microdialogue'* that determines the peculiar character of Dostoyevsky's verbal style.
>
> (*PDP*, 40)

The dialogical is, then, a relationship among all the parts of a novel but it also works within each part – within each word, in Bakhtin's hyperbole. It is present within authorial prose as it frames the speech of characters, and present within each character's speech as it incorporatively reacts to others' speech. In Dostoevsky, for example, a character's speech is not only doubled by the author's intonations but doubles itself. In *The Brothers Karamazov*, 'Ivan is disputing not with Alyosha but above all with himself, and Alyosha is not disputing with Ivan as an integral and unified voice but rather intervenes in his internal dialogue, trying to reinforce one of its rejoinders. And there can be no talk here of any sort of synthesis; one can talk only of the victory of one or another voice, or of a combination of voices in those places where they agree' (*PDP*, 279; so much for polite and permanent competition of ideas!)

Dialogism is a principle of all three of Bakhtin's discourse categories, and can be shown to be at work in Lawrence's authorial prose and in the speech of his characters. But it is in the third category of the doubly-oriented discourses that the dialogical novelist distinguishes himself, strategically deploying its modes in the large movements of his fiction, rather than merely resorting to them for local effects. It is the third category that is Bakhtin's stamping ground, and an adequate review of Lawrence's achievement would require illustration of his achievement in most of the modes listed in Bakhtin's 'discourse typology': not only stylization but 'narrator's narration' (the lightly characterized omniscient narrator found later in *St Mawr*), first-person narration generally and as parodied (this, admittedly, Lawrence eschews), parody at large and especially of colloquial story-telling (parodistic *skaz*), 'discourse of a character who is parodically represented', (one need only think of Hermione, Halliday, *et al.*), hidden internal polemic (as in Loerke's exposition of his aesthetic doctrines), polemically coloured autobiography (a fair characterization of the *roman à clef* elements of *Women in Love*), and hidden dialogue, to be illustrated below (*PDP*, 199ff.).

While Bakhtin does not say that all these modes are necessary to the polyphonic novel, some at least would seem to be required for the novel-type Bakhtin distinguished as the carnivalesque. Lodge closes his accounting of Lawrence's achievement by considering the novelist's approximation of this sub-genre. He sees it as an essentially comic form, albeit of the 'reduced laughter' class that allows even the somber Dostoevsky to enter. Lodge recognizes that it is 'the carnivalesque subversion of orthodox hierarchies' (p. 104) that marks the freewheeling inclusiveness of this form of prose fiction. (It is akin to Northrop Frye's 'anatomy' – both Frye and Bakhtin employing the model of Menippean satire.) Yet he remains doubtful that such un-comic novelists as Dostoevsky and Lawrence can fully qualify, and belatedly brings in an unfinished but markedly comic novel as his example of the carnivalesque. To this we may offer two rejoinders: if *Women in Love* were to be found sufficiently wide-ranging in its dialogical modes and subversive in its effects on orthodox hierarchies of life and art, it would stand as a great exemplar of the carnivalesque novel. And – to overcome the lesser objection – doesn't it provide comedy enough?

From the first page, we are aware of a dialogical relation to language. In place of the panoramic omniscient narration in the initial scene-setting of *Sons and Lovers* and equally removed from the elaborate stylization of pulsing prose rhythms in *The Rainbow*'s bravura opening, we get:

> 'Ursula,' said Gudrun, 'don't you *really want* to get married?' . . .
> 'I don't know,' she replied. 'It depends how you mean.'
> Gudrun was slightly taken aback. She watched her sister for some moments.
> 'Well,' she said, ironically, 'it usually means one thing! – But don't you

think, anyhow, you'd be –' she darkened slightly – 'in a better position than you are in now?'

Here is 'discourse with an orientation toward someone else's discourse' *con brio* – not only the author but the characters taking up the question of what words mean with a practised self-consciousness. Before they emerge as individuals, the sisters are dialogically presented as two representatives of the 'New Woman' model of the time, distinctly legible by their speech. The modish emphasis on *really* is only the first in a series of such items, which grows to include 'the *experience* of having been married', '*Really!* . . . Have you *really?*' and 'Do you *really* want children, Ursula?' There's internal character dialogism, too, as Gudrun employs a set of phrases from the conventional middle-class argot to test her sister's degree of liberation from them: 'in a better position' is soon followed by 'You wouldn't consider a good offer?' and 'imagine him coming home to one every evening, and saying "Hello," and giving one a kiss.'[4]

The larger enterprise in which this dialogism is recruited is one of the standard operations of the third discourse category: parody. The opening chapter of an English novel, entitled 'Sisters', places two young women 'in the window-bay of their father's house', embroidering and sketching and talking of marriage – and explodes a mine under the whole shebang, the subject of English novels from Jane Austen down to romantic pulp. The entire scene is orientated not only towards its referential object, the characterization of two individualistic heroines, but towards the models of social language and behaviour from which they are trying to extricate themselves. It is also one of the funniest scenes in fiction since Austen herself.

Women in Love's claim to be a great dialogical novel does not rest, of course, with its abundant illustrations of Bakhtin's third category of modes. Moreover, what makes it a work of Dostoevskian stature is only in part that it is a novel of ideas, in which characters with some claim to be called intellectuals debate in formal session. What makes it polyphonic is that all its discourses are double-voiced: the characters talk not only about people and ideas but about words, they quote those words when making their own responses, other speakers chime in with their own rhetorics – and so on, so as to constitute a world of words. Things do happen in this world, of course, and they are often of the grotesque sort that happen in Dostoevsky novels – a hysterical woman's blow with a paperweight, a double drowning, scenes of degenerate *demi-mondaine* cafe life, that sort of thing. But through it all, the protagonists go on talking – and we listen, rapt, for longish chapters, as we do to Shatov and Dmitri Karamazov and Myshkin. The fascination of men and women who, as Bakhtin puts it, do not 'coincide' with themselves is irresistible, because they are precious and rarely presented in fiction.

Gerald Crich is Lawrence's Dmitri and 'The Industrial Magnate' chapter one of his grand exercises in dialogical characterization:

He looked around. There lay the mines. They were old, obsolete. They were like old lions, no more good. He looked again. Pah! the mines were nothing but the clumsy efforts of impure minds. There they lay, abortions of a half-trained mind. Let the idea of them be swept away. He cleared his

brain of them, and thought only of the coal in the under earth. How much
was there?

(XVII, 223)

These are the sounds of a mental process, inner speech, that has been studied
by Soviet psychologists in ways comparable to those in which Bakhtin describes its literary representation.[5] The variety of speech modes – interjection
or expletive, optative construction ('Let the . . . be swept'), interrogative – as
well as the semantic peculiarities of his metaphoric diction ('old lions',
'abortions', 'under earth') suggest that we are made privy to an internal
conversation. Here rhetorical virtuosity and hyperbolic vehemence are put to
service by a man trying to convince himself of a fresh conception of his life.

Yet the same technique can also signal a mind wavering and inept in
self-awareness: 'The devil of it was, it was so hard to keep up his interest in
women nowadays. He didn't care about them any more. A Pussum was all right
in her way, but she was an exceptional case, and even she mattered extremely
little. No, women, in that sense, were useless to him any more. He felt that his
mind needed acute stimulation, before he could be physically roused' (XVII,
233). The prose tracks a man in transition from ruling-class self-assurance and
its accompanying tone ('The devil of it was', 'all right in her way') towards
more intellectual values – the emphasis on '*mind*' representing his awkward
sense of them. Unfortunately, Gerald is not to the intellectual manner born,
and persists in making rationality and intellection merely instrumental in
behalf of crudely egoistic goals ('useless to him', 'stimulation, before he could
be physically roused'). The half-baked qualities of Gerald's thinking – and, at
other places in the chapter, the demonic destructiveness and self-
destructiveness that propel him – are amply displayed in the double-voiced
prose which reports it.

The chief exhibitions of a divided mind in action are, of course, the longish
chapters devoted to Rupert Birkin's oral lucubrations. What is perhaps most
remarkable about these Hamlet-like excoriations of himself and his world is
that, apart from his assault on the moon's reflection, they are not staged as
soliloquies. So thoroughly dialogical is the way of life depicted in the novel –
quite apart from the dialogical method of that depiction – that Birkin seems to
be able to explore his own ideas only by expounding them to others. While
Gerald is a fairly passive respondent to his notions of male bonding, soon won
over to its active expression and metaphysical implications, Ursula is a full-
fledged other to his expositions of male and female relations. This is what
makes their love-talk so piquant: neither a debate between differing ethical
positions which eventually come to adjudication (the classic model of *Pride and
Prejudice*), nor simply a clash between a domineering male and a female
maintaining her integrity (of which *Jane Eyre* is the prototype), these encounters are a dialogue of voices each of which is doubly orientated, playing on
the words of the other. To put this in Lawrence's (or Birkin's) terms: their
dialogues are already an enactment of the star-equilibrium which is the
ostensible goal of their striving – a condition in which the lovers are alone
together, communicating but different, dynamic but enduring.

A brief example from the skein of Birkin–Ursula discourses will illustrate the process. In the 'Moony' chapter he declares his desire for 'that golden light which is you' and goes on to explain:

> 'I don't mean let yourself go in the Dionysic ecstatic way,' he said. 'I know you can do that. But I hate ecstasy, Dionysic or any other. It's like going round in a squirrel cage. I want you not to care about yourself, just to be there and not to care about yourself, not to insist – be glad and sure and indifferent.'
>
> 'Who insists?' she mocked. 'Who is it that keeps on insisting? It isn't *me!*'
>
> There was a weary mocking bitterness in her voice. He was silent for some time.
>
> 'I know,' he said. 'While ever either of us insists to the other, we are all wrong. But there we are, the accord doesn't come.'

(XIX, 251)

Birkin's conclusion is, of course, premature, for it is precisely by the process their dialogue traces that they reach the enduring – or at least promising – accord of later chapters.

In the present phase, we find Birkin laying down a rule of conduct based on his disdain of a competing norm – in this case, 'Dionysic ecstasy', presumably of the spurious kinds indulged in at the Pompadour Cafe, at Hermione's Breadalby, or in Gudrun's arty Dalcroze movements. Having repeated the offending word, 'Dionysic', with mounting ire, he wipes it away with a homely simile: 'like going round in a squirrel cage.' He then turns to a non-mannered style that aims at personal truthfulness by using almost exclusively monosyllabic words which have juxtaposed clauses. (Even this anti-rhetorical style is itself conventional and uses rhetorical figures.) Among the few non-monosyllables is, however, that loaded word 'insist', and it generates a new phase of dialogical activity. Ursula picks up Birkin's word and repeats it in two rhetorical questions. She reverts to the mannered, italicized emphasis we've observed in the novel's opening dialogue, the stress falling on that key-word of egoism and the exact antagonist of Birkin's diatribe: *me!* But this regression is not an entire setback, for Birkin draws in his horns, meditates on what has been said, and redeems the offending word: 'While ever either of us insists to the other, we are all wrong.' Not a bad day's work, on which a usable maxim is produced.

The thrust of these observations will doubtless be granted even by those with differing views of the dialogical: Lawrence writes much of *Women in Love* in double-voiced discourses, particularly when representing the thought-speech of divided protagonists, in mutually incorporative dialogues between them, and in parodic scenes even broader than the one I have cited. But the sticking point remains his conduct of authorial discourse. *Women in Love*, as critics from Leavis on down have appreciated, is a massive critique of English society and culture in the first decades of this century, and on behalf of that critical dissection the dialogical modes are put to powerful service. But it also marks the start of Lawrence's long dedication to the use of fiction as doctrine: to expostulate on marital relations, not omitting the sexual; to lay out rules of personal conduct almost as particularized as Robinson Crusoe's; to indulge in the kind of racial abstractions and cosmic predictions usually restricted to gospel texts and theories of history.

How can the dialogical approach to Lawrence help to exonerate him from charges of dogmatic prosing, authorial intervention or 'monological' novel writing, and yet avoid relegating his outbursts of authorial assertion to the margins? Like them or not, they make up a large chunk of *Women in Love* and, I would submit, a measure of its greatness. What I wish to urge is that these apparently monological passages are themselves governed by the operations of dialogical writing. It is not only in depicting character thought and speech, nor only in satirizing social speech and behaviour, that Lawrence directs language towards other people's language, but in his 'own' discourses as well.

I take as my text the well-known passage that follows Gerald's suicide, which considers and rejects his alternative option of taking 'the great Imperial road leading south to Italy':

> [Birkin] turned away. Either the heart would break or cease to care. Best cease to care. Whatever the mystery which has brought forth man and the universe, it is a non-human mystery, it has its own great ends, man is not the criterion. Best leave it all to the vast, creative, non-human mystery. Best strive with oneself only, not with the universe.
>
> 'God cannot do without man.' It was surely a saying of some great French religious teacher. But surely this is false. God can do without man. God could do without the ichthyosauri and the mastodon. These monsters failed creatively to develop, so God, the creative mystery, dispensed with them. In the same way the mystery could dispense with man, should he too fail creatively to change and develop. The eternal creative mystery could dispose of man, and replace him with a finer created being. Just as the horse has taken the place of the mastodon.
>
> (XXXII, 478–9)

Efforts to justify such essayistic passages usually take the form of locating them in character discourse; indeed, Lawrence makes a feeble attempt of this kind in the sentence following: 'It was very consoling to Birkin to think this.' And of course it is possible to argue that the habit of speculating on evolution in the specialized diction of 'ichthyosauri' and 'mastodon' suits very well a school supervisor who had earlier been seen making sharp points on teaching biology to the novice Ursula (Ch. III). But no one is fooled by this and like texts; this is the author speaking and no mistake. Yet when an author speaks, how many voices are heard?

Let us keep count. 'He turned away': this is Lawrence speaking as ultimate source, together with the constructed narrative voice we still call 'omniscient narrator'. 'Either the heart would break or cease to care': we hear the narrator and the character simultaneously, for the mode of reporting this thought is free indirect style (Bakhtin's term for it is 'quasi-direct discourse').[6] The specific marker of this mode is the tense change from the appropriate 'will' to the modulated 'would'; i.e., Birkin's thought would normally take the form, 'Either the heart will break', but it is modified to 'would break' to conform to the narrator's non-proximate deictics (to employ the linguists' terminology). The hallmark of free indirect style is that character and narrator are heard simultaneously, in the peculiar ventriloquism that has been called 'the dual voice.'[7] 'Best cease to care': this is a direct response to the preceding sentence, marking the passage as a 'hidden dialogue' by a bitter speaker/thinker, but here, too, we would be hard put to demonstrate that it is either Birkin or Lawrence who is speaking and not both at once. And so with the remaining sentences of this paragraph.

The two voices (or three, if we maintain the initial duality of author and narrator) are joined by another in the next paragraph. This curious 'free-floating quotation' is followed by a rather cavalier attribution to 'some great French religious teacher'. The paradox itself is a variant of a Voltairian dictum that has gone through many cultural variations – even before Voltaire.[8] The passage thus voices not only Lawrence, Birkin and the 'religious teacher', but carries echoes of a long chorus of sceptics. The quoted authority and his *bon mot* are, however, set up only for argument's sake, for subsequent sentences are framed in the same form with directly opposed content ('God can do without man', etc.).

Yet even in Lawrence's reversal of others' witty inversions, asserting his apparent conviction with gnomic pithiness, there is continued dialogical tension. Having passed beyond the sceptics' sly taunts against religious anthro-pomorphism, he is not inclined to uphold the opposite image of divine self-sufficiency and priority. God (it is not, of course, clear what the term denotes for Lawrence except in its dialogical function, 'for argument's sake') is posited as independent of man primarily to signal man's aloneness in the world; man's non-necessity and the contingency of all his works are urged here with Nietzschean brusqueness. But along with threats of extinction comes a challenge: the imperative to the individual, as to the race, to evolve his own nature, his own future.

Now we are beginning to savour the true dialogical, which often resembles those conversations – sometimes remaining among the most memorable of one's life, and of which one cannot recall a word – in which everyone is talking at once. And out of this Babel come . . . words of relative simple-mindedness ('Just as the horse has taken the place of the mastodon') . . . words of future-oriented wisdom ('The eternal creative mystery could dispose of man, and replace him with a finer created being'). This orientation returns us to the issue of the carnivalesque novel, raised earlier.

In a number of his works, Bakhtin elaborated a sweeping theory of the history of the Western novel, in which the world-overturning, socially subver-sive and comically exhilarating spirit of medieval–Renaissance carnival en-tered into literary tradition in the form of 'carnivalized genres'. Sure signs of such carnival energies at work in the novel from Cervantes onwards are the presence of 'Menippean' dialogues both serious and mock-serious, of parodic inversions and doublings of characters, and of the inventive word-play and verbal satire for which Rabelais is Bakhtin's exemplar. Lawrence does not indulge in these ludic activities in the degree that would make his novels classics of the carnivalesque. But they evince a number of the traits of language-criticism, social-hierarchy subversion, and generic mixing and dis-tortion that are distinctly in the tradition of the carnivalized novel. Although I cannot make a systematic review of these features of *Women in Love* in the present venue, one can adduce – at the opposite end of the novel from its comic opening – the near-closing passage of authorial prose we have been considering.

It is not alone the multi-voicedness of this writing that makes it dialogical or carnivalesque, just as the explicit authorial doctrine does not indelibly brand it as monological. Bakhtin's values in life and in fiction resemble but go beyond the ecumenical norms of his recent followers; like Lawrence, he stands for something fairly specific. After speaking of the dialogical writer's avoidance in his own voice of dogmatic seriousness, one-sided views and conclusive dialogues, he adds:

> the carnival sense of the world also knows no period, and is, in fact, hostile to any sort of *conclusive conclusion*: all endings are merely new beginnings; carnival images are reborn again and again.
>
> . . . *nothing conclusive has yet taken place in the world, the ultimate word of the world and about the world has not yet been spoken, the world is open and free, everything is still in the future and will always be in the future.*[9]

(PDP, 165–6)

Lawrence's sense of the future extends beyond his leaving his principal characters in mid-passage, without guarantees of their after-careers; it is not a matter of mere open endings. Nor is his dialogical deployment of antithetical doctrines merely a relativistic bow to their equal truth or value; it is not that they are undecidable, or that he is indecisive about them, but that they have not yet been decided. For Lawrence, the openness of the future is to be taken literally and is expressed in our chosen passage as a negative principle, even a doctrinal one: 'Whatever the mystery which has brought forth man and the universe, it is a non-human mystery, it has its own great ends, man is not the criterion.' It is this sense of mystery, both as to origins and ends, that makes *Women in Love* not merely a dialogically multiple but a carnivalized novel, subversive of our human norms and welcoming a larger evolutionary prospect.

Notes

1 I have made my own approach to this project in 'He do the polis in different voices: Lawrence's later style,' in Peter Balbert and P. L. Marcus (eds), *D. H. Lawrence: A Centenary Consideration* (Ithaca, NY, 1985), 162–79.
2 Mikhail Bakhtin, *Problems of Dostoevsky's Poetics*, ed. and trans. Caryl Emerson, intro. Wayne C. Booth (Minneapolis, 1984 [1929]). This edition will be cited here, as it is in David Lodge's article, as *PDP*.
3 Lodge also discusses another category 3 mode, the stylization of the oral-narrative style called *skaz*, in describing a late Lawrence story, 'Things' (pp. 101–4).
4 All quotations in this paragraph are from the first three pages of *Women in Love*.
5 See Caryl Emerson, 'The outer word and inner speech: Bakhtin, Vygotsky, and the internalization of language,' in G. S. Morson (ed.), *Bakhtin: Essays and Dialogues on His Work* (Chicago and London, 1986), 21–40. This volume also contains a neo-Marxist rejoinder to current uses of Bakhtin for purportedly liberal ideological functions – Ken Hirschkop, 'A reply to the forum on Mikhail Bakhtin', 73–9 – from which the present argument must carefully be distinguished.

6 V. N. Volosinov (*sic*), *Marxism and the Philosophy of Language*, trans. Ladislav Matejka and I. R. Titunik (Cambridge, Mass. and London, 1973 [1929]), pt. III, ch. 4. The experts' discussion of Bakhtin's authorship of this book, while showing no signs of abating, seems to have reached consensus.

7 Roy Pascal, *The Dual Voice: Free Indirect Speech and its Functioning in the Nineteenth-Century European Novel* (Manchester, 1977). See my article (n. 1 above) for other useful references on this subject.

8 Even this relatively innocuous 'discourse with a sideward glance at someone else's word' introduces a characteristic expansion of multiple-voiced discourse, for the quoted words bear the marks of a long process of repetition for varied ends. The Cambridge editors cite Ludwig Feuerbach's 'God is nothing without man' (*The Essence of Christianity*, in George Eliot's translation), with a reference to the French skeptic Pierre Bayle as the prototype; they also give other Lawrence uses and abuses of the formula (pp. 584–5). The novel's 'hidden polemic' calls, however, for treatment more general than that of a source-hunt. The first witty reversal of normal expectations in god-and-man sentences seems to have occurred in an ancient pseudo-Platonic dialogue, 'Sisyphus': 'He was a wise man who invented God.' Thomas Hobbes had thoughts on this subject, while Voltaire's more famous 'Si Dieu n'existait pas, il faudrait l'inventer' itself became the object not only of quotation but of discussion in the nineteenth century; a locus classicus is *The Brothers Karamazov*, bk. V, ch. 3 – textbook example of Dostoevskian dialogism. The linguistic turn remained popular in turn-of-the-century theorizing, e.g., Nietzsche's 'Is man only a blunder of God, or God only a blunder of man?' (*Twilight of the Idols*), or Samuel Butler's 'An honest God's the noblest work of man' (reversing Pope). Lawrence plays his role in this dynamic verbal process at this point.

9 Lodge quotes part of this passage with respect to Lawrence's open endings (p. 98), but avoids contextualizing it in Bakhtin's exposition of the carnivalesque. Elsewhere, the discussion of *Women in Love* as a 'philosophical adventure story whose chief characters are questing' (p. 97) speaks to the issue, without naming it as such.

10 *Sons and Lovers*: the price of betrayal

Malcolm Pittock

One of the most obvious signs in Lawrence's work of unresolved conflict is the existence of a central paradox: that, though from his own experience he knew the pressures exerted by the social and physical environment on the patterns and possibilities of living and is quite capable of conveying that knowledge in his fiction, yet he is equally likely to ignore it if he finds it convenient to do so. On the one hand, there is the Lawrence who stresses the precise relationship between location, rent and status involved in the Morels' tenancy of an end house in the Bottoms: '[Mrs Morel] enjoyed a kind of aristocracy among the other women of the "between" houses, because her rent was five shillings and sixpence instead of five shillings a week' (*Sons and Lovers*, Penguin edn, 36),[1] and, on the other, there is the Lawrence who can present, with ludicrous insouciance, the spectacle of a grammar school mistress (Ursula) and a LEA inspector of schools (Birkin) giving up their respective jobs: ' ". . . I'm thinking we'd better get out of our responsibilities as quick as we can. . . . We must drop our jobs, like a shot" ' (*Women in Love*, Penguin edn, 397; Camb. edn, 315). Lawrence can be so absorbed in writing of what he feels strongly about – 'the relations between men and women' (*Collected Letters*, Camb. edn, I, 546) – that he blots out any properly consistent awareness of the way all acts necessarily take place in a social context, so that some 'confounded fact' can 'start up and knock the whole thing over' independently of our convenience. Thus he does not try, for instance, to make the 'confounded fact' that the Brangwen inheritance was partible ('the patrimony was divided every time', *The Rainbow*, Penguin edn, 41; Camb. edn, 9) square with the other 'confounded fact' that 'at the Marsh, there was ample'.

Lawrence lacks, in fact, a certain allegiance to the haecceity – the this-ness – of the real world: allowing it to dim out like the lights in a theatre when his gaze is elsewhere. This weakness in the very heartland of his strength is a manifestation on the surface of his fiction of a deep-seated conflict. On the one hand, he had an emotional bias which needed, if occasion demanded it, to remake the world in its own self-interested image, and, on the other, he could, at the same time, never quite conceal from himself what he was doing and why he was doing it: material and social circumstances had impinged altogether too closely on his working-class environment for that to be possible.

One interesting relationship between fictional distortion and an underlying, though consciously unacknowledged, awareness is manifested in the odd fact that in Lawrence's major fiction, involving characters of primary creative interest to him, no woman, however many times she has sexual intercourse, ever gives birth to a child out of wedlock (or a child not the husband's born in wedlock). One could plausibly attribute this to the adoption of contraceptive practices about which the novelist was merely reticent – and Lawrence had used condoms (see Neville, *A Memoir of D. H. Lawrence*, 85–6). However, I do not think it is to be so simply explained. Lawrence's leading ladies can become pregnant as the result of an affair, as Helena in *The Trespasser*, Ursula and Constance Chatterley do – but still no baby is allowed to be born: in the cases of the first two there are miscarriages, while, in that of Connie, the novel ends before the confinement can begin. Although I do not want to press the matter here, there seems, on the face of it, a significant relationship between this odd motif and Lawrence's all too probable sterility and his equally probable awareness of it. There could be no doubt that Frieda was fertile: nor did she and Lawrence appear to practise contraception ('I do not believe, when people love each other, in interfering there', *Letters*, I, 402). To have as one's confessed life work 'sticking up for the love between man and woman' (ibid., I, 492), while trying to keep at bay the knowledge that one cannot father children, is likely to lead to a compensatory attempt to isolate sexuality itself as a locus of value, and, in certain contexts, to divide it from its normal consequences. It was more possible for Lawrence to do this as there were clear, usually medieval, precedents (and Lawrence had some acquaintance with medieval romance). The relationship between Troilus and Criseyde, for example, is puzzlingly infertile, though, in this case, the biological artificiality of the story is a concomitant of its conscious moral heresy (exposed by Chaucer at the end of course) in attempting to transvalue sexuality in contexts where it would normally be condemned by the prevailing culture as fornication.

I want to argue that the example just given of the relationship between reality deformation in Lawrence's fiction and suppressed emotional distortion within himself is itself the consequence of an earlier and crucial repression which prevented his ever facing reality with complete honesty. Lawrence never came to terms – he never could come to terms – with his betrayal of Jessie Chambers and the serious damage he had done her. One sign of his guilt is the lifelong animus he had towards her (like Paul who as a child 'seemed to hate the doll [Arabella] so intensely, because he had broken it', *Sons and Lovers*, 97). It ranges from the emotional coarseness of his letter to Edward Garnett of 2 May 1913 ('It's all very well for Miss Chambers to be spiritual – perhaps she can bring it off – I can't. She bottled me up till I was going to burst. . . . God bless her, she always looked down on me – spiritually', *Letters*, I, 545) right through to Mellors–Lawrence's thinly disguised tirade against her in *Lady Chatterley's Lover* ('"We were the most literary-cultured couple in ten counties. . . . The serpent in the grass was sex. She somehow didn't have any; at least, not where it's supposed to be. . . . So there we split. I was cruel, and left her"', Penguin, 209). The rather perfunctory admission of culpability does not conceal the continuity of tone with the letter of fifteen years earlier. It is significant, too, that the revisions of his poems which Lawrence made for the *Collected Edition* of

1928 are usually towards greater harshness when Jessie is the subject. The most interesting example is the addition of Sections VI and VII to 'Two Wives' which had originally appeared as late as *New Poems*, 1918. This is a curious poem in which wife one (obviously Jessie Chambers) mourns over the corpse of her dead husband (obviously Lawrence) only to be bitterly attacked by the mistress (Frieda). It is these attacks which are not added until 1928 and in them Lawrence can indulge his animosity more freely since he can hide behind a persona of the opposite sex:

> 'But do not touch him, for he hated you
> To touch him, and he said so, and you knew.'
> (*Complete Poems*, ed. Pinto & Roberts, Penguin, 158:
> for changes in the text see ibid., 988)

The whole poem, which in its transposed fantasy mode is very revealing, is of considerable interest and has been surprisingly neglected.

Lawrence's brittle hardness towards Jessie Chambers is the more significant in that it contrasts with his ability to apologize abjectly to Louie Burrows ('I want to say that it grieves me that I was such a rotter to you', *Letters*, I, 479). Undoubtedly, he treated her badly too, but their mutual involvement was not so intense. That the real pain of guilt lay behind the hardness is, indeed, indicated most tellingly in Willie Hopkin's letter to Harry Moore describing Lawrence's last visit to Eastwood:

> He and I went over the old ground. When we reached Felley Dam he stood looking over at the Haggs. I sat down by the pool and when I turned to look at him he had a terrible look of pain on his face. When we got back I asked him when he would come again, and he said, 'Never I hate the damned place.'
> (cited Moore, *The Priest of Love*, Penguin, 530)

When, too, in 1913 he had read Jessie Chambers's *Eunice Temple* (subsequently destroyed), which she sent to him as 'a matter of honour' (quoted *Letters*, I, 525), it had made him so miserable that he 'had hardly the energy to walk out of the house for two days' (*Letters*, I, 551).

Though I would not go so far as Jessie Chambers when she says of *Sons and Lovers* 'his mother conquered indeed, but the vanquished one was her son' (*A Personal Record*, 1935, 202), I think she was justified in her complaint to Helen Corke that 'The Miriam part of the novel is a slander, a fearful treachery' (quoted *Letters*, I, 531). Far from representing a naive failure to discriminate between art and life, her approach to the novel seems – quite apart from the question as to the acceptability of her particular judgement – aesthetically valid. She realized – to use a current terminology – that *Sons and Lovers* was a particularly intimate speech act in which Lawrence was endeavouring through fiction to make sense of his early life so that he could suffuse it with some general, more impersonal significance. The fact that Lawrence showed Jessie the first incomplete draft of the novel, took her advice as to how it should be changed, asked her to provide notes for a later draft, submitted the draft to her piecemeal and further changed it in certain respects in the light of her comments, all point to the absurdity of treating *Sons and Lovers*, as some commentators try to do, as an artefact separate from its creator, with a disembodied narrator who is distinguishable from and critical of his protagonist. After all, even the final form of the novel was given to it by an editor, Edward Garnett.[2]

Nor, of course, did Lawrence himself subscribe to a formalist aesthetic. Indeed, in *Women in Love* he sees a non-speech act view of art most tellingly off. For when Loerke defends his statuette on the grounds that

> '. . . that horse is a certain form, part of a whole form . . . it is part of a work of art,'
>
> (p. 525; Camb. edn, 430)
>
> 'Do you see, you *must not* confuse the relative work of action, with the absolute work of art'
>
> (p. 526; Camb. edn, 431)

Ursula's reply clearly has Lawrence's authority behind it (and, moreover, is nearer the bone than he was perhaps altogether aware):

> 'It isn't a word of it true, of all this harangue you have made me, . . . This horse is a picture of your own stock, stupid brutality, and the girl was a girl you loved and tortured and then ignored. . . . The world of art is only the truth about the real world, that's all – but you are too far gone to see it.'
>
> (p. 526; Camb. edn, 431)

The most blatant evidence of Lawrence's emotional dishonesty in *Sons and Lovers* is the discrepancy between the interpretation of the Miriam sections of *Sons and Lovers* which Lawrence offers to Edward Garnett and what the novel itself tells us ('Never trust the artist'):

> The next son gets a woman who fight for his soul – fights his mother. The son loves the mother – all the sons hate and are jealous of the father. The battle goes on between the mother and the girl, with the son as object. The mother gradually proves stronger, because of the tie of blood.
>
> (*Letters*, I, 477)

This brief description puts the failure of the relationship between Miriam and Paul at Mrs Morel's door. But this is by no means how the novel always presents it. Take the following, for example:

> Sometimes, as they were walking together, she slipped her arm timidly into his. But he always resented it, and she knew it. It caused a violent conflict in him. With Miriam he was always on the high plane of abstraction, when his natural fire of love was transmitted into the fine stream of thought.
>
> (*Sons and Lovers*, 224)

Far from the 'violent conflict' being represented as the result of his mother's sexual hold on him, it is Miriam and her 'high plane of abstraction' who is the real culprit – even though she has taken a *physical* initiative. Obviously she can't win.

To bring the argument round to the point with which I began, I now want to show that the desire to denigrate Jessie Chambers can be related to faults in the novel which are ultimately manifestations of a failure to appreciate the complex reality of circumstance. It is a failure which, interestingly enough, is not present in *A Collier's Friday Night*, the only one of Lawrence's early works which can challenge direct comparison with *Sons and Lovers*. A dramatic masterpiece, *A Collier's Friday Night* (importantly for my argument) was composed before the final break with Jessie Chambers.[3]

There have been other critics, of course, who have claimed that in *Sons and Lovers* Lawrence falsely objectifies his situation. In his chapter on *Sons and Lovers* in *The Novels of D. H. Lawrence: A Search for Integration* (1971), which also contains a valuable examination of those critiques of the novel which have a similar thrust to his own, John E. Stoll justly says:

> In identifying with his characters, Lawrence the artist succumbs to Lawrence the man, a fissure opens between intention and performance, and 'the sickness was not healed, the emotion not mastered, the novel not perfected.' Behind the work and unconsciously distorted within it is an unrecognised neurosis . . .
>
> (p. 67)

Without getting involved in psychoanalytic criticism (and Stoll shows how this has been the burden of those who do not regard the novel as an integrated artistic whole), what I want to show is that omissions and distortions in the representation of reality in the novel can be reasonably interpreted as signs of a desire for moral evasion.

Lawrence's adaptation of the facts of his own and his family's life when creating the Morels reveal clear signs of imaginative slovenliness. Lawrence was the third son and fourth child in a family consisting of five children – three boys and two girls. The others were George, b. 1876; Ernest, b. 1878; Emily Una, b. 1882; and Ada, b. 1887. In *Sons and Lovers* Paul is the second son and third child in a family of four (three boys and one girl). Nor do any of the Morel children have a corresponding position on the grid to the Lawrence children. Of the three sons, George, the eldest, becomes Arthur the youngest. Like Arthur, George lived from an early age in Nottingham, where he was apprenticed (Moore, *The Priest of Love*, 41; *Sons and Lovers*, 213, 232); though, unlike Arthur, George did not go into the army, he must have tried to since Neville speaks of his being 'rescued' from it (*Memoir*, 181). Ernest, the second son, becomes William, the eldest, though still as much older than Paul (seven years) as Ernest was than D. H. Lawrence (*The Priest of Love*, 41; *Sons and Lovers*, 37). Emily Una and Ada form the composite sister Annie, who has some of Ada's characteristics (she becomes a teacher) but, like Emily, is older than Paul. Emily, however, was only three years older than Lawrence, while Annie is five years older than Paul (*The Priest of Love*, 41; *Sons and Lovers*, 37). It is Arthur whose age relative to Paul's more or less corresponds to Ada's to D. H. Lawrence's. (Ada was 21 months younger than her brother: *The Priest of Love*, 41; Arthur is 17 months younger than Paul: *Sons and Lovers*, 85.)

Though all the Morel boys can be related to the Lawrence brothers – even if their relative positions are different – only Ernest Lawrence has been transferred without any significant alteration from life to fiction. With George and D. H. Lawrence the situation is different: thus – to take some of the more obvious features – Arthur, unlike George, wins a scholarship to Nottingham Grammar School (*Sons and Lovers*, 158). Paul, unlike Lawrence, does not, and instead of leaving Haywood's (the Jordan's of the novel) he continues to work there. Nor is Paul a poet and novelist but a painter (though in his youth D. H. Lawrence did, of course, copy paintings).

There is nothing necessarily wrong in making adaptations like this if the adapted character and his circumstances have been consistently re-created. Arthur, however, is not presented as academic and intellectual in any way ('He hated study,' *Sons and Lovers*, 157), and yet he is the one who wins a scholarship! In transferring to Arthur what is essentially his own achievement, Lawrence has done so quite inertly. There is no attempt to indicate why it was Arthur rather than Paul (let alone William) or why, with such an advantage over his brothers, he should have become a tradesman rather than a clerk. This comparatively small but none the less significant point is an indication of Lawrence's imperfect command of objective reality.

This impression is strengthened if we look at Lawrence's treatment of Annie. With Arthur he must have been aware of what he was doing, however implausibly he did it: with Annie he has no settled grasp at all. Although in age she clearly belongs with William, being, as I have indicated, actually two years older than Emily Una, Lawrence seems incapable of remembering this self-imposed imaginative fact with any consistency. Because he has identified Annie with his younger sister Ada in occupation and temperament, he treats her for much of the time as if she was Ada's age as well. Indeed she forms a group with Arthur and Paul, referred to as 'the children'. 'The children played in the street' (p. 98); 'The children lay silent in suspense' (p. 99); 'The three children said not a word. Annie began to whimper with fear' (p. 181). This last occurs when William's corpse is brought home. Since William was twenty-three when he died, Annie should now be twenty-one!

As this last example suggests, the substitution of memory for objectified re-creation leads to a serious distortion in the presentation of Annie's relationship to William. Thus, when William, already the young man about London town, returns to Bestwood for Christmas, we are told, 'The three children could scarcely go into the waiting-room for fear of being sent away, and for fear something should happen whilst they were off the platform' (pp. 120–1). Since William's adult status is insisted on ('The two men [i.e., William and his father] shook hands', p. 122), the incongruity of Annie's being referred to – and behaving – like a child is all the more patent. This is not, however, as flagrant an incongruity as the following:

> . . . Paul never forgot coming home from the Band of Hope on Monday evening and finding his mother with her eye swollen and discoloured, his father standing on the hearthrug, feet astride, his head down, and William, just home from work, glaring at his father. There was a silence as the *young children* entered, but none of the *elders* looked round.
>
> William was white to the lips, and his fists were clenched. He waited until *the children were silent, watching with children's rage and hate* . . .
>
> Morel danced a little nearer, crouching, drawing back his fist to strike. William put his fists ready. A light came into his blue eyes, almost like a

laugh. He watched his father. Another word, and the *men* would have begun to fight. Paul hoped they would. *The three children sat pale on the sofa.*

(pp. 97–8; all italics mine)

If it were not for the last sentence one might be tempted to suppose that Lawrence was thinking only about Paul and Arthur. The realization that Annie is, indeed, included comes as a shock.[4]

So far I have given instances of Lawrence's lack of consistent grasp of the actual where there appears no obvious emotional interest in manipulating reality to his own advantage. But the changes which Lawrence introduces in his own life history when creating Paul clearly cannot, even on the surface, be interpreted as without *parti pris*. In Paul's relations with Miriam, Lawrence aims to reproduce his own with Jessie Chambers as he saw them. In actuality, the particular quality of this relationship had been partly dependent on the existence of four factors:

1 That Lawrence's education was superior to Jessie's so that in the earlier phases he could act as mentor (he had a grammar school education; she had not).
2 That Lawrence had sufficient leisure to see Jessie and her family regularly. The long holidays and short hours of a teacher were important in securing this.
3 That he and Jessie shared a common professional interest – she became a teacher, too, and thus, since they attended the same pupil–teacher centre, had an additional opportunity of meeting.
4 That Lawrence's gifts and interests were primarily literary – so there was much shared reading and Jessie, who had talent herself, could give informed and crucial help at a time when he was finding his feet.

Paul Morel, however, does not go to grammar school and, throughout virtually the whole action of the novel, has a position in an artificial limb factory, though Lawrence himself worked in one only for the first three months after leaving school. Further, Paul is not a writer, but a painter. As for Miriam, she appears to have no profession. And in making these, objectively speaking, unnecessary changes, Lawrence runs into difficulties which could have easily have been avoided had he kept more closely to his own life history.

We have already had a foretaste of them in the seemingly gratuitous transference to Arthur of Lawrence's own grammar school education. This is not only profoundly unsatisfactory as far as Arthur is concerned, as we have seen, but it leaves Lawrence with no readily acceptable explanation of how Paul came to know such non-board school subjects as Algebra and French. Lawrence 'solves' the problem by casually inserting the following in quite different sections of the text: 'Paul, also very clever, was getting on well, having lessons in French and German from his godfather' (p. 93), and 'he knew some French and German and Mathematics that Mr. Heaton had taught him' (p. 130). But this bald information only makes more puzzling why Paul, rather than Arthur, remained at the board school in the first place.

By making Paul continue to work at Jordan's, Lawrence runs into a further series of problems. For the hours taken up by work and travelling occupy most of the day. Paul is represented as leaving home at quarter to seven in the morning (p. 143) and, after working a twelve-hour day (p. 151), arriving home at twenty past nine (p. 151). This corresponds no doubt to Lawrence's actual experience of Haywood's and it is no wonder that Lawrence in life, as Paul in the novel, became seriously ill, particularly since this punishing regimen was shadowed by Mrs Lawrence's trauma following the death of Ernest. Mrs Lawrence made sure that after his illness Lawrence never went back to Haywood's – naturally. And so by making Paul return to Jordan's Lawrence is faced with two pressing problems: to make Mrs Morel's behaviour credible and to allow Paul the leisure to see Miriam and her family which continued employment at Jordan's would have denied him.

Not only can it not be said that he succeeds in making Mrs Morel's behaviour credible: he does not even try to do so. Mrs Morel's anxious and guilt-ridden inquiry of the doctor: '"Might he never have had it [i.e., the illness] if I'd kept him at home, not let him go to Nottingham?"' receives a far from reassuring reply. '"He might not have been so bad"' (p. 186). This, I should think, probably approximates to an actual exchange. And such a woman, in fiction as in life, would hardly have burdened her conscience by exposing a son who had already nearly died to further risks.

Indeed, all that Lawrence can think of to meet both of the problems he has created for himself, that of sufficient leisure time and Mrs Morel's acquiescence at Paul's return, is to alter the working hours at Jordan's in a way which is as incredible as it is perfunctory. Even before Paul's illness, we are suddenly informed that Paul had a regular half-holiday on Monday afternoon (p. 165); it had never been mentioned before and is never mentioned again. An unlikely enough practice, which would doubtless have amused Arnold Bennett. The context shows that it is a mere convenience to enable Paul and his mother to visit the Leivers for the first time. (Lawrence was still at Nottingham High School when he first met Jessie at the Haggs – *The Priest of Love*, 55.) Presumably – if we can take it seriously – this half-holiday is still in force on Paul's return to Jordan's, when we are briefly informed:

> . . . the conditions of work were better. He had Wednesday off to go to the Art School – Miss Jordan's provision – returning in the evening. Then the factory closed at six instead of at eight on Thursday and Friday evenings.[5]
>
> (p. 208)

Naturally we have not heard of Miss Jordan before; and behind this implausible early experiment in industrial day release (and probably the half-holiday too) is the adapted memory of Lawrence's own attendance at a pupil teacher-centre.

Why does Lawrence make the changes that he does in his own life history even though they lead to discrepancies and implausibilities which are ultimately sustained by bald and barefaced subterfuges? I think it was to minimize his debt to and involvement with Jessie Chambers so that he could mitigate the consciousness of betrayal. She was aware of it, of course:

> But to give a recognizable picture of our friendship which yet completely left out the years of devotion to the development of his genius . . . seemed to me like presenting *Hamlet* without the Prince of Denmark.
>
> (*A Personal Record*, 203)

I believe the more significant manifestation of this is his failure to provide Miriam with any profession. Why couldn't she have been represented as the schoolmistress Jessie actually was? Because this would have made her a less isolated and less dependent figure. But Lawrence would hardly have been expressly motivated by so discreditable a reason. I have no doubt that in terms of conscious intention it can be regarded as mere forgetfulness, as with the changing age of Annie. But as with the treatment of Annie, what Lawrence allows himself to forget may be significant.

Lawrence's ability to change, ignore, suppress or muddle material facts when he wanted to justify himself can be paralleled by a significant inability to take realistic account of the wider cultural context. Because Lawrence wants to stress, for example, that, unlike Miriam, Clara is not a threat to Mrs Morel's psychic dominance, he shows the latter entertaining her amicably to tea ('Mrs Morel measured herself against the younger woman, and found herself easily stronger' (p. 386); 'Miriam realized that Clara was accepted as she had never been' (p. 388)). In doing so, Lawrence is falsely abstracting Mrs Morel from the period moral and social attitudes which a real life Mrs Lawrence would and did have (see *A Personal Record*, 117. '"To think that *my* son should have written such a story"' – of an early version of *The White Peacock*; ibid., 126: 'His mother had said how terrible might be the consequences of only five minutes' self-forgetfulness'; ibid., 152, '"Yes, I was glad when I knew there was a baby. It will keep him pure"').

That a woman like Mrs Morel, from a highly respectable Nonconformist Victorian middle-class background, would have been prepared to entertain a married woman separated from her husband with whom her son was friendly was hardly likely even if she was unaware of the erotic character of the relationship: But as Mrs Morel is certainly so aware (Paul actually tells his mother, '"She's fearfully in love with me"', p. 417), hospitality on her part is inconceivable. Since for Lawrence the psychological antithesis between Mrs Morel's attitudes to Clara and Miriam is everything, in search of a false emotional essentialism he schematizes the complex attitudes of a real Mrs Morel. Even when Paul is beaten up by Baxter Dawes and he tells his mother (p. 436), her distress seems unrelated to any moral disapproval.

But not only is Mrs Morel's attitude unrealistic, Lawrence ignores completely the likely reactions of the local community – their behaviour, indeed, is as curious as that of Sherlock Holmes's dog in the night-time. Paul's involvement with Clara would have provided a particularly juicy piece of scandalous gossip and caused Mrs Morel endless embarrassment and humiliation. For it certainly cannot be claimed that it could have been kept secret. When Dawes assaults Paul and Mr Jordan, the latter brings a court case in which Paul's involvement with Clara comes out clearly enough for the magistrate to remark 'Cherchez la femme' (*Sons and Lovers*, 416). Lawrence chooses to 'forget' once more an inconvenient consequence of a situation he has brought into fictional being.

The evidence for Jessie Chambers's belief that Lawrence suppresses crucial aspects of his experience in *Sons and Lovers*, 'He was aware . . . and he refused to know' (*A Personal Record*, 202), the consequences of which I have been tracing on the level of novelistic coherence, emerges more clearly and yet most subtly in his delineation of Miriam. The most obvious case is the presentation in Chapter XI, 'The Test on Miriam', of the consummated relationship between Paul and Miriam. For what is missing from Lawrence's account – and it is a correlative of Mrs Morel's unscandalized acceptance of Clara – is any substantially felt awareness on the part of Paul or his creator of the emotional difficulty for a respectable young woman brought up in late Victorian times, when sexual frigidity was a feminine ideal, of becoming a mistress rather than a wife – and not only because of the risk of an unwanted pregnancy either (though this was important too). It was consequently quite unfair to imply that Miriam's inhibited behaviour in the role of mistress was a sign of a permanent sexual disability. Of course, Lawrence really knew the score: Louie Burrows and her parents had been fussily insistent on observing current proprieties in the year in which he was engaged to her. And, moreover, there are the astonishing anecdotes told by George Neville, which, if he is to be believed, show us a Lawrence who was shocked by Jessie's quiet acceptance of Alan Chambers's information 'that one of the cows . . . was ready for the bull' (Neville, *Memoirs*, 72). As Neville explains: 'At the farm, subjects which in Lawrence's young life had always been strictly taboo were treated as simply coming into the natural order of things' (ibid., 72). And it was a Lawrence, moreover, who became hysterical when he learned that women had pubic hair, attacking Neville and gasping ' "You dirty little devil. It's not true. It's *not* true, I tell you" ' (ibid., 82).

Since in the passages where Miriam is seduced we are approaching the heart of the matter, we should expect that this would be a more complex case than that of Clara, in that in order to engage in suppressions and denials the more effectively, it was imperative for Lawrence to negotiate the admission of a simulacrum of what was being suppressed: a false Florimel of apparent concessions to Miriam's feelings. Consequently there are passages which seem to raise relevant issues – but do so only in an evasive way. Thus Paul makes a remark which is clearly meant to reassure Miriam about the possibility of her becoming pregnant:

'I know it's a lot to ask . . . but there's not much risk for you really – not in the Gretchen way. You can trust me there.'

(p. 344)

It is ironical (though I don't think Lawrence allows himself to see this) that Paul should be so inhibited as to come out with so coyly euphemistic a literary reference (but one that perhaps shows a subliminal awareness on the part of his backward-looking creator of responsibility for betrayal and abandonment) while not properly allowing for the more obviously well-grounded inhibitions that a woman might have.

Even so, Paul has admitted that there is a risk even if he seeks to minimize it. But there is insufficient awareness in the case of either Paul or Lawrence as to just how generous and tactful Miriam is being, particularly in the face of such indefiniteness, when she replies: ' "Oh, I can trust you". The answer came quick and strong' (p. 344). She has, I think, grasped that he must be proposing to engage in coitus interruptus or to use condoms. (And Lawrence does not allow for the extra strain on a woman of Jessie's background of the use of such methods even though, as we have seen, he was to express distaste for them himself.)

Nor can Lawrence bring himself to do more than hint broadly at other and more complex supra-personal inhibitions on Miriam's part in her '"Don't I want your children"' – '"But we must be married to have children"' (p. 352). This has to do duty for what clearly must really have been at work: a strong social inhibition against engaging in extramarital intercourse (after all, even in 1935, Jessie could not bring herself to be explicit about her sexual relations with Lawrence though there was no rational motive for trying to conceal something that had already been revealed). And part of this inhibition – though having a much more obviously natural basis – is the desire to procreate and nurture – just what extramarital sexuality aims necessarily to frustrate ('"You can trust me there"').

So considerable distortion is involved in exhibiting Miriam's frigidity as a permanent, purely personal defect quite independent of circumstances. For these were surely quite enough of themselves to imply clearly that it would have been very difficult for Miriam to have given herself to Paul outside marriage in any other way than by a self-sacrificial act of will which naturally left her tense and frigid. Paul's reproach to her for not feeling desire is cruel: '"That doesn't alter the fact that you never *want* it"' (p. 352), as is his response to her '"Don't I want your children"': '"But not me"' (p. 352).

It might be argued (nowadays it is the kind of thing that always is argued) that Paul's inability to appreciate Miriam's situation is dramatic and involves no necessary complicity on the author's part. But such an apologia is not borne out by the fictional method. Most of the crucial sequence (pp. 344–52) is presented in terms of Paul's feelings: those of Miriam are seldom delineated independently of Paul's apprehension of them – in fact, only in the paragraph beginning 'Miriam plunged home over the meadows' (p. 345) and the two sentences beginning 'She relinquished herself to him' (p. 348). If Lawrence had wanted to show us a Paul who was blind to Miriam's real feelings, he would have been at far greater pains to establish what these were.

Further, from time to time, Lawrence provides 'authoritative' summings up which are clearly biased in favour of Paul. For example:

> He spent the week with Miriam and wore her out with his *passion* before it was gone.
>
> (p. 352)

> And after a week of *love* he said to his mother suddenly one Sunday night just as they were going to bed . . .
>
> (p. 353) (italics mine in both cases)

Lawrence obviously does not want to use 'lust' which, though more appropriate than the words he has used, would be far too unfavourable to Paul. So he speaks inappropriately of 'passion', which is just what Paul's feelings for Miriam has been shown not to be, and even more euphemistically of 'love' – the kind that lasts only a week apparently. Then, of course, there is the tell-tale title of the chapter, 'The Test on Miriam'. It could have been just as objectively titled, 'The Test on Paul.' Finally, it is significant that Paul's attitude to Miriam in the fiction is the same as that expressed by Lawrence towards the flesh and blood Jessie Chambers. 'You are shapely, you are adorned / But opaque and null in the flesh' (Collected Poems, Penguin, 111) he says in his 'Last Words to Miriam', where the use of Jessie's fictional instead of her actual name is of obvious importance for my argument.

Lawrence had to pay a high price for his betrayal of Jessie Chambers (compounded as it was with other betrayals: Louie Burrows, Ernest Weekley, and his and Frieda's children). What mattered was not so much the abandonment of her but the emotional dishonesty of the projective recriminations with which he concealed from himself his own real awareness of the intensity of her suffering and the extent of his responsibility for it. Having had to deform reality in order to sustain his repressions, he could never, in any of his subsequent fiction, consistently view the social environment as having solidity rather than being, when occasion demanded it, frail and plastic, while at the heart of his fiction is a good deal of emotional dishonesty. The full price that could be exacted is revealed most clearly in The Plumed Serpent which is self-indulgently stupid in its attempt to project fantasy on to an actual society. Only someone who was capable of reducing the complexities of stubborn social realities to a mere congeries of manipulable ideas could possibly have perpetrated it.

And there is the very real achievement of A Collier's Friday Night to show that Lawrence could have been honest in Sons and Lovers. For in this play Lawrence has selected and arranged the material of his life with a much surer hand: because there he was aware only of the problem, he did not have to justify the betrayal too; that was still in the future. In A Collier's Friday Night (which is closely related to Sons and Lovers, 249–69), Lawrence has provided Ernest Lambert with one sister only, Nellie (Ada). But Ernest and Nellie Lambert's relationship is presented convincingly and without confusion. Similarly Ernest Lambert is represented as being at college as Lawrence, of course, was. Not only is Lambert's resentment against his son thereby given a new dimension, but Ernest's brittle student slang and artificiality of manner convey not only his immaturity but the class elements involved in the situation. As a consequence the play is juster to Arthur Lawrence than the novel and the sense of a profound emotional impasse persisting under the daily routine of domestic life is beautifully rendered in an ending which has been earned by the complex analytic grasp of the situation that the play has revealed. Lawrence's even-handed method allows us to realize why the relation between Ernest and Maggie can never succeed. That Lawrence subsequently wrote off the play as 'most horribly green' (see Sagar, Life into Art, 35) may not be without significance either: for the success of its premiere at the Royal Court in 1965 showed that such a judgement had no objective basis. It is indeed the best play that Lawrence ever wrote. But what was the reason for his animus against it and the pretence that it had been completed much earlier than it clearly was? (In its present form it cannot be earlier than 1909.) We are back where we began.

Notes

1 All subsequent references are to this edition.
2 See Keith Sagar, *D. H. Lawrence: Life into Art* (Harmondsworth, 1985), ch. 3, '"A Great Tragedy": the genesis of *Sons and Lovers*' for a full account of Jessie Chambers's role.
3 See Sagar, *Life into Art*, 36–44.
4 To make matters even more unsatisfactory, there are times when Lawrence does remember that Annie is supposed to be older than Paul. Thus she 'was now studying to be a teacher' (p. 93) when Paul is still at school. Again (p. 96) we are told that 'Paul was towed round at the heels of Annie'. Annie also marries before the end of the novel, when Paul is nearly 23, though Ada did not marry until 1913 (*Letters*, I, 27). However, it is clear that Lawrence is not thinking of Emily Una's marriage since this had taken place as early as 1904 (*Letters*, I, 36). One sign of this is that Annie's marriage is treated as premature and unseemly ('Morel called her a fool for getting married . . . Paul could not quite see what Annie wanted to get married for', p. 301). It would be rather difficult to represent the marriage of a mature woman of twenty-eight in this light!
5 It is not clear whether this closing at 6 p.m. on Thursday and Friday is a new practice. Certainly, like the half-holiday, we have not heard of it before. Moore, *The Priest of Love*, 59, says of Haywood's, 'sometimes work finished about two hours earlier on Thursdays and Fridays'. It is not clear where he obtained his information other than from the very passage discussed.

*

This essay first appeared in *Essays in Criticism*, XXXVI (July 1986). It has been slightly shortened.

11 Craftsman before demon: the development of Lawrence's verse technique

Christopher Pollnitz

The account Lawrence gave of the development of his verse technique in the 'Note' to his *Collected Poems*[1] – tying it to his own personal development, and describing it as a fight to free 'his demon' from a self-censoring 'young man' – has received general acceptance. Not only have apologist commentaries, like Vivian de Sola Pinto and Warren Roberts's introduction to *The Complete Poems* (*CP*, 1–21), linked the evolution of his work to the concept of a biographical self-liberation, but even critics determined to attack the poetry have attributed its failure to this identification of the man who suffers with the man who creates. Thus, while R. P. Blackmur set out to change the terms of Lawrence's 'Note' – the 'young man' was for him the 'poet as craftsman', while the demon represented those passions which, undisciplined by craft, led to sentimental self-expression – he too discussed the poems in relation to the career of the young man and his infirmities of character.[2] The legacy of these early studies persists even in the most recent: his verse-craft is still only discussed in relation to Lawrence's life or sense of life.[3]

The advantages of studying Lawrence's changing technique in isolation (the pages that follow trace this process up to the shaky technical maturity achieved in *Birds, Beasts and Flowers*) are more than just novelty. Since the 1970s the critical estimate of Lawrence's poetry has risen, as has the number of studies appearing; but these appraisals have proceeded in a technical limbo. While doubts are sometimes raised as to whether Lawrence's verse is even poetry,[4] there has been no sustained debate about the kind of poetry it is.[5] These pages attempt to open such a discussion, relying only on the familiar terms of diction, tone and genre, and of classically derived prosody. The discussion throws into question, not the fact that for Lawrence the achievement of a distinctive poetic voice was something that had to be lived through and fought for, but his description of the voice as that of a 'demon'. Lawrence's mature voice is less an inversion of the Protestant Inner Light, less the one voice divinely and unescapably given, than it is a collage of voices needing to be invented, assembled and constantly remade. Finally, the analysis that follows has the advantages of reading Lawrence's verse in the context of other Modernist poetry, and of revealing the extent of the antagonism between Lawrence's individual talent and any preceding tradition.

The first phase of Lawrence's verse-composition ends in 1912, but includes poems Lawrence continued to revise until 1918. The antagonism in these early poems is to a much earlier poetic generation, to the 'gem-like lyrics of Shelley and Keats' (*CP*, 182); but the bulk of the verse Lawrence produced in reaction to their lyric 'finality and perfection' nevertheless accords well with the loosening of accentual-syllabic metre practised by the generation preceding his own. Four different verse-styles, one close to Shelley's, others to those of other later nineteenth-century practitioners, can be distinguished in this first period.

The first of these styles, the staple of the verse designated *Rhyming Poems* in *Collected Poems*, is a long-lined discursive style, usually broken into quatrains. Most lines are hypermetric, a mix of iambs and anapaests.[6] The lines are also hypermetric in the sense that, within a given poem, they may extend from tetrameter to heptameter or even beyond. The opening stanzas of 'Dreams Old and Nascent', Lawrence's first published poem, are representative:

```
x x  /  x   x   /  x x   /   x  /   x  x  /
I have opened the window to warm my hands on the sill
    x   x  /   x     /   x x   /    x  /x  /
Where the sunlight soaks in the stone: the afternoon
x  / x    /       x /   x   /   x x  /
Is full of dreams, my love; the boys are all still
x x  /  x   /    x  / x   /
In a wishful dream of Lorna Doone.

   x   /   x x   /  x   /  x x  /    x  /
The clink of the shunting engines is sharp and fine
  x   /  x   / x   /  x x  /   x x  /
Like savage music striking far off; and away
x  (x) x  / x    x   /  x  /     /   /  x     /
On the uplifted blue Palace, light pools stir and shine
   x    x   /  x  /    ‖ x x   /   x   /
Where the glass is domed   up the blue, soft day.
```
                                                    (*CP*, 922)

The scansion would be altered by a different reading of the last two lines, but as they stand, 'pools stir' is a lingering spondee made possible by the uncertainty of the metrical beat, and the eighth line is two half-lines, each echoing the other as the dome of the Crystal Palace mirrors the sky. Although Lawrence manages some interesting local effects, however, the style *en bloc* is undistinguished. The irregular accenting throws emphasis on the rhymed line-endings, which are marred, in most of these early poems, by a quota of gratuitous fillers. Few do not include at least one stanza of halting McGonagallese.[7]

Easier on the ear are the short-lined early poems – 'Dog-Tired' for example – cast in lyric stanzas of irregular line-length but otherwise modelled on the taut stanzas and free rhythms of Shelley's lyrics.

Lawrence made a trial of the capacity of free verse to mimic kinetic movement in a sequence of early poems, collected in his first College notebook (Ferrier, MS 1) under the title 'Movements'.[8] These poems deserve to be considered as a third style of verse, one which Lawrence evidently found too limiting to use in more than this handful of prototypes. But the delicacy with which he renders a toddler's running or the vigorous cadences which mime adult motion in 'A Man at Play on the River' show what a versatile free-verse technician Lawrence could be as early as 1909:

A swift, dexterous man, plying the slender pole,
His body pulsing with play
His full, fine body bending and urging like the stress of a song,
Darting his light punt with the quick-shifting fancy of verse,
Among the shadows of blossoms and trees and rushes,
In-weaving the bright thread of his joy
Flashing his bright, brown arms as he leans on the pole,
His blue shirt glimmering in the water among the shadow of trees,
Threading the round joy of his white-flannelled hips full of play,
Up the river, under the trees,
Down the river, in the gleam of the sun,
Across the river, bending low
In one swift bound to the house-boat.

(*CP*, 871)

While the rhythms imitate the stresses of punting, the verse relies for structure on its parallel participial constructions. Such parallelism, and the focus on the active male body, point to the impact of Whitman on Lawrence's verse-writing.

Just prior to 'Movements' in Lawrence's first College notebook may be found 'A Still Afternoon in School', a poem in which Whitman's influence irrupts into Lawrence's verse-style. 'A Still Afternoon' is the first version of a poem already quoted, 'Dreams Old and Nascent'. Lawrence begins this first draft in ink and rhyming quatrains, abandons ink for pencil after the fourth stanza, after the fifth stanza abandons rhyme, and after the ninth stanza abandons quatrains. There is evidence, that is, that Lawrence is composing directly into the notebook and is being carried along, at speed, by the release into free-verse and the impulse of Whitmanian ideas.

Here in my class is the answer for the Great Yearning
Eyes where I can watch the swim of dreams reflected on
    the molten metal of dreams
Watch the stir which is rhythmic, and moves them all
    like a heartbeat moves the blood
Here, in the swelling flesh the great activity working
Visible there in the change of eyes and the face

Oh the great mystery and fascination of the unseen
    shaper,
Oh the power of the melting, fusing force
Heat, light, colour, everything great and mysterious in
    One swelling and shaping the dreams in the flesh

> Oh the terrible ecstasy of the consciousness that I am
>   life
> Oh the unconscious rapture that moves unthought with
>   Life
> Oh the miracle of the whole, the wide spread labouring
>   concentration of life
> Swelling mankind like one bud to bring forth the fruit
>   of a dream
> Oh the terror of lifting the innermost I out of the
>   sweep of the impulse of Life
> And watching the Great thing labouring through the
>   whole round flesh of the world

There are some affinities with 'the procreant urge of the world' called on by Whitman in 'Song of Myself', but probably the main text Lawrence is translating, from Brooklyn to Croydon, is 'I Sing the Body Electric', with its paeans to the flesh and to homoerotic passion. Yet one interest of this outcropping of Whitmanesque free verse in Lawrence's early work is its rarity.

Lawrence's notebooks suggest that he did not discover Whitman for the first four years of his practice as a poet, and show that he did not write again in this parallelist mode, with any frequency, until 1915. Here, then, there are indications of a fear of influence, and inferences may be drawn as to why, for Lawrence, the fear was acute. Lawrence as poet is not a stylist. He did not find in Whitman a detachable freedom of poetic organization, but rather a demagogic verse-form inseparable from the American's political, erotic and religious enthusiasms. For Lawrence to have said, 'Let there be commerce between us',[9] would have been for him to surrender his own sensibility to Whitman's imperializing embrace. So the young poet took his 'innermost I' back to writing long-lined quatrains and Shelleyan lyrics.

In mixing feet and freeing accent from syllable-count, Lawrence was following a trend among later nineteenth- and earlier twentieth-century poets, a trend he endorsed in Meredith and Hardy as 'the brutalising of English poetry'.[10] The deregulation of accentual-syllabic verse was taken to its extreme by scholarly poets like Hopkins, who evolved a new, purely accentual metric from the extinction of the old. When Lawrence had his mimesis and metric under control, he could produce tautly sprung lines, like the opening stanza of 'Discord in Childhood'. Yet his verse-form lets down many promising early poems: why could Lawrence not produce, from his own irregular metric, verse with the poise of Hopkins', Hardy's or Meredith's? The much revised early notebooks suggest that it was not so much neglect of his craft as a particular ignorance.

Lawrence defended the form of his early poems in a series of letters to the Georgians' editor, Edward Marsh. His first line of defence was to claim that his irregular rhythms imitated shifts of emotion in the way 'A Man at Play on the River' had mimed bodily motion.[11] By 18 November 1913, however, Marsh's arguments had driven him on to less subjective, more contestable ground. He speculated that his poetry might be read 'more by length than stress', and went on to repeat his concern that both rhythm and verse-reading should enunciate lyric emotion:

It all depends on the *pause* – the natural pause, the natural *lingering* of the voice according to the feeling – it is the hidden *emotional* pattern that makes poetry, not the obvious form. . . . It is the lapse of the feeling, something as indefinite as expression in the voice, carrying emotion.

(*L*, II, 104)

What Lawrence appears to have been feeling his way towards was a free verse, the governing principle of which would be speech-rhythm. But, having beside him a volume of Ernest Dowson, he also attempted to apply his speculations to one of the 1890s' best-known poems. He scanned four lines from the third stanza of Dowson's 'Non Sum Qualis Eram Bonae Sub Regno Cynarae':

```
x x   x x   /   /  x x   /   x   x   /
I have forgot much, Cynara! gone with the wind,
   x   / x   / x   /   x x x   x      /
Flung roses, roses riotously with the throng,
   /   x    x x x   /   x   / x  [x] [x]  /
Dancing, to put thy pale, lost lilies out of mind;
   x x x   / x x    x  /  x x   /   / x
But I was desolate, and sick of an old passion. . . .[12]
```

Lawrence may have had the impression that Dowson arrived at the striking rhythms of this, his finest and freest poem, by imitating quantitative metre, the metre of the Horatian ode from which he drew his title. In fact, Dowson's 'experiment' was the result of imitating Lionel Johnson's imitations of the French Alexandrine.[13] Dowson allows himself certain un-French liberties with syllable-count and caesurae, but the important liberation he achieves, experimenting with English dodecasyllabics, is a controlled uncertainty about when the next accent will fall. Breaking away from iambic metres and casting out of his verse 'those energetic rhythms, as of a man running', Dowson is still, in 'Non Sum Qualis' and a number of other poems, crossing his 'passionate prose' with the 'ghostly voice' of a metrical norm. The result is 'vivid speech that has no laws except that it must not exorcise the ghostly voice'; it is vivid accentual verse that a longer-lived member of the Rhymer's Club from whom I have been quoting, W. B. Yeats, would make the hallmark of his style.[14]

Turning back to Lawrence's scansion of Dowson's lines, I can find only one of Yeats's two voices represented. Lawrence registered the spoken stress he would place on these lines, but remained deaf to the 'ghostly voice' of metrical accent. Eager to throw off the shackles of tradition, Lawrence was simply unaware of how some metrical regularity, in the case of Dowson and of other late nineteenth-century experimenters, was essential to producing the impassioned accent he heard in their work. The fault in Lawrence's poetic equipment was his failure to appreciate the vital tension in verse between speech-rhythms and metre. It is the falling apart of this tension in Lawrence's longer-lined irregular verse that leads to stanzas of trudging versification or rhyming prose. Given his lasting insensitivity to this creative tension, the way forward for Lawrence's poetry lay in verse-forms freed from metre, but forms that were less overwhelming than Whitman's in their potential influence.

Lawrence was introduced to Anna Hepburn or Anna Wickham, to use her *nom de plume*, in the summer of 1914, and from August to December in 1915 was her near neighbour in Hampstead.[15] During these months he tried to interest Marsh and Harriet Monroe in a number of her poems, which were eventually published in *The Man with the Hammer*. Wickham's epigrams advocating free verse appear in this same volume, her 'Note on Rhyme' for instance –

> Rhymed verse is a wide net
> Through which many subtleties escape.
> Nor would I take it to capture a strong thing,
> Such as a whale.

– and her 'Comment':

> Tone
> Is utterly my own.
> Far less exterior than skill,
> It comes from a deep centre of the will:
> For nobler qualities of Song,
> Not singing, but the singer must be strong.[16]

Although some of Wickham's satires, like the wonderful 'Nervous Prostration', do look forward to Lawrence's *Pansies*, neither the bulk of her verse nor the centre of her achievement – the brief, gnomic lyrics of *The Man with the Hammer* and the Hardyesque reminiscences of *The Little Old House* – much resemble Lawrence's free verse. Most of her free verse is rhythmically conservative: pegged out with iambic lines, as if to prevent its erosion into prose. As for her superior handling of line-length and rhyme, there was no reason for Lawrence to learn these from Wickham's verse when he had not learnt them elsewhere.

The rapport Wickham claimed to have with Lawrence as a man was based on class, on her understanding of his experience of board school education and on their shared religious heritage: 'Lawrence asked two things of me: that I should talk to him, and sing hymns with him, the lovely hymns of our grandfathers. . . .'[17] The importance of that Nonconformist heritage to Wickham's own work is evident in its emphasis on 'will', strength and the individual soul or 'innermost I'. For Wickham the appropriate speech of that soul was the core vocabulary of the hymn-tradition, the purified diction of Blake's *Songs*. Her gift to Lawrence was perhaps to reintroduce him to the possibilities of his religious upbringing when it came to refashioning his verse, and, more particularly, his diction. To her influence can be attributed the advice Lawrence gave to Catherine Carswell, early in 1916:

> I *do* wish . . . you didn't use metre and rhyme. . . . The essence of poetry with us in this age of stark and unlovely actualities is a stark directness, without a shadow of a lie, or a shadow of deflection anywhere. Everything can go, but this stark, bare, rocky directness of statement, this alone makes poetry, today.
>
> (11 January 1916, *L*, II, 502–3)

The work of Lawrence's own which fulfils this new poetic of 'stark directness' includes such uncollected war poems, written in 1915, as 'Resurrection' and 'Erinnyes', and such later poems from *Look! We Have Come Through!* as 'New

Heaven and Earth' and 'Manifesto'. After 'A Still Afternoon at School', these are the most Whitmanesque poems Lawrence ever allowed himself to write. Permission would probably not have been granted, had he not believed he was synthesizing Whitman's 'barbaric yawp' with the diction of his native Nonconformism.

Yet late poems from *Look! We Have Come Through!* like 'Craving for Spring', with its Whitmanesque trans-Atlantic gesturings, Shelleyan syntax and Non-conformist diction, do not point the direction of Lawrence's mature free verse. Lawrence, the irrepressible mimic, was not to find his own voice in trying to isolate an ancestral diction. The better poems in *Look! We Have Come Through!* are the shorter-lined lyrics from early in the sequence, where Lawrence allows rhyme or conventional rhythms to determine the shape of the line and even the stanza. 'Gloire de Dijon', with its description of a woman's 'swung breasts . . . like full-blown yellow / Gloire de Dijon roses', contains some fine imagery and relaxed rhythms:

> She drips herself with water, and her shoulders
> Glisten as silver, they crumple up
> Like wet and falling roses, and I listen
> For the sluicing of their rain-dishevelled petals.
> In the window full of sunlight
> Concentrates her golden shadow
> Fold on fold, until it glows as
> Mellow as the glory roses.

(*CP*, 217)

The pentameter of the first and third lines is enjambed into rhythms miming the kinesis described; the last four lines pick up a trochaic momentum and dipodic lilt that are quite sensitively handled. But the rhyme and the inverted verb in their main clause remain Georgian, conjuring awkward shades of Walter de la Mare into the sunlight.[18]

Compare, however, the uncertain technique behind 'Gloire de Dijon' (one of a series of poems probably inspired by a distaste for Yeats's *Rose* sequence)[19] with H.D.'s 'Sea Rose':

> Rose, harsh rose,
> marred and with stint of petals,
> meagre flower, thin,
> sparse of leaf,
>
> more precious
> than a wet rose
> single on a stem –
> you are caught in the drift.
>
> Stunted, with small leaf,
> you are flung on the sand,
> you are lifted
> in the crisp sand
> that drives in the wind.

Can the spice-rose
drip such acrid fragrance
hardened in a leaf?[20]

An oblique tribute to the subtlety of the alliterative and assonantal patterns
which knit together each of H.D.'s early poems, from the first to the last page of
Sea Garden, is that they have passed virtually unnoticed. Alliteration in 'Sea
Rose' is supplemented by half-rhyme ('harsh'/'sparse', 'stint'/'thin') and
strings of consonantal clusters ('stint'/'stem'/'stunted', 'drift'/'drives'/'drip').
But the poem's main acoustic impetus is imparted by assonance, by the
denaturing of the deep *o* of 'rose', the pushing of vowels higher and further
forward in the mouth, till all that remains is 'crisp sand / that drives in the
wind'. This is a technique in full possession of itself.

H.D.'s poetry, the product of long and arduous revision,[21] is arguably the
most technically demanding free verse produced by any English or American
Modernist. She should have had little cause to wonder that, 'when it came to
one, any one, of her broken stark metres, he [Lawrence] had no criticism to
make':[22] if only by withholding his advice, Lawrence was admitting that here
was a poetry he could learn from. Contrariwise, H.D., though finding little to
admire in the poems of *Look! We have Come Through!* ('[she] says they won't do
at all; they are not *eternal*, not sublimated', Lawrence puzzled),[23] was herself
puzzled by the freedom of self-revelation in Lawrence's work, and surprised by
his powers of sympathy and vision. From a memory of 'Gloire de Dijon' she
developed a private mystical term, the *gloire*, for a numinous halo cast around
certain objects or events.[24] Yet the importance of their creative collaboration,
as of Lawrence's friendship with Anna Wickham, has been obscured by the loss
of the correspondence. In H.D.'s case, her letters from Lawrence were burnt by
Richard Aldington; in Wickham's, they were destroyed by a fire-bomb in the
Second World War.[25]

Despite different backgrounds, Wickham and H.D. could both feel themselves unaccepted in England's literary establishments, for more reasons than
their gender. Wickham's class background and Australian upbringing were
matched by H.D.'s American nationality and Moravian religious training.
Himself a congenital outsider to the lettered classes he liked to move among,
Lawrence had particular interest in the quarrels writers like these, or like
Katherine Mansfield, had with orthodox forms. His own remaking of English
fiction was actuated less by the Modernist's stylistic passion to make it new
than by a conviction that the fictional mould he inherited had to be broken and
recast to accommodate the new range of experience he brought to it. His
eschewing accentual-syllabic conventions from his earliest work (one of the
few poems in which he attempted conventional euphony, 'Tease', has a
decided parodic edge to it) bespeaks a similar unwillingness to dress his raw
materials in metres which would conventionalize their rawness. A poet like
H.D., with both an *outré* background and a passion for a personal, stylistic
precision, was well qualified to influence Lawrence's poetic technique. The
oblique but powerful sexual component of her poetry was an added lure.

Initially, pagan classicism may have attracted H.D. as a means of distancing
herself from her sexually charged but repressive Moravian background; later,

Hellenism and Imagism became the means of externalizing a repressed mysticism and sexuality. In 'Hermes of the Ways' the broken sand-grains are made receptive by the wind to 'the great waves' advancing over the leagues towards them, and a similar receptivity attends the persona's passive waiting for 'him / of the triple path-ways, / Hermes', a god who suffers yet seems to orchestrate these greater elementals. Early H.D. poems invoke and identify with small objects that lie at the mercy of, and in waiting for, a self-destroying, oceanic power. And in the sexual mysticism of these Imagist lyrics Lawrence heard a deep calling to his deep. His response upon meeting H.D. –

> I was at dinner with Miss Lowell and the Aldingtons last night, and we had some poetry. But, my dear God, when I see all the understanding and suffering and the pure intelligence necessary for the simple perceiving of poetry, then I know it is an almost hopeless business to publish the stuff at all, and particularly in magazines. It must stand by, and wait and wait. . . . Mrs Aldington has a few good poems.
>
> (*L*, II, 203)

– is proof enough that he was able to recognize in her a fellow, inwardly searching and driven artist. At this stage anything less than a religious vocation in a poet seemed to Lawrence to be trifling with the externals of poetry, to be 'piffling', to use one of his favourite pejoratives. Indeed, as the war progressed, a banned and persecuted Lawrence turned away from his earlier, intimate lyrics to verse as guardedly impersonal as H.D.'s, with its esoteric symbolism and hierophantic tone.

In *Bid Me to Live* the H.D. character, Julia, recalls which of her poems the Lawrencian 'Rico' preferred:

> He liked her flower poems. He had particularly liked the blue iris-poem, that day at the top of the Berkeley, overlooking Green Park.
>
> (*Bid*, 141)

The second and concluding part of H.D.'s 'Sea Iris' asks:

```
x   x   / x  /  x
Do the murex-fishers
    /     x  x  x    /
drench you as they pass?
x   x   /    /  x  /  x
Do your roots drag up colour
   x    x   /
from the sand?
   x    x    /     /   x   x   x
Have they slipped gold under you –
  /   x x   /
rivets of gold?

   /   x / x  /   x
Band of iris-flowers
x  /    x    /
above the waves,
```

```
     x    x    /   x   /
```
you are painted blue,
```
     /   x   x   x   /      /
```
painted like a fresh prow
```
     /       x   x   x   /      /
```
stained among the salt weeds.

(SG, 40)

Like Anyte of Tegea, whose inscription to Hermes provided the model for
'Hermes of the Waves',[26] H.D. adopted the basic mode of the inscription or
invocation for her Imagist poems. The vocative syntax that results leads to
frequent falling rhythms and heavy, spondaic stressing. H.D.'s free verse is best
described – using a term from Pound's Imagist manifestos[27] – as 'cadenced', as
patterned by characteristic rhythms or cadences the frequency and character of
which are not easily represented by the usual English feet.

Such cadenced verse is quite different in its movement to the irregular verse
Lawrence produced prior to meeting H.D., but similar cadences begin to
appear, some six years later, in the short-lined passages of *Birds, Beasts and
Flowers*. This verse-paragraph from 'Almond Blossom' reproduces both H.D.'s
mode of address and her rhythm, as Lawrence describes by invoking the
colours of the flower before him:

```
     /   x   /   ‖ /      /   x x
```
Knots of pink, fish-silvery
```
     x   /   x x   /   x      /   x
```
In heaven, in blue, blue heaven,
```
     /   x   /   x   /   x      /   x   /   x
```
Soundless, bliss-full, wide-rayed, honey-bodied,
```
     /   x   x   /
```
Red at the core,
```
     /   x   x   /
```
Red at the core,
```
     /   x x   /   x x /   x   /      /
```
Knotted in heaven upon the fine light.

(CP, 307)

The scansion could show more spondees than have been marked, but even as
represented, there is still much close stressing linked by runs of lightly stressed
syllables. Comparison shows that Lawrence's syntax in his flower poems is
freer than H.D.'s; it has room for more speech-structures and rhetorical
fragments, but it has the same vocative formations and a very similar
cadencing.

If all the lineaments of H.D.'s invocations cannot be found by rummaging
through the *Greek Anthology*, there is a genre closer to hand which supplies the
remaining characteristics – the Romantic ode. Shelley's 'To a Sky-Lark', with
its invocations and long series of images, is an apposite model. As does Shelley
in the ode, H.D. in her poems both addresses and questions her objects, the
interrogatives diversifying a syntax that might otherwise become monot-
onous. Most of the questions are rhetorical, as in 'Sea Iris', where the closing

lines merely reassert the frail beauty that has been questioned. But the interrogatives open the possibility of disclosures about subject as well as object. Is there not a touch of whimsy, of the American ingenue perhaps, in the question about rivets?

Such whimsy and such interrogative syntax are found throughout the more expansive free-verse odes in *Birds, Beasts and Flowers*:

> On he goes, the little one,
> Bud of the universe,
> Pediment of life.
>
> Setting off somewhere, apparently.
> Whither away, brisk egg?

('Tortoise Family Connections', CP, 356)

It is worth remembering that Robert Bridges, in 'A Passer-By', had asked of a 'splendid ship' under sail 'Whither away, fair rover?',[28] but also noting that parody is only part of Lawrence's breezy humour here. The prevalence of such humour throughout *Birds, Beasts and Flowers* is the most important marker of tonal difference between Lawrence's and H.D.'s poetries. Yet for Lawrence comic banter may cohabit with a hierophantic seriousness. His interrogative formations serve equally well for both:

> What is it?
> What is it, in the grape turning raisin, .
> In the medlar, in the sorb-apple,
> Wine-skins of brown morbidity,
> Autumnal excrementa:
> What is it that reminds us of white gods?

(CP, 280)

After-dinner pleasantries may be transformed in an instant into eerie catechisms, and vice versa.

Both poets vary tone through their interrogations of objects. In 'Sheltered Garden' H.D.'s questionings lead not to whimsy but to searchingly earnest conclusions:

> Why not let the pears cling
> to the empty branch?
> All your coaxing will only make
> a bitter fruit –
> let them cling, ripen of themselves,
> test their own worth,
> nipped, shrivelled by the frost,
> to fall at last but fair
> with a russet coat.
>
> Or the melon –
> let it bleach yellow
> in the winter light,
> even tart to the taste –
> it is better to taste of frost –

the exquisite frost –
than of wadding and of dead grass.

For this beauty,
beauty without strength,
chokes out life.

(SG, 18–19)

The question initiates a chain of vitalist moral injunctions, the dogmatism of which is only deflected by their being couched in symbolism. This strategy is one so familiar to readers of Lawrence's work that one may cast around at first for some suggestion of Lawrence's influence on H.D. Yet there is none, I think, in this passage. Rather it is corrective to realize that another Modernist writer, having produced the effect, could choose not to reproduce it thereafter. And though the pattern is frequent in Lawrence's work, it is not always used to prophetic effect: it may both set up and modulate moral pronouncements. Consider the interrogative endings of 'Figs', or 'Bare Almond-Trees', or 'Pomegranate':

Do you mean to tell me there should be no fissure?
No glittering, compact drops of dawn?
Do you mean it is wrong, the gold-filmed skin,
integument, shown ruptured?

For my part, I prefer my heart to be broken.
It is so lovely, dawn-kaleidoscopic within the crack.

(CP, 278–9)

Here, in one of Lawrence's swiftest and most beautiful tonal shifts, he at once retreats towards a vulnerable selfhood and reasserts his purchase on a universal truth.

As Richard Aldington remarked, 'anyone can see from his *Collected Poems* . . . Lawrence was for a time influenced by H.D.'[29] It takes only slightly more perspicacity to pick where that influence was first exerted. It is discernible in the revisions Lawrence made, in April 1918, when preparing early poems for publication in the inappropriately named *New Poems*. In 'Embankment at Night Before the War: Charity' he attempts a rhyme-scheme more flexible and a cadence subtler than the old *abab* iambic-and-anapaestic quatrains. Also from *New Poems*, 'Parliament Hill at Evening' is an example of a short descriptive poem lifted out of a long early sequence so that it becomes an Imagistic fragment.[30] The impact of H.D.'s work is even stronger in the in-more-than-name new poems Lawrence composed about this time and published in *Bay* – poems which, their urban settings suggest, Lawrence wrote in late 1917 while staying in H.D.'s flat. 'Bombardment' and 'Town in 1917' have a freer cadencing and evolve from a single image in a manner that would be more like H.D.'s, were it not for the retention of rhyme and the eruptions of tittering humour:

London
Used to wear her lights splendidly,
Flinging her shawl-fringe over the River,
Tassels in abandon.

And up in the sky
A two-eyed clock, like an owl
Solemnly used to approve, chime, chiming
Approval, goggled-eyed fowl!

(CP, 170)

Bay is Lawrence's least considerable volume of poetry. The critical biographer's problem is to explain how, in under three years, its adolescent humour and unstable technique were transformed into Lawrence's mature verse.

In a solidly illuminating chapter on *Birds, Beasts and Flowers* from *Life into Art*, Keith Sagar has revised his chronology of that volume's composition. Retracting his former suggestion that the first poem written was 'The Mosquito', Sagar now proposes that

> the earliest poems are probably a group of three short and untypical poems, 'Tropic', 'Peace' and 'Southern Night', written at the beginning of June.[31]

Living in Taormina, Sicily, in June 1920, having put his friendship with H.D. and the 'nightmare' of the war firmly behind him, Lawrence began to write poetry again in a manner almost totally H.D.'s. Compare 'Southern Night' –

> Come up, thou red thing.
> Come up, and be called a moon.
> The mosquitoes are biting to-night
> Like memories.
>
> Memories, northern memories,
> Bitter-stinging white world that bore us
> Subsiding into this night.
>
> Call it moonrise
> This red anathema?
>
> Rise, thou red thing,
> Unfold slowly upwards, blood-dark;
> Burst the night's membrane of tranquil stars
> Finally.
>
> Maculate
> The red Macula.

(CP, 302)

– with H.D.'s 'Oread':

> Whirl up, sea –
> whirl your pointed pines,
> splash your great pines
> on our rocks,
> hurl your green over us,
> cover us with your pools of fir.[32]

Both poems are mystic and sexual incantations. Like H.D.'s mountain nymph, Lawrence's white European consciousness entreats rape by a looming elemental power. The differences lie only in temperature profiles and levels of explicitness. The imperative syntax ('Come up' or 'Whirl up') and the Imagist technique (the superimposing of forest and sea, moonrise and erection) are identical. Freed from rhyme, Lawrence's cadences at last assume those falling rhythms, with sudden clusters of stress, that characterize the passages of invocation-and-description in *Birds, Beasts and Flowers*. Looked at in terms of his development 'Southern Night' is the poem in which Lawrence assimilates the lessons of Imagism.

The vatic stance of Lawrence's little incantation is undercut at one point only, by a line of pure prose-consciousness that contributes to the symbolism only as an afterthought: 'The mosquitoes are stinging tonight / Like memories.' H.D., constantly revising and marshalling her tonal intensities, would have been incapable of such a broadening, as well as flattening, breach of decorum. This is the line singled out by Marjorie Perloff, in her pioneering article on the 'theatrical role playing' in *Birds, Beasts and Flowers*,[33] as giving a sense of the performing artist, a sense that he may be going to wear more than one mask, that he may enter wearing his pyjamas instead of his cape. It may not be a grace-note, but the mosquitoes sound the note of the reality principle, and it was this note, of nagging persistence and wry admission, that enfranchised Lawrence's free verse.

What remains is to trace how Lawrence came to elaborate from this note the tonal complexity which is essential to *Birds, Beasts and Flowers* and which makes it not a pale imitation of *Sea Garden* but very much Lawrence's own, and his best, volume. While not the first poem in the volume to be written, 'The Mosquito' is, Sagar remains certain, one of the first, possibly datable to August 1920.[34] I suggest it is the odd key which opened the door to Lawrence's mature verse.

The new dictional resource that Lawrence the realist poet draws on in 'The Mosquito' is the vernacular. He discovers that he can use the language of his familiar letters, and the wit of his conversation, in his poetry. The simultaneous discovery of this in his essays makes it plausible that it was the experience of living abroad, for the first time since 1914, which re-alerted Lawrence to the untranslatable nuances and possibilities of English idiom. 'The Mosquito' opens with a playful touch of English xenophobia and English idiom: 'When did you start your tricks, / Monsieur?' It recalls a notable vernacular witticism: 'I heard a woman call you the Winged Victory / In sluggish Venice'. And it puns on colloquialism and cliché at its close:

> Are you one too many for me,
> Winged Victory?
> Am I not mosquito enough to out-mosquito you?

> (*CP*, 334)

If the juxtaposition of this mock-heroic 1920s banter with the arcane chantings of the Lawrencian blood-mysteries produces some peculiar moments, 'The Mosquito' is a no less curious performance in its larger effects.

The poem is both a narrative, about a one-sidedly life-and-death game played between a man and a Sicilian mosquito, and an Ode to a Mosquito, an insect that, because it is as representative as Keats's nightingale, should not be 'born for death'. The odic address to the Mosquito ('I heard a woman call *you* the Winged Victory / In . . . Venice') is undercut by the narrative address to the rival mosquito ('Come then, let us play at unawares, / And see who wins in this sly game of bluff'). It can hardly, narrative logic reminds us, have been the same mosquito in Venice that is playing bluff in Siracusa. This anomaly is played on within the poem ('Are you one too many for me'?) and in the conspicuous definite article of the title. The killing of *the* mosquito terminates the ode. Indeed, the narrative denouement exposes the factitiousness of odic discourse, the intrinsic falsity of questioning an inarticulate life-form and ventriloquizing its answers. A Romantic ode (this is Lawrence's point in his essay, 'The nightingale')[35] robs the object addressed of its otherness, or blood-being, more insidiously than squashing the life out of it. Better to be a narrative protagonist than a sneaky odist: you will at least have to confront 'the infinitesimal faint smear' left behind when you physically destroy the other.

Lawrence does more in 'The Mosquito' than enliven the narrow tonal band of H.D.'s Imagism with contemporary talk. He also explodes the august Romantic dialectic of subject and object, but explodes it, I would maintain, in order to reconstitute it on his own epistemological terms, terms which are in some ways still Romantic, in others postmodernist. 'The Mosquito' does appear to be the breakthrough, the poem in which he finally secedes from the Imagist and Romantic ode and produces a new mode. Generically, it is at once narrative, lyric and metapoetic; formally, it combines both cadenced and spoken rhythms; tonally, it plays a game with a reader's expectations as subtle, if not as deadly, as that played with its nominal addressee.

By autumn 1920 'Peach' illustrates the tonal and formal richness of Lawrence's mature verse:

Why, from silvery peach-bloom,
From that shallow-silvery wine-glass on a short stem
This rolling, dropping, heavy globule?

I am thinking, of course, of the peach before I ate it.

Why so velvety, why so voluptuous heavy?
Why hanging with such inordinate weight?
Why so indented?

Why the groove?
Why the lovely, bivalve roundnesses?
Why the ripple down the sphere?
Why the suggestion of incision?

Why was not my peach round and finished like a billiard ball?
It would have been if man had made it.
Though I've eaten it now.

(CP, 279)

The acoustic patterns are as intensely worked as in an H.D. poem. Worth mentioning are the assonance on the hard *o* that fills the mouth in 'This rolling, dropping, heavy globule'; the labiodental alliteration beginning with '*velvety*' that sinks teeth into the flesh of even the silent reader; and what I have heard called the Shylock hiss of 'incision'. A reverence for otherness and the creative principle is part of the burden of these lyric lines, as is a mythopoeia of blood-sacrifice. But this is only half the story. The story itself is a transparently simple one, of a man's eating of a peach. The lyric cadences and odic questions are cut across by the humorous asides of the narrative protagonist ('I am thinking, of course, of the peach before I ate it'). The speech-rhythms in these asides contribute a new dimension of plebeian insouciance. A final voice that chimes in is that of the moral orator, with his large questions and prepared, predictable answers. But no voice, certainly not his, has the last say in this comedy of manners.

Generically, 'Peach' is a monologue, not an ode; the 'you' addressed is a silent auditor. But to call it only a monologue would be to miss the generic and tonal interplay of this dialogic poetry. Lawrence as novelist, Lawrence as moral prophet, Lawrence as pagan and Protestant mystic: these are the moving forces in Lawrence's psychological make-up which could not be satisfied within the genre of lyric, and which impelled him to the creation of this new and composite verse-style, a 'lyric theatre' as Marjorie Perloff has called it. This was the poetry in which he satisfied his Protestant artistic conscience not by isolating and speaking with his innermost voice but with the voices of all his known selves.

It would be too much to say of each of these voices that it brings with it not only its own tone but its own inalienable syntax and rhythm, making the verse a conglomerate of these. But scansion of 'Grape' or 'Almond Blossom' reflects what happens in these poems in terms of content and tone: they begin with cadenced invocation, then turn off into the spoken terrain of moral discursiveness and mythopoeic speculation, before at last returning to lyric cadences. A full description of the rhythms of *Birds, Beasts and Flowers* would need to take into account not only the linear cadences and speech-rhythms but the larger, circular patterns of theme and image. These too recur according to what Lawrence called 'the old pagan process of rotatory image-thought',[36] a process which informs both his essays and poems in the 1920s.

As a final, and surely superfluous, defence of Lawrence's poetry as poetry, it can be observed that the rhythmic structures of *Birds, Beasts and Flowers* are fundamental to the volume's discourse. Instead of the superimposition of rhythm on metre found in accentual-syllabic and accentual verse, what Lawrence contrives in this volume is a fundamental juxtaposition of cadence and speech rhythms. The juxtaposition signals how the poetry must be read: dialogically. Any voice apparently speaking with authorial conviction will have its authority challenged a few lines, or a few poems, later. If the volume were rearranged by order of composition, it might be possible to show the elaboration of this dialogic method, from early work like 'The Mosquito' to a later poem like 'Purple Anemones', where the complex vocal collage is made up of carefully distinguished elements.

The poems of *Birds, Beasts and Flowers* are a paradox, polyphonic lyrics. While Browning might be invoked as an antecedent, it is clear that this conglomerate poetry could not have been written, had its author not been a novelist with a novelist's concern for social realism and manners, any more than *The Rainbow* could have been written, had its author not been a poet with a poet's concern for symbol and mythopoeia. Yet the synthesis achieved in *Birds, Beasts and Flowers* was, in the hands of the novelist-poet who achieved it, unstable. In *Pansies* it was shattered again into different voices and distinct modes. It is worth remembering that Lawrence arrived at this synthesis through irreverent poetic parody, and that, as a novelist in' the 1920s, his concern was not to remake but to unmake English fiction. No doubt he would have prescribed for the health of English poetry what he prescribed for the health of English fiction, a bomb. Tremors of his iconoclastic impatience can already be felt stirring in the shifting metapoetic foundations of *Birds, Beasts and Flowers*.

Notes

1 *The Complete Poems of D. H. Lawrence*, ed. Vivian de Sola Pinto and Warren Roberts, 3rd edn (London, 1972), 27–8. Future references to this edition are shown as *CP*.

2 R. P. Blackmur, 'D. H. Lawrence and expressive form', in *Language as Gesture* (London, 1954), 286–300; published previously in *The Double Agent* (New York, 1935).

3 See M. J. Lockwood, *A Study of the Poems of D. H. Lawrence* (London, 1987), 13.

4 See, for example, Philip Hobsbaum, *A Reader's Guide to D. H. Lawrence* (London, 1981), 135–6.

5 One study – Hebe Riddick Mace, 'The achievement of poetic form: D. H. Lawrence's *Last Poems*', *D. H. Lawrence Review*, XII (1979), 275–88 – has focused on Lawrence's later prosody. Mace's premiss, that free verse must have 'metrically, a clearly identifiable pattern', leads her to devise a system of nineteen 'extended feet', to which further variants are added. Her assumptions are not followed here.

6 With some very irregular lines it may be necessary to admit paeonic feet (one stressed and three unstressed syllables), if scansion by feet is maintained.

7 [The name of McGonagall is not always familiar to North American readers. He was a charmingly bad Scottish verse-maker of the last century, addicted to hypermetric feet. *Ed.*]

8 See Carole Ferrier, 'D. H. Lawrence's pre-1920 poetry: a descriptive bibliography of manuscripts, typescripts, and proofs', *D. H. Lawrence Review*, VI (1973), 333–59. The poems in the 'Movements' sequence are 'A Baby Running Barefoot', 'A Baby Asleep after Pain', 'The Body Awake' (later 'Virgin Youth'), 'A Man at Play on the River' and 'The Review of the Scots Guards' (later 'Guards').

9 See Ezra Pound, 'A Pact', *Collected Shorter Poems* (London, 1952), 98.

10 See Carl E. Baron, 'Two hitherto unknown pieces by D. H. Lawrence', *Encounter*, XXXIII (August 1969), 4.

11 *The Letters of D. H. Lawrence*, ed. James T. Boulton *et al.* (Cambridge, 1979–87), II, 61, 18[–20] August 1913. Future references to this edition are shown as *L*.

12 *L*, II, 103. Lawrence's use of the symbols of quantitative prosody has been changed, two syllables he omitted to scan are added, and the scansion is placed over the text of Dowson's lines as punctuated in the standard edition, namely, *The Poetical Works of Ernest Dowson*, ed. Desmond Flower (London, 1967), 52.

13 The metre of the Horatian poem from which Dowson's takes its title (*Odes*, IV, i) is the Third Asclepiad, which cannot be imitated in accentual verse. For Dowson's imitation of the French and his debt to Johnson, see *The Letters of*

Ernest Dowson, ed. Desmond Flower and Henry Maas (London, 1967), 184, [7 February 1891].

14 W. B. Yeats, *Essays and Introductions* (London, 1961), 163, 524.

15 *L*, II, 208, 17 August 1914; and David Garnett, *Great Friends* (London, 1979), 85.

16 Anna Wickham, *The Man with the Hammer* (London, 1916), 14, 13.

17 *The Writings of Anna Wickham*, ed. R. D. Smith (London, 1984), 366.

18 Cf. de la Mare's 'All That's Past', in *The Listeners* (London, 1914).

19 See *L*, I, 488, 17 December 1912: 'Thanks for the Yeats. . . . He seems awfully queer stuff to me now – as if he wouldn't bear touching.'

20 H.D., *Sea Garden* (London, 1916), 1. Further references to this edition are shown as *SG*.

21 See Barbara Guest, *Herself Defined: The Poet H.D. and Her World* (London, 1985), 10.

22 H.D., *Bid Me to Live* (London, 1984), 80. There is warrant for reading the account of relations between Julia and Rico in this novel as H.D.'s memoir of her relationship with Lawrence. Further references to this edition are shown as *Bid*.

23 *L*, III, 102, [9 March 1917].

24 *Bid*, 168, 176.

25 See Robinson, *H.D.; The Life and Work of an American Poet* (Boston, 1982) 122; and Wickham, *Writings*, 23.

26 Guest, *H.D.*, 40; and see Peter Jay (ed.), *The Greek Anthology* (Harmondsworth, 1981), 74, 78.

27 See 'A retrospect', from *Literary Essays of Ezra Pound* (London, 1954), 3–14.

28 See Robert Bridges, *Poetical Works* (London, 1913), 244.

29 Richard Aldington, *Life for Life's Sake* (London, 1968), 127.

30 'Evening', an earlier draft of 'Parliament Hill in the Evening', had been the first part of a sequence entitled 'Transformations' in Ferrier, MS 5. See *DHLR*, VI (1973), 345.

31 See Keith Sagar, *D. H. Lawrence: Life into Art* (Harmondsworth, 1985), 208; and cf. Sagar, *D. H. Lawrence: A Calendar of his Works* (Manchester, 1979), 101.

32 H.D. *Collected Poems*, ed. Louis L. Martz (Manchester, 1984), 55.

33 Marjorie Perloff, 'Lawrence's lyric theatre: *Birds, Beasts and Flowers*', in Peter Balbert and Philip L. Marcus (eds.), *D. H. Lawrence: A Centenary Consideration* (Ithaca, NY, 1985), 108–29.

34 Sagar, *Life into Art*, 216.

35 *Phoenix* (London, 1936), 40–4.

36 *Apocalypse*, ed. Mara Kalnins (Cambridge, 1980), 95.

12 *Birds, Beasts and Flowers*: the evolutionary context and an African literary source

Christopher Heywood

In the course of his Mediterranean tour of 1920–1, Lawrence met Jan Juta, the South African artist who contributed illustrations to *Sea and Sardinia* (1921) and whose portrait studies of Lawrence are among the most striking ever made of him. At Anticoli, where the Lawrences visited Juta from 2 August 1920, Juta lent Lawrence a copy of an important African literary text, *Specimens of Bushman Folklore* (1911), by W. H. I. Bleek and Lucy L. Lloyd, a book which remains in his collection.[1] The impression made by this work on Lawrence's mind remained with him eight years later when Brewster Ghiselin notes that he spoke about 'some translations of stories by Bushmen that he had once read'[2]. My purpose here is to suggest that the power of Lawrence's most important collection of poems, *Birds, Beasts and Flowers* (1923), owes much to the impact on his imagination of this mythological, cultural and poetic treasure-house.

Bleek's *Specimens*, a selection from the notebooks of a pioneer of African literary studies, remains to this day a principal source for knowledge of San ('Bushman') lore, language and literature. The work of Bleek and his family circle culminated with the posthumous publication in 1956 of the *Bushman Dictionary* by his daughter, Dorothea Bleek (1867–1948), Reader in African Languages at the University of Cape Town.[3] Of studies in various aspects of the extensive San and Khoi ('Hottentot') language group, Professor Ernst Westphal has written: 'very little remains of an authoritative and comprehensive kind that cannot be ascribed to members of the Bleek family'.[4] Bleek's work in South Africa as translator, interpreter and founder of modern studies in African languages has extensive roots in the liberal intellectual movement in Germany, where his father, Heinrich Bleek (1793–1859), was a professor of theology at Bonn from 1829. The family circle included W. H. I. Bleek's cousin, Ernst Haeckel (1834–1919), the evolutionary writer whose *The Riddle of the Universe* (1901) was read by Lawrence in 1908.[5] The kinship between the two men was probably not known to Lawrence, who may also not have known that Haeckel wrote a preface to another of Bleek's important works, *The Origin of Language*.[6] Nevertheless, *Birds, Beasts and Flowers* is a recapitulation and summation of Haeckel's evolutionary thought and a bridge between his modern scientific positivism, which Lawrence guardedly espoused, and the visionary, mythical world which was mediated by Bleek's African text. Indeed, in the thinking underlying Lawrence's enigmatic section 'The Evangelistic Beasts', San literary tradition supplies clues to Lawrence's meaning.

The *Specimens* comprises some eighty texts, many with variants and all with close documentation relating to their provenance. The texts are selected from the many hundreds of oral texts which Bleek and his sister-in-law, Lucy Lloyd, collected from authentic sources during the years 1870–85.[7] Despite his early death in 1875, his sister-in-law, by then adept in the language, the performances and the transcription methods which produced the texts, continued the work for a further decade, finally bringing her selection to light in the volume of 1911. A further selection by Dorothea Bleek, who had assisted her aunt in preparing the volume for printing, was published in 1923.[8] Care was taken from the outset to maintain exceptionally high standards of collection, transcription and presentation. San speakers of outstanding achievement were recruited with permission from successive colonial governors, Sir Harry Barkly and Sir Philip Wodehouse. A small, displaced community which simulated the numbers and conditions of traditional San family groups was established in the Bleek household. That these individuals were recruited from the prison community of a population on the brink of extermination emphasizes the sense of urgency and the devotion the Bleek family brought to their work and underlines the quest for authenticity which underlay the task, the first and last of its kind to be undertaken among the now extinct San population of the Cape. The documentation of oppression and suffering is a poignant ingredient in these texts, which foreshadow many elements in the subsequent literature of South Africa. Of the procedure of writing down the oral narratives of the principal performer, ‖Kabbo, one of the eight narrators who provided texts, Lucy Lloyd later writes: 'He was an excellent narrator, and patiently watched until a sentence had been written down, before proceeding with what he was telling. He much enjoyed the thought that Bushman stories would become known by means of books' (*Specimens*, x). The gravity and explicitness of his material are in contrast with the work of another narrator, Dia!kwain, who is more notable for the imaginative colouring he gives to his exposition of transformations, dreams and astronomy. A great measure of certainty can be accorded to the probable impression made on Lawrence by the performances of the boy narrator !Nanni, which appear as an Appendix (*Specimens*, 405–33) and which were collected by Lucy Lloyd. Besides offering the most concentrated instances in the volume of the transformation lore which is predominant in the San tradition and which Lawrence recalled fairly accurately in his discussion with Brewster Ghiselin, the songs of !Nanni include the 'Prayer to the Young Moon' (*Specimens*, 414–15), in which aspects of Lawrence's late poem 'Invocation to the Moon' are foreshadowed. Most striking of all is the foreshadowing of Lawrence's poem 'Snake' which occurs last in the volume in the narration by !Nanni: 'A Certain Snake, which, By Lying On Its Back, Announces a Death in The Family, And Which Must Not, Under These Circumstances, Be Killed' (*Specimens*, 431–3).

Lawrence's handling of nature, evolution and natural life in *Birds, Beasts and*

Flowers (a text omitted by Roger Ebbatson from his study of Lawrence's relation to evolutionary thought) has a strong affinity with Haeckel's cosmogony in *The Riddle of the Universe*, but differs from it in crucial points.[9] These points of difference are charged with values stemming not so much from Bleek himself as from the literary tradition which he interprets and mediates. Lawrence and Haeckel concur in invoking a cataclysm overtaking European social and religious life and in proposing a Coleridgean remedy which would entail a return to ancient roots and the oneness of man, nature and the universe. *Birds, Beasts and Flowers* invokes categories of human awareness and existence which the poet apprehends and which stem from his reading and experience: but from which his own lamented upbringing, itself a product of the cataclysm, drags him back, as Mephistophiles drags Faust to an omnipresent hell. Denunciation of a negation entails, as Blake found, traffic with defilement. Perhaps giving Lawrence more credit than he would have given himself for escaping from the maelstrom of modern ironic negativism, Sandra Gilbert expresses the problem thus: 'He focused his mind with the meditative intensity of a medieval mystic, consciously hurling his poems like so many inkwells at the "cold devil" of nerve-brain irony who threatens the dark gods of the intuitional unconscious.'[10]

Though the framework of Lawrence's thought in the volume stems from Haeckel, the drift of the work is toward a mythic view of the world. As he saw it, this view is obscured to modern man but retrievable through patience, study and instructive encounters with natural phenomena. *Birds, Beasts and Flowers* forms, as Professor Warren Roberts has observed, 'a literary bridge between Europe and America'.[11] But when he was contemplating his Mediterranean visit as a first stage of the pilgrimage, Africa was in Lawrence's mind, and Jan Juta was pressing him to make a visit.[12] In one of the meditative passages in *Sea and Sardinia*, Lawrence reveals his view of the interchangeability of the American, African and Mediterranean experiences of the suppression of ancient religions: 'She [Eryx Astarte] is a strange goddess to me, this Erycina Venus, and the west is strange and unfamiliar and a little fearful, be it Africa or be it America.'[13] In her supplementary study of Lawrence's poetry, Sandra Gilbert characterizes this cycle of poems as Lawrence's descent into a newly found underworld, 'a botanist's or zoologist's Black Mass'.[14] In this infernal journey, Lawrence arrives at a vision of America as an extension of the world of negation in which his own education had implicated him. Self-correction figures largely in his journey through hope and despair: 'so that for us to go to Italy and to *penetrate* into Italy is like a most fascinating self-discovery, back, back down the old ways of time.'[15] In the moral wilderness created by the egotism, irritability and negativism of which he accuses himself in 'Snake', 'Bat' and 'Man and Bat' (animals with strong representation in the San repertoire), Lawrence reaches out to the *Specimens* as a repository of the integration of man, nature and magic. Whereas Haeckel offers scientific method as the escape route towards a universality of human interests, Bleek offers instead the more appealing message of language and myth as the underlying feature in all human life. Whereas Haeckel sees Africa as the haunt of human forms scarcely evolved beyond simian forms – 'auf der tiefsten Stufe menschlicher Entwicklung . . . am wenigsten von den Affen entfernt'[16] –

Bleek sees language as 'the cement that binds together all the parts of the gigantic organism of humanity, and the expressions of this endowment bear a certain analogy to the circulation of the blood in the animal body'.[17] Bleek points especially to the vanished art of the San as a major repository of a mythic vision of the world: 'The main importance of this Bushman literature lies in the mythological character of the stories . . . in which animals and heavenly objects are personified' (*Specimens*, 445). Lawrence's vision of a supranormal perception of the world – and his identification of it with San culture in opposition to the brutalization of the American continent by the European heritage – is illustrated in his introduction to Edward Dahlberg's *Bottom Dogs*, a work written around the time of his 'Invocation to the Moon' and the interview with Ghiselin. In his introduction Lawrence emphasizes the 'most brutal egoistic self-interest' of the form of the hero Lorry's 'minimum of human consciousness', a depth 'far lower than the savage, lower than the African Bushman'.[18] Thus, of the two ingredients of the German heritage of romantic liberalism, it is the mythic rather than the scientific element which acts as a release to Lawrence's imagination in his romantic quest for self-knowledge.

In the cycle, the strongest evidence of Lawrence's involvement with San imaginative themes occurs at the time of his contact with Jan Juta, when the *Specimens* first became available to him. Of the forty-eight poems in the printed text of *Birds, Beasts and Flowers*, five were written before the contact with Juta. These poems, 'Mosquito', 'Trees', 'Tropic', 'Southern Night' and 'Humming-Bird', lack all evidence of the San preoccupation with magic transformation, the feature which Lawrence remembered best when he spoke to Ghiselin and referred to 'stories by Bushmen . . . in which the qualities of things seemed to be in continual change'.[19] The poem written about his encounter with a snake in the hot weather of July 1920 carries, in contrast, the strongest available evidence of literary indebtedness. Lawrence was receptive to African influences at this time, since in June, before meeting Juta, he had written in the poem 'Tropic' about '. . . my hair twisty and going black. / Behold my eyes turn tawny yellow / Negroid' (*CP*, 301). In 'Snake' Lawrence records an incident which followed Juta's visit to Taormina during the hot weather of July which immediately preceded Lawrence's visit, on 2 August, to Juta's house at Anticoli, where the copy of the *Specimens* lay in wait for him. The exact sequence and duration of the composition of 'Snake' cannot be determined; nevertheless, parallels with !Nanni's narrative 'A Certain Snake', which occurs last in the *Specimens*, point strongly to the presence of the newly found San literary source in Lawrence's new phase of composition. By the end of September, Lawrence had composed a total of twenty-four poems and, in November, he arrived at his title. Although by this date the 'Flowers' sequence had yet to be composed, the 'Fruits' had been written in September. The inclusion of plant life as a major theme is an inevitable consequence of the title, taken from Sabine Baring-Gould's hymn, and of the strongly evolutionary cast, taken from Haeckel, which Lawrence gave to the cycle of poems.

Thus, whereas the vision of animal life before his encounter with San tradition was entirely Haeckelian, after his contact with the *Specimens*, Lawrence's picture of animal life adopted African characteristics. In 'Humming-bird', the only 'Bird' poem written by the time the title came to him, Lawrence looked to this phylum as a latecomer in an evolutionary chain whose beginnings were among reptiles. He invokes a time when the various bird species were still undifferentiated, when there were 'no flowers', and 'probably he was a jabbing, terrifying monster' in 'that most awful stillness' (*CP*, 372). This positivist, Wellsian view is abandoned in the vision of the snake as a 'lord of life' whom he wrongly wished to kill. The San view of nature, in which the snake is a guardian and messenger (as in other African traditions), is graphically illustrated in various rock paintings[20] and in !Nanni's 'Snake' narrative. Commenting on the peculiarities of San custom, Lucy Lloyd provides the exact accent of Lawrence's 'education', from which he strives to emancipate himself:

> On one occasion I saw a snake close to the coping of a burial place; and showed it to !Nanni, expecting him to destroy it. He merely looked at it in rather a strange way, and allowed it to depart uninjured; saying something about its being near a grave; which, at the time, I did not clearly understand.
>
> (*Specimens*, 431)

In his explanatory narrative !Nanni explains how a certain harmless snake species, normally killed by women, must be left alone if it exposes its belly:

> (If, when) we strike it, it does in this manner with its belly, [that is, turns the under side of its body upwards] it gives us its belly, we fear it, and go away, and return home; while (we) do not kill it. For (we) let (it) alone; and it lies, lies; arises, (and) goes away altogether. . . . Another day, we see it, (when) it is in the water – tree water [that which is in the hollow of a tree] we are near it, we think that it will drink water, we see its body, (when) it is in the water, (and) it sees us, it quickly goes out of the water, and lies upon the ground. We think that we will strike it, and it gives us its belly, we turn back, we go away, and it alone lies (there) . . .
>
> (*Specimens*, 430–3)

This foreshadowing of Lawrence's poem, the self-confessed original incomprehension of the editor and her eventual recognition of another level of apprehension about snakes, the water-drinking and the indecision of the narrator about whether to strike or not, the association of the animal with life and death, all point to the strength of the impression made by this work on Lawrence. Lawrence's repetitions, 'And truly I was afraid, I was almost afraid' and 'I . . . must wait, must stand and wait', the 'hot, hot day', etc., catch the accent of San speech, as in !Nanni's 'and it lies, lies, lies' and 'we approach it, approach it, approach it' (*Specimens*, 433).

In a late poem, 'Invocation to the Moon' (*CP*, 695–6), Lawrence returned to the spirit of !Nanni's 'Prayer to the Young Moon', in which the San doctrine of the ambiguous relationship between life and death is obliquely referred to. The date of composition of this poem, which appeared in *Last Poems*, is uncertain, but it clearly falls near Brewster Ghiselin's visit, an event which prompted Lawrence's long meditative reflection with him on African culture and art, and his perceptive recollection of the *Specimens*. In his long poem, Lawrence invokes a being who will, he hopes, as death approaches, 'give me back my lost limbs' and make of him 'a healed, whole man, O Moon!' Lawrence's prolonged fascination with moonlight as a marker of transitional states in the social integration of the individual has been frequently noted; but as Sandra Gilbert observes, a new quality enters into his image of the moon at this point: 'Her power and her beauty reside in the very remote and radiant spirituality that the younger writer saw as deadly.'[21] A new strand among the many known mythological sources of Lawrence's literary obsession can accordingly be found in the 'Prayer to the Young Moon', recounted by !Nanni and explained by Dia!kwain in one of the finest performances, 'The Origin of Death; preceded by a Prayer Addressed to the Young Moon' (*Specimens*, 414–15 and 56–65). The San doctrine of death and immortality is contained in these texts. According to the tradition, the principle of mortality and immortality resides in the moon, since – unlike the sun – it disappears and reappears. In another narrative, 'Habits of the Bat and the Porcupine' (*Specimens*, 246–53), Dia!kwain links it to the powers of the nocturnal hunter, upon whose skill survival may depend. The moon is the origin of death, since the hare – at the time when all creatures were men – doubted the immortality of his mother, made his doubt known in a complaint to the moon, and incurred the moon's wrath. As a result, the hare received a blow on the lip and was reduced to a lesser creature; other animal species, which had been men, emerged; and men entered into mortality. Nevertheless, the moon is constantly invoked as the guarantor of regeneration for the individual. The belief in a moon with ambiguous powers of destruction and regeneration appears with singular force in Lawrence's poem. The directness and colloquiality of his 'Invocation' and its 'lapses into cuteness or vulgarity, as fairy tales may', noted by Sandra Gilbert,[22] probably stemmed from the *Specimens*. The special obsession of the hare with his mother's mortality reappears in Lawrence's 'Spirits Summoned West', the last but one of his poems in *Birds, Beasts and Flowers*, in which he appears as a pilgrim making a progress toward his mother's grave. In the 'Invocation', now facing his own death, he appeals to the moon's healing powers and asks to be taken to her dwelling:

> Be good to me, lady, great lady of the nearest
> heavenly mansion, and last!
> Now I am at your gate, you beauty, you lady of all nakedness!
> Now I must enter your mansion, and beg your gift
> Moon, O Moon, great lady of the heavenly few.

> (*CP*, 695)

!Nanni's song foreshadows this theme:

> Young Moon! Speak to me! Hail, Hail,
> Young Moon!
> Tell me of something.
> Hail, hail,
> When the sun rises,
> Thou must speak to me, that I may eat . . .

> (*Specimens*, 414–15)

The narrative by Dia!kwain illustrates the versatility of San narrative styles at work on similar thematic material. Here the same theme appears in personal, descriptive and interpretative terms which come closer to Lawrence's phrasing:

We, when the Moon has newly returned alive, when another person has shown us the Moon, we look towards the place at which the other has shown us the Moon, and when we perceive it, we shut our eyes with our hands, we exclaim: 'kabbi-a yonder! Take my face yonder! Thou shalt give me thy face yonder! Thou shalt take my face yonder! That which does not feel pleasant. Thou shalt give me thy face, (with) which thou when thou died thou dost again, living return, when we did not perceive thee, thou dost again lying down come, – that I may also resemble thee – for, thy joy yonder, thou dost always possess it yonder, that is, that thou art wont again to return alive, when we did not perceive thee; while the hare told thee about it, that thou shouldst do thus. Thou didst formerly say, that we should also again return alive, when we died.'

(*Specimens*, 56–9)

The numerous parallels of theme and intention point strongly to Lawrence's recollection of the *Specimens* in his 'Invocation', as in 'Snake'. In verse technique, however, Lawrence retains his stance as a romantic explorer of individual experience and makes no attempt to imitate the role of the traditional oral poet, whose function is to transmit imperatives relating to an environment in which survival is dependent on skills or community values invoked in the poems.

*

In his recollection to Brewster Ghiselin, Lawrence paid especial attention to the mobility of species and the doctrine of transformation, a feature with particularly abundant representation in San oral tradition. Lawrence recalled stories 'in which the qualities of things seemed to be in continual change: now the giraffe would seem to be large, now small, now vague and far, now looming over.'[23] Though the recollection of a giraffe is erroneous, since no giraffe appears in the *Specimens*, Lawrence here probably misremembered an equally stately species, the hartebeest, which figures in the first narrative in the *Specimens*, 'The Mantis Assumes the Form of a Hartebeest' (pp. 2–16). In this story, ‖Kabbo portrays the divine spirit, the insect god 'Mantis', who 'cheated the children, by becoming a hartebeest, by resembling a dead hartebeest', triumphing with divine cunning over their efforts to dismantle his carcass. Moving around the near and far distances, he transcends death and frustrates his inexperienced pursuers:

He was as if he was dead; he was (afterwards) opening and shutting his eyes; he afar lay talking (while the children were running off). He talked while he mended his body; his head talked, while he mended his body. His head talking reached his back; it came to join upon the top (of his neck).

He ran forward; he yonder will sit deceiving (at home) while we did cut him up with stone knives (splinters). a-tta! he went feigning death to lie in front of us, that we might do so, we run.

(*Specimens*, 15)

The spirit of cunning in the divine trickster appears in Lawrence's narrative of the bat and its triumph over its would-be captor in 'Man and Bat'. The animal eludes capture and appears in a number of metaphorical guises, a 'beast in air', 'big as a swallow', a 'clot with wings', 'a prayer', and eventually reveals itself as instructor to his captor and liberator: 'I am greater than he' (*CP*, 340–7). This transforming, humanized power of the animal world reappears in the portrayal of the 'Evangelistic Beasts', the enigmatic group of poems which, together with the 'Tortoise' sequence and the greater part of the 'Fruits' group, formed Lawrence's main output of verse in September 1920. In that month, the tour of Sardinia was completed, and Lawrence's return to the mainland was the occasion for an outburst of writing in which the technical and intellectual themes of the *Specimens* had been assimilated, appearing with greater oblique-ness than the direct indebtedness of 'Snake'. The Haeckelian themes occur again, especially in the portrayal of reptiles other than the snake species. Thus, the tortoises recapitulate the evolutionary struggle of man, rising from 'non-life' in 'life's unfathomable dawn' through the 'primeval rudiments of life' in a quest which enacts and foreshadows the Passion of Christ: they are 'crucified into sex' (*CP*, 353–64). Here, Haeckel's distinctive doctrine, 'ontogenesis recapitulates phylogenesis' (that is, the individual's embryonic development re-enacts the development of the phylum and its families of species), provides the intellectual base from which Lawrence works. But in other poems written in September, Lawrence reverted to the contrary pressure exerted by San traditional animal lore.

In the 'Evangelistic Beasts' series, another distinctive framework taken from Haeckel – his crusading view of the corrupting influence of Christian ortho-doxy – provides no more than a framework for a San picture of animal and divine transformation. San theology involves a belief in the divine presence in insect form, in the person of the predatory 'Mantis'. The Greek name for this family of species indicates Mediterranean acknowledgement of their peculiar watchful intensity, and Germanic vernacular names in southern Africa, 'Hotnotsgod' and 'Hottentot-god', have registered the indigenous reverence for these creatures' cunning, skill and expressively human cast of features. Known variously as ‖kaggen and !Xue, this representative of the divine essence is capable of impersonating all the forces of nature. He is, however, subject to fits of incomprehension and pride and frequently suffers adversities from natural rivals who understand and exploit his weaknesses. !Nanni's sequence of texts includes the striking narrative of !Xue, who appears as a San equivalent of Lawrence's own emblem, the phoenix: '!Xue as Water and Other Things. In his Own Form, he Rubs Fire and Dies' (*Specimens*, 405–13). Here, Mantis appears in successive transformations as fruit, a tree, the Man Omuherero, a fly, water, a lizard, a hunter, a winged creature, a fire-maker and fugitive from his father in his mother's country. In a study making more use of San tradition than most recent investigations of African literary art, Richard Karutz writes of the 'divine grasshopper Mantis, the image of the metamorphoses of the spiritual life, which occurs in hundredfold forms'.[24] Recognition of this central doctrine underlies Lawrence's use of this theme, which is apparent from the *Specimens*, as the basis for a polemical reading of Christian orthodoxy in the 'Evangelistic Beasts' section. An answer to Sandra Gilbert's question, not attempted in her study, 'Why have the "Evangelistic Beasts" been placed between "Flowers" and "Creatures"?',[25] can be offered: insects fall in the evolutionary chain between plant and vertebrate life, and Lawrence endows his evangelists with the transformational potency of the insect manifestations of the deity according to San tradition. Accordingly, the appearance of Matthew as man, winged creature, fish, bat and lark; of Mark as lion and sheep; of St Luke as a wall and bull; and of St John as eagle and phoenix is another of Lawrence's literary adaptations from San tradition. A pivot for this treatment of orthodox doctrine occurs in Haeckel, whose Chapter 17 in *The Riddle of the Universe*, 'Science and Christianity' (pp. 316–38), includes a satirical portrayal of the Council of Nicaea as well as a denunciation of the exaggerated importance of the four Evangelists and their Gospels in post-Athanasian Christian tradition.

*

Any attempt to measure Lawrence's drift towards San poetics is fraught with difficulties. The quest presents more elusive problems than the thematic topics noted above. R. M. Dorson cogently warns that 'The relation of folklore to literature is a problem that can properly be studied only by a critic trained in folklore as well as in literary studies,'[26] but his dismissive listing of Bleek in a group of amateurs including Richard Burton, Mary Kingsley 'and other intrepid missionaries and travelers',[27] and his omission of the San repertoire from his conspectus of traditional African literary forms, weaken the authority of his survey. Lawrence's receptivity to oral literary forms began in Eastwood, and thus his discovery of the San poetic corpus extended his already wide literary experience. 'The creative writer has often found nourishment in folk narrators and folk bards,' Dorson notes.[28] Lawrence is one of many writers and artists in Europe and America who borrowed from African sources. San verbal art offers a complex, pictorial rather than narrative, evocation of critical transitions, encounters and perceptions, and is the product of a society without hierarchy and formal division of social or ecological roles, beyond the assignment of hunting to male and plant gathering to female groups. Materials are interchangeable among sex and age groups; accordingly, as we have seen in the evocations of the moon, themes can be transposed into varying forms according to the occasion of the performances, in which encounters, reminiscence, anecdote, instructional imperatives and magical transformations are freely mingled. The verbal structures are schematized, and the overall effect is to present an event outside the sequence of ordinary time. Lawrence's reminiscence to Ghiselin obliquely suggests his receptivity to these peculiarities. Once again, the record of his poetic composition after the contact bears out the strength of the impression made on him by the texts.

Repetition, the key to oral performance, is strongly imprinted in Lawrence's poetic composition after his contact with Juta and *Specimens* in the summer of 1920. Juta's copy of *Specimens* bears no trace of intensive reading or marking, and thus Lawrence's reading was probably selective and rapid, but (as his clear memory of it suggests) absorbent. Repetition is especially strong in the poems of September 1920; it makes a far more tentative appearance in poems written before July. A performance by Dia!kwain, 'Habits of the Bat and Porcupine' (*Specimens*, 247–53), provides examples of techniques of the type which appear to have impressed Lawrence, who made use of these species in three subsequently written pieces. Dia!kwain's performance has eight topics. Of these, two occur once only, and six have four repetitions apiece. In the former group, subservience of man and animals to the stars concludes the second half of the performance, the half devoted to the father's voice and experience. In the first half, the mother's voice predominates, insisting on the magical powers of the porcupine. This section is jointed to the second by Dia!kwain's expression of subservience to his father's example at his mother's behest; this item occurs once and thus acts as a double link, between the 'mother' and 'father' parts of the exposition and the two groups, one with repetition and the other without, which compose this numerically symmetrical artefact. The six elements which have repetitions are: the voice of the mother; the habits and practical cunning of the porcupine; the supernatural capacity of this animal to lure the apprentice huntsman into sleep and thus to elude capture; its exceptionally acute sensory powers and shunning of daylight; the hunter's need to stay awake; and the father's example as a skilled huntsman. This closely woven yet seemingly formless mode of composition has the close patterning of poems such as 'Aire and Angells' or 'The Collar'. The components are hinged in the phrase: 'For mama was the one who told me that I must do as father used to do, when father watched for the porcupine' (*Specimens*, 251). Collected by Bleek in his last month of life, this work was handed to Dia!kwain in performances by his father as well as his mother; it enacts the cyclic, magical and instructional, family-based configuration of San society and art and has the formal characteristics of an ideogram rather than of narrative or image.

Lawrence's receptive response to this mode of composition can be gauged from his intensified use of repetition and the pictorial qualities of natural encounters from 'Snake' onwards. 'Bat', 'Man and Bat' and 'Reflections on the Death of a Porcupine' make use of the only fauna, in the *Specimens*, which Lawrence knew well; in turning down Juta's invitation to accompany him to Africa, he restricted the range of animal species he could share with San tradition. As in Dia!kwain's 'Habits of the Bat and Porcupine', Lawrence's written works are built around opposing principles which receive numerous repetitions and resolving insights which occur once only. The patterning in Lawrence's work is less minutely schematized, but the principle of San composition appears to have been thoroughly grasped and explored. In 'Bat' four principal components receive between four and six repetitions, and the resolving insights, two in all, occur once only. A more diversified 'trickster' narrative form prevails in 'Man and Bat', and in 'Reflections on the Death of a Porcupine' the Haeckelian argument about survival and extinction of species is revived. In 'Bat' the four repeated components are: the transition from daylight to dark (six repetitions); the natural and architectural setting (five repetitions); flying animals (six repetitions); the illusion that these are swallows (six repetitions); the discovery that these are bats (five repetitions). A single linking phrase hinges the two main groups: 'at a wavering instant the swallows give way to bats' (*CP*, 341). The final reflection, the poet's inability to accept an Oriental attitude to these animals, which he finds repulsive, occurs once. Clearly, Lawrence and the San artist share a general human propensity towards argument, contrast and repetition as the basis of communication, and too much should not be made of the formal resemblance, which could be fortuitous. The difficulty in such an argument, however, would be that Lawrence did not have this style before his exposure to San art. A better explanation would be that he responded with intuitive skill to the inner musculature of a newly found type of performance. In 'Man and Bat' the narrative mode of ‖Kabbo's 'Mantis' performance appears to be the more probable model. The bat adopts the voice of an instructor in the last lines, and twenty-one preceding components of the poem are given varying amounts of repetition: eleven for the crazy flight of the bat in captivity, five for the poet's efforts to eject the animal, seven for its refusal to enter the daylight, eight for its fatigue, eight for the voice of the poet's negative response, four for its religious scruple and submission. In its general configuration, the poem adopts the San attitude towards animals, which manifests the shifts of human conscience in its quest for divine guidance in human affairs.

To sum up: from the summer of 1920 onwards, when he had read *Specimens of Bushman Folklore*, Lawrence drew on San themes – such as divine transformation, the moon in relation to death, and the snake which is not to be killed. These items all represent essential aspects of San literature, life and thought, and are strongly represented in this major African literary text. In the composition of *Birds, Beasts and Flowers*, Lawrence developed a strongly evolutionary argument, particularly noticeable in such works as the 'Tortoise' sequence, 'Kangaroo' and 'Humming-Bird'. This encapsulating framework is clearly different from the material of his African source, but yet is related to it, since Bleek's work was motivated by interests shared with his cousin Ernst Haeckel, Lawrence's principal source of evolutionary ideas. Diverging from Haeckel and obeying his interest in the mythic literature of preliterate society, Lawrence urged the restoration of modes of thought and feeling stemming from traditional views of nature, animals, death and regeneration, and the transformations of the divine spirit. His literary technique underwent a change and showed receptivity to the characteristics of San oral art, especially in its use of repetition in performances which assert the interdependence of man and nature.

Notes

1 *Specimens of Bushman Folklore*, collected by W. H. I. Bleek and Lucy C. Lloyd, ed. Lucy C. Lloyd (London, 1911; facsimile reprint, Cape Town, 1968). All subsequent references to this edition will be cited parenthetically within the text by *Specimens* and the page number. I thank the staff of the University of Cape Town for assistance in consulting the Bleek collection; my colleague Dr John Widdowson and members of the African Literature seminar at Sheffield University for hearing a first exploration of the subject and making suggestions; and Jan Juta. See also Jan Juta, *Background in Sunshine* (New York, 1972).

2 *D. H. Lawrence: A Composite Biography*, ed. Edward Nehls (Madison, 1957), III, 285–98 (p. 296).

3 Dorothea Bleek, *A Bushman Dictionary* (New Haven, 1956). See also Otto H. Spohr, *Wilhelm Heinrich Immanuel Bleek: A Bio-Bibliographical Sketch* (Cape Town, 1962).

4 *A Preliminary List of Publications Referring to the Non-Bantu Click Languages*, comp.

Leah Levy (Cape Town, 1968), part 2, p. 1. Subsequent studies include the following: Lorna Marshall, *The !Kung of Nyae Nyae* (Cambridge, Mass., 1976); Richard B. Lee and Irven DeVore (eds), *Kalahari Hunter-Gatherers: Studies of the !Kung San and Their Neighbours* (Cambridge, Mass., 1976); Patricia Vinnicombe, *People of the Eland* (Pietermaritzburg, 1976).

5 Ernst Haeckel, *The Riddle of the Universe*, 2nd edn, trans. Joseph McCabe (London, 1901). All subsequent references to this edition will be cited parenthetically within the text and indicated by the abbreviation *RU* and the page number.

6 W. H. I. Bleek, *Ueber den Ursprung der Sprache*, herausgageben mit einem Vorwort von Ernst Haeckel (Weimar, 1868).

7 University of Cape Town Libraries.

8 Dorothea Bleek, *The Mantis and His Friends: Bushman Folklore* (Cape Town, 1923).

9 Roger Ebbatson, *Lawrence and the Nature Tradition: A Theme in English Fiction 1859–1941* (Brighton, 1980).

10 Sandra M. Gilbert, *Acts of Attention: The Poems of D. H. Lawrence* (Ithaca and London, 1972), 160. See also Sandra M. Gilbert, 'Hell on Earth: *Birds, Beasts and Flowers* as subversive narrative', *DHLR*, 12 (Fall 1979), 256–74. See also D. H. Lawrence, *The Complete Poems*, ed. Vivian de Sola Pinto and Warren Roberts (Harmondsworth, 1979). All subsequent references to this edition will be cited parenthetically within the text and indicated by the abbreviation *CP* and the page number.

11 Warren Roberts, *A Bibliography of D. H. Lawrence* (London 1963), 69. For dates of composition see Keith Sagar, *D. H. Lawrence: A Calendar of His Works* (Manchester, 1979), 101ff.

12 Jan Juta, letter of 17 October 1917.

13 D. H. Lawrence, *Sea and Sardinia* (New York, 1921), 81.

14 Gilbert, 'Hell on Earth', 257.

15 *Sea and Sardinia*, 216.

16 Haeckel, 'Vorwort' to Bleek, *Uber den Ursprung der Sprache*, iv.

17 W. H. I. Bleek, preface to *On the Origin of Language*, ed. Ernst Haeckel, trans. Thomas Davidson (New York, 1869), cited in Spohr, *Bleek*, 30.

18 D. H. Lawrence, introduction to Edward Dahlberg, *Bottom Dogs* (London, 1929), iii–ix (p. xvi).

19 *Composite Biography*, III, 296.

20 For graphic representations, see Tim Maggs (ed.), *Major Rock Paintings of Southern Africa* (Cape Town, 1979), 102; Kathe Woldmann, *Das Wahre Gesicht des Buschmannes* (Basel 1938), 33 ('Ein geflugelter Schlangenmensch . . .').

21 Gilbert, *Acts of Attention*, 286.

22 ibid., 290.

23 *Composite Biography*, III, 296.

24 Richard Karutz, *Die Afrikanische Seele* (Basel, 1938), 34.

25 Gilbert, 'Hell on Earth', 260.

26 *African Folklore*, ed. Richard M. Dorson (Bloomington, Indiana, 1972), 24.

27 ibid., 13.

28 ibid., 24.

*

[The reader's attention is drawn to Dr Keith Sagar's reference to this essay in ch. VI of his always indispensable study, *D. H. Lawrence: Life into Art* (Harmondsworth, 1985), 209, 232–3. *Ed.*]

13 Lawrence's politics

Rick Rylance

Lawrence's political reputation has interestingly reflected some of the major shifts in cultural attitude in our century. Vilified in his own day as obscene, and suspected by the Home Office of moral corruption and treachery, he was attacked throughout his career by the right-wing patriotic press, saw two of his books banned, his paintings confiscated and his poems seized in the mail. His last novel – *Lady Chatterley's Lover* – could not legally be read in Britain for thirty-two years. These persistent difficulties followed directly from his scathing attitudes to the settled English life of his time, not least his outspoken opposition to the First World War and to industrial culture generally.

Yet it became easy to lose sight of Lawrence's dissidence as his reputation fell away sharply among younger, more consciously aligned (mainly Marxist) critics in the 1930s. Although many attempted reasoned refusals, Lawrence came to be widely regarded, as Mark Spilka put it, as 'a sex-mad homosexual fascist, a mindless and misguided genius scarcely worth attention'.[1] But Lawrence's reputation was not to stiffen in the mould in which the 1930s had cast it. F. R. Leavis recruited some of the novels for his 'Great Tradition' of morally engaged English fiction; and by the late 1950s and 1960s Lawrence's sensually-based critique of the mainstream culture of industrial capitalism was appealing to elements of the counterculture of the period (as is emphasized in Ken Russell's 1969 film of *Women in Love* for instance). Lawrence's status and prominence in the curricula of the educational system at all levels owes much to the Leavisian values whose inculcation has been so prominent a feature of literary study in Britain.

More recently, however, there has been a fresh reassessment. The old authoritarian Lawrence of the 1930s rose again in the 1970s and 1980s. Several critical movements combined to produce this feminism – the most lively critique of Lawrence yet – has called necessary attention to the habitual phallocentric organization of Lawrence's political imaginations; while there has also been (poststructuralist influenced) rejection of the so-called 'organic' and 'realist' forms of Lawrence's writing so valued by Leavis. The most common political account of his work today sees Lawrence, like several of his major contemporaries, as too closely associated with right-wing authoritarian ideologies of the 1920s. In sexual as in social politics, Lawrence is widely thought to be tainted with fascism: another rightist pessimist, like Eliot, Yeats, Lewis or Pound.

However, it is these attitudes – an orthodoxy of late – that I wish to re-examine here. For the very volatility of Lawrence's political reputation is itself an accurate reflection of a voice that continues to challenge.

I

Accusations of proto-fascist politics began early, with Bertrand Russell an influential voice. Russell and Lawrence were enthusiastically friendly for some months in 1915, united by their opposition to the war and perception of the wide-reaching crisis of which, they believed, the war was symptomatic. Initially, the politics of this opposition was liberal–left, even socialist, and Lawrence himself had grown up in the milieu of working-class, Nonconformist dissent, which at the turn of the century had a political orientation towards the left, or at least towards a reformist liberalism.[2] Russell, by contrast, hailed from one of the great aristocratic liberal families, well used to articulate dissidence and the language and assumptions of conventional political discourse. It was thus a socially ill-sorted alliance; nevertheless, they planned together a lecture-series on the 'Principles of Social Reconstruction'. Lawrence, however, quickly turned against Russell and his Cambridge and Bloomsbury world. The lecture plan – and their friendship – was ended.

In rejecting Russell, Lawrence shifted ground politically to the right. In angry letters he attacked Russell's draft lectures for their failure to add radical moral and spiritual substance to the reform of the mere political apparatus.[3] He demanded that Russell withdraw from all 'external' organizations, such as the Independent Labour Party and the Union of Democratic Control (the leading anti-war organization among intellectuals) and harangued him about his support for the Labour Party after the Welsh miners' strike of 1915.[4] Instead of Russell's mealy-mouthed reforms, Lawrence urged the case for a 'Caesar for England', firm leadership to pull the country round from imminent class war and government on the debilitating French principles of liberty, equality and fraternity. 'You must have a government based upon good, better and best.'[5]

Russell subsequently recalled the sudden about-turn in Lawrence's views in his *Portraits from Memory*. Lawrence, he claimed, shockingly abandoned rational discourse on political questions. He became in effect a fascist fellow-traveller whose ideas would lead to the concentration camps. According to Russell, these views governed Lawrence for the rest of his life, and his authoritarianism came from a megalomaniac's baulked will, a small-minded egotism and a neglect of real political problems. Russell pictured Lawrence as a petty and frustrated dictator, isolated in a New Mexican desert bullying a few empty-headed disciples.[6]

There is, initially, some plausibility to Russell's view, which others have taken up. For over a decade Lawrence was proudly anti-intellectual, and sometimes frankly irrationalist; and he did flirt with ideas which have disturbing destinations. But Lawrence's situation in 1915 was difficult. Whereas Russell conceived of reform within the framework of a secure, if oppositional, intellectual tradition with reliable institutional affiliations, Lawrence, mad-deningly for Russell, remained beyond the liberal dissenting consensus: an outsider to the society whose renewal he sought. This, I feel, is a key issue in the events of 1915; for Lawrence's personal disenchantment with Russell followed the well-known visit to Cambridge in March and is part of his wider rejection of the class-based forms of even dissident English political, intellectual and artistic culture in the 1910s.

In Cambridge Lawrence was uncharacteristically tongue-tied and mutin-ously moody: he seems understandably to have been socially intimidated, despite Russell's good offices. He returned in a black mood dreaming of beetles – always a bad sign. Accounts frequently refer to his shocked encounter with homosexuals like J. M. Keynes, but he was clearly equally unsettled by the demanding social mores of Cambridge. His distress thus has an important *class* dimension, which combined with the other crises in his life – ill-health, financial and marital worries, the stresses of the war for a man with a German wife and a suspect reputation, the banning of *The Rainbow*, and the struggle to find outlets for his writing – to push his opinions to fierce extremes. Though Lawrence may have wished to *appear* comfortable in this 'advanced' intellectual-bohemian world, there remained an unsettled edge to his rel-ations with it. It was a world to which he never returned after the war, and to which he never thought of himself as belonging.[7]

The aggressive, oppositional element in Lawrence's views is important; for, frequently, they are what they are in reaction to the orthodoxies he found around him. As a working-class man who lived little of his adult life among the working class, he was in some senses a stranger to his most intimate formative processes, and certainly to the habits of that culture's adult life. At the same time he was, too, awkward among those with whom he next came into contact as an 'artist': that is, the dissident fraction of English intellectual life, centred on Lady Ottoline Morrell's circle at Garsington, which championed his early work. And it is in quarrel with the forms of dissidence available to him that Lawrence's political views were formed. In his quarrel with Russell, this meant a reaction to liberalism, though not a return to the politics of the working-class communities, which he saw as dominated by the wage-scramble and the irrelevancies of parliamentary representation.

We need, then, to specify how Lawrence developed his ideas, for he did not, contrary to Russell's account, leap into jack-boots. How did he take his distance from mainstream English dissent, and what did he propose as an alternative? His proposals, occasionally formulated but more usually *explored* in his fiction and other imaginative writing, *sometimes* have an authoritarian cast (though it is necessary to specify the context of these moments). Throughout, though, his thinking has a number of central emphases. These include: first, a denigration of the culture of the advanced industrial nation-state, including its most prevalent political form, democracy; second, a lively interest in alternative cultural modes, explored and imagined in terms of vanished, and regretted, primitive cultures and ways of feeling (hence one reason for his emphasis on sexuality); third, the interpretation of social collectivities in terms of individual experience rather than notions such as 'the general good'; and fourth, a restless – and consistently rather thoughtless – flirtation with ideas of phallocentric authority in both state and home, where women especially were to submit to patriarchal government. Running through these were a number of variables, most significantly the degree to which Lawrence understood the predicament of the times to be reversible. Here he moved between utopianism and blank despair, dependent on contingent factors produced by his restless movements about the world and the dramatic social changes of the 1920s. Among these were the rise of fascism in Europe, which he experienced while living in Italy and on which he commented widely, directly and always negatively, and the related political crisis in Britain in the same period. (Both are considered in the final section of this essay.)

Lawrence's wartime and post-war writings can be savage in tone. They suggest, in formal attitude and manner of expression, a sensibility alienated from its immediate personal acquaintance and from the culture in which – though dissident – that acquaintance participated. This acerbic alienation is found in the major novel of this phase, *Women in Love*, which savagely indicts the intellectual and artistic culture of the war years. Lawrence's manner of formulating his ideas in this period, however, was not always so accusatory. He could adopt a comic mode – and *Women in Love* is too little commented upon in this light – and he could be more patiently expository, as in the long essay 'Democracy' (1919), which sets out clearly and, on the whole, temperately Lawrence's views at this time.

The immediate target of the essay is Walt Whitman, a favourite among dissident intellectuals of the period. Edward Carpenter, who is sometimes claimed to have had an influence on Lawrence, for instance, wrote his long prose-poem *Towards Democracy* in a Whitmanesque manner and with Whitman's ultra-democratic and libertarian views in mind. It went through several editions, and circulated widely among younger 'progressive' intellectuals on both sides of the Atlantic. It was admired, for instance, by the young Havelock Ellis and other members of the 'Progressive Association' (a forerunner of the Fabian Society), and there was a thriving Whitman Club in Bolton, Lancashire from 1885 which spread Whitmanesque ideas in the North.[8] Lawrence's essay, then, in challenging Whitman, challenged yet another faction of dissident intellectual life in Britain. Nor was this casual. Whitman's politics were also hammered in *Studies in Classic American Literature* (begun 1917, published 1923). Ostensibly a book of literary criticism, the *Studies* are in fact a sustained attack on the values of the purely commercial-democratic culture America, in Lawrence's view, had become. This use of literary criticism as an opportunity for political pronouncement is frequent in Lawrence.

'Democracy' is an across-the-board dismissal of the political apparatus and assumptions of capitalism: 'Politics – what are they? Just another, extra-large, commercial wrangle over buying and selling – nothing else.'[9] For it is not only electoral democracy that is rejected, but all the other political 'contrivancies' – left and right – of the post-war world: socialism, nationalism, internationalism, conservatism, liberalism, imperialism, republicanism, bolshevism and the League of Nations are all mentioned. For Lawrence, the faith placed in some of these 'contrivancies' by Whitman and other modern democrats involves a category mistake: the mechanics of the provision of material needs (food and shelter) are confused with the goals and ideals of proper social and spiritual living. Democrats assume, quite correctly, that each should, without discrimination, have access to material necessities. But whereas all may be equal in basic need, men are *unequal* 'in Spiritual and Mystical needs' (p. 75): each individual is unique. Modern industrial societies err because they cannot grant the individual self the opportunity to flourish, and instead these societies confer a factitious and distorting social identity 'like identity-medals on wretched khaki soldiers' (p. 81) – a simile which places this essay among Lawrence's bitter wartime experiences. This false, khaki identity wrecks individual vitality and potential, and thus societies die through the 'superimposition of the abstracted, automatic, invented universe of man upon the spontaneous creative universe' (p. 80). Each man carries his social identity as a hard disfiguring weight or rind – hence one of Lawrence's most persistent images for the damage done by industrial societies: the incubus, or shelled, scaly or carapaced creature routinely and mindlessly going about its horrible business. This image is used widely in *Women in Love*. In 'Democracy' Lawrence pictures men carrying around millstones fancifully decorated with modern delusions of belonging and mutuality: nationalism, patriotism or equality.

Lawrence's perception of this disordering, unhealthy, conformism is of course a central concern of much English romantic and post-romantic literature, and of political thinking within the Marxist and radical liberal traditions (for example Bertrand Russell). However, a problem in Lawrence's account emerges as he considers the relationship between individuality and the collective provisioning mechanisms. Lawrence's emphasis falls on individual self-realization rather than on a consideration of collectively defined benefit or a sense of mutual purpose or good. The collective becomes not a possibility to be realized but a threat to be resisted. Thus social matters are turned almost entirely into matters of individual psychology, because 'the highest collectivity has for its true goal the purest individualism, pure individual spontaneity' (p. 77). This creates a tension in Lawrence's politics which he never resolved. On the one hand we have a recommendation for spontaneous individual growth; but on the other hand Lawrence recognizes the necessity for mutuality and collectivity in the provisioning system and for the satisfaction of key drives and needs, principally love. At the same time as he embraces a fierce individualism, he also resists, in his intransigent opposition to industrial capitalism, the most prevalent argument (then as now) for 'free' individualism in 'market' conditions.

Lawrence has no clear means of resolving the dichotomy between individual and collective such as that possessed by theorists of the free market. The latter argue that maximum general benefit is enabled by releasing competing individuals as freely as possible on to the market. The market thus operates as the resolving force between the individual and the general good. In Lawrence, however, individuals do not have this kind of participation in collective systems, for these systems tend to be thinly abstracted in his account, thus distancing real social experience. For example, the question of the provision of material needs – an urgent one in post-war Britain (e.g. housing) – is airily offered as self-solving. The essay's remoteness from concrete social experience is of a piece with Lawrence's angry and alienated mood. The rightwards drift of Lawrence's thought is continuous with his increasing separation from his own social origins and experience.

Lawrence's views have other complex consequences. They imply for instance a biological, or at least ecological, optimism, which is counterposed with the destructive social world. At its heart, 'Democracy' assumes two countervailing forces: the possibility of natural grace, health and renewal, and the bleak recognition of a worsening social system producing the 'present state of unspeakable barbarism' (p. 93). His writing gains its characteristic vigour when describing the latter: mechanical lusts, disintegrating amorphousness, fragmentation, and a rhetoric of doom, 'the end' and 'the last phase'. This language is used, too, in *Women in Love*, one of whose early titles was 'Last Days'.[10] Moreover Lawrence does not discriminate between the use of this language in collective or individual psychological contexts. They are, after all, one and the same for him – hence some of the more disorientating and initially puzzling effects of a novel like *Women in Love*. Beetles are at work in psyche *and* society, and the rhetoric characteristically blurs the boundaries between 'character' and 'milieu'. This is part of Lawrence's political message. Lawrence further distinguishes between *activity* and *creativity*. The former describes typical behaviour in modern societies, the latter its desired alternative. Individuality is the release of a creativity whose mode of expression is love and whose motor-force is desire. Activity, though, is an expression of the social personality and the ego which is constructed from units 'of the material world of Force and Matter' (p. 87), that is, of the social-industrial world. Its typical mode is the exercise of power and the unhealthy pursuit of abstractions like the equality of man.

'Democracy', then, is precariously poised between a bleak rejection of the direction of modern social systems and a more positive comprehension of man's natural potential. But because Lawrence cannot reconcile his opposed ideals of social harmony *and* spontaneous individuality, he cannot conceive of a coherent alternative form of social organization and is forced into anxious redefinition and unconvincing restatement. Thus he ends saluting a 'new Democracy', but this appears to be simply an aggregate of differentiated individuals associated in the (vague) 'strange recognition of present otherness' (p. 92): in other words in the kind of anarchistic syndicalism which, interestingly, became Bertrand Russell's position in 1918.[11] As for social arrangements, 'all settlement of the property question must arise spontaneously out of the new impulse in man' (p. 95). It is a weak argument.

'Democracy' is a telling indication of the strengths and difficulties of Lawrence's political thought. As Raymond Williams has argued, the essay contains elements that look to a democracy more openly responsive to the needs of the masses of individuals who compose and enable it.[12] However, the line of thought in which it participates – the conservatively-coloured tradition of nineteenth-century organicism (the theory that the state is like, and functions as, a natural organism) – appears bankrupt, for Lawrence can describe no real community to replace the vanished, often feudal, forms of village and nation which this tradition celebrated. The result is that when read from the perspective of the individual, as it were, the essay seems coherent; but when read from the perspective of the collective, it seems depressingly baffled and rhetorical. Traditional forms of mutuality or belonging – nationhood, for instance – are pictured as falling apart, and the essay is riddled with images of haphazard breakdown: of the human body in pieces, and of buildings that are not homes but hotels, hostels, tourist agencies and houses of commerce. It is a portrait of an atomized culture whose separations are symptoms of its decline, though these separated individuals are, at the same time, to be the agents of recovery. The deliberately disordered forms and the scrambling search for better lives, which are features of many of Lawrence's novels, reflect this ideological stalemate. Hence the mood, structure and substance of the novels of the period after *The Rainbow* (1915), which deal repeatedly with displaced and alienated individuals (*Women in Love, Aaron's Rod*), with flight and escape (*The Lost Girl, The Plumed Serpent*), and with wandering and search, as in *Kangaroo*.

However, 'Democracy' does *not* find a solution to its political difficulties in ideas of hierarchy. Later this did become a temptation, and it is easy to see why. If one posits a radical separation of the individual from the collective (as Lawrence does in this essay and in the plots and situations of the novels); and if one further posits as nugatory, or takes for granted, the contributions the collective makes to the satisfaction of the material needs of individuals (something which Lawrence ceases to describe in fiction, by and large, after *The Rainbow*); and if one also emphasizes the *negative* features of living in collectivities – then the political temptation is to remake desired collectivities in the image of the exceptional individuals who are thought to escape social conditioning. In other words, one ends with a theory of *élites*; and Lawrence did at one stage involve himself in such theories. The rhetoric he then deployed – and the fiction rendered by it (one thinks particularly of the chilling *The Plumed Serpent*, 1923–5) – is exceptionally disturbing. The mixture of sexual violence, leadership politics and the fevered excitement of the denunciations tempts one to reject him wholly. Instead of the proud assertion of individual selves which is the founding (and welcome) central value of 'Democracy', it is *submission* that is urged. Contact with charismatic individuals will remake the social identities ruined by modern capitalist states. This is the condition of the Irish-American Kate Leslie in *The Plumed Serpent*. The nasty, modern, wilful, American part of her (as it were) needs to be eliminated; and the submerged racial fire of her Irishness needs to be recovered. This can be done, it seems, through the macho glamour of the revolutionary religious organization with which she involves herself.

In the 1930s *The Plumed Serpent* was seen as clear evidence of Lawrence's proto-fascist leanings. W. H. Auden described its politics in 1939. *The Plumed Serpent* is politically ridiculous because it 'treat[s] the modern state as if it were a tiny parish and politics as if it were an affair of personal relations'. Thus whilst Lawrence can offer 'admirable advice to lovers', that advice almost always means, in politics, 'Beat up those who disagree with you'. Auden's account is illuminating:

One of the strongest appeals of Fascism lies in its pretence that the State is one Big Family; its insistence on Blood and Race is an attempt to hoodwink the man-in-the-street into thinking that political relations are personal. The man-in-the-street whose political education is confined to personal relations, and who is bewildered by and resentful of the impersonal complexity of modern industrial life, finds it hard to resist a movement which talks to him so comfortingly in personal terms. One of the best reasons I have for knowing that Fascism is bogus is that it is much too like the kinds of Utopias artists plan over café tables very late at night.[13]

Auden thus identifies two central problems in Lawrence's political thought: the blurring of the categorical and experiential differences between the personal and the collective, and the attempt to recast the collective in terms of a unitary personal image rather than the difficult, plural realities of community. The closing reference to café utopias is also pertinent, for Auden sees the connection between Lawrence's socially alienated existence (as an artistic bohemian) and his reach for fables which would marry individual and collective but at a remove from the actual conditions of living for most people. Hence the appeal of remote locations like New Mexico, where he wrote *The Plumed Serpent*. In New Mexico he felt he could leave the corrupt world and, new-born, imagine a better.[14]

II

There is a difficulty, of course, in writing like this about *The Plumed Serpent*. Emphasizing its ideological line perhaps obscures its specificity as a literary text, i.e., the degree to which it is a self-interrogating work, exploring the limits of its own argument even as it advances it. Personally, I do not believe *The Plumed Serpent* is open to this kind of reading. The upsetting feature of the novel is the ferocity of its message. But other texts by Lawrence from this period do seem open to such interpretation. *Kangaroo* (1923) is an example.

Kangaroo is a political novel, in part about fascism. In it Lawrence describes the formation of a fascist group in Australia from the disappointed expectations of returning soldiers, the disgruntled claims of the 'small man' against big business, the growth of nationalism and racial prejudice, and the resulting emphasis on the power of the Will, athletics, male bonding and the charisma of a male leader, Kangaroo. (This powerfully suggestive socio-political scenario is clearly indicated and understood.) The action, such as it is (for it is a discursive rather than a plotted book), turns on the encounter between Kangaroo and the English writer Richard Lovat Somers. Somers is partly a self-portrait (he is given, for instance, Lawrence's wartime experiences), but also an ironic portrait of a contemporary type: the artist searching the seas for a more meaningful life – like, for instance, R. L. Stevenson, whose initials Somers shares. This ironic mode is established early and is sustained, partly through the wry perspective on Somers given by his wife, Harriet.

He had passed 'Elite' and 'Très Bon' and 'The Angels Roost' and 'The Better 'Ole'. He rather hoped for one of the Australian names, Wallamby or Wagga-Wagga. When he had looked at the house and agreed to take it for three months, it had been dusk, and he had not noticed the name. He hoped it would not be U-An-Me, or even Stella Maris.
      'Forestin,' he said, reading the flourishing T as an F. 'What language do you imagine that is?'
      'It's T, not F,' said Harriet.
      'Torestin,' he said, pronouncing it like Russian. 'Must be a native word.'

'No,' said Harriet. 'It means *To rest in.*' She didn't even laugh at him. He had become painfully silent.[15]

As Somers associates these suburbs with the sprawl of 'modern democracy', his silly error has a nicely judged political resonance, and mocks Lawrence's own craving for 'the primitive'. Somers, therefore, is another of Lawrence's ironized versions of himself which are a consistent feature of his fiction. He is, like Rupert Birkin, a study of the searching artist-intellectual attempting to find a cultural home.

Politically, the novel is about the lure of fascism for the displaced intellectual, and shows Lawrence's alert sense of how the private and the public, the personal and the political, might be confused. As Auden noticed, Lawrence can confuse these; but *Kangaroo* carefully separates the appeals made to Somers in his encounter with ultra-rightist politics. He is enticed both personally and ideologically; and it is the personal appeal, of love and comradeship, which Somers finds difficult to resist, though he eventually does so. Meanwhile, ideologically, Somers is in utter confusion, and a range of options are held in tense opposition until none appears finally attractive: sprawling suburban democracy is opposed to the beautiful natural world (though the natural world itself also appears frighteningly empty and unsolacing); unionist socialism is opposed to rightist authoritarianism; commitment to freedom; marriage to male bonding; love to violence and the pursuit of political power. Thus hopeless social ideals and ideological certainties are juxtaposed with Somers' engrossed, uncertain self-assessment. The book is an ideological hall-of-mirrors typical of Lawrence's fictional procedures. One thinks, for example, of the binary groupings of *Women in Love* which pair against each other the two men, the two women, the two couples, the locations, the life-styles, and so on, in order to release its meanings. What this difficult dialectical method does to the politics of a novel like *Kangaroo* is to scupper any sense of a firm solution. The form of the book reflects this. It is tellingly non-linear in narrative, and moves disconcertingly in time, tone and perspective. It brings together diverse bits of writing to jostle against each other. (One chapter is actually called 'Bits', and the title is very apposite.) *Kangaroo* is like *The Waste Land* in prose; a critical cultural inquiry whose shape comes from the distress of its personally felt predicament.

Kangaroo thrives as a novel because it dramatizes its political problem so intently and plays off settled conviction (generally pictured as misguided) against Somers' bewildered searching. Competing political options are put at arm's length because they cannot be integrated with personal need. Revealingly, the dominant and recurrent image is of voyaging and, specifically, of the sea. Everything is at sea – the Somerses' marriage, Lovat's convictions, the narrative's close – and the last words seem forlornly to echo Matthew Arnold's deployment of an image (so dear to sad English intellectuals generally) in 'Dover Beach' or the Marguerite poems: 'It was only four days to New Zealand, over a cold, dark, inhospitable sea.' Yet the tone is not merely dismayed, for the book is written in a mode of Romantic irony usually associated with Byron or Keats; that is, *Kangaroo* subverts, yet understands, its ironically conceived central character's predicament and unsteady venturing.

Kangaroo's ironic mode, then, is in sharp contrast to the ruthless solutions of *The Plumed Serpent*. But the important point about *The Plumed Serpent's* politics is that these solutions are *mythicized*, rather than set in testy dialogue with personal circumstances or realistically conceived environments. When Lawrence does attend to such circumstances, or sets himself to picture such environments, then the ideological character of his work changes. Lawrence cannot, finally, commit himself to any political programme which is not mythically distanced, and his ideological imagination is characteristically restless.

Some of Lawrence's non-fictional work of the mid-1920s shows these same features – for instance the Epilogue (written, but not published, in 1924) to his school textbook *Movements in European History*. The Epilogue attacks capitalism and socialism in a language reminiscent of fascism in the same decade: the 'cancer' and 'stranglehold' of the financiers, the 'swindle' of industrial capitalism, the spiritual beggary and roguery of Russian communism, the demand for 'Great Men'. Yet the harangue is pulled-up short as Lawrence considers really-existing fascism in Italy. He recalls the 'bullying' of the preceding socialists, then the worse bullying of the fascists in 1920, and there begins an uneasy alternation in the pronouns used – from the hectoring demands of '*We* must . . .' to the resistant, querulous voice of 'I' who opposes bullying and stands for individual potential.[16] It is the same tension as in 'Democracy'. There we remarked upon the political *disadvantage* of Lawrence's failure to imagine collectivist forms to enable his individualist vision. Now it is that very individualism which divides him from the most ghastly collectivist errors and the tyrannies embraced by too many of his contemporaries and juniors: Pound, Lewis, Williamson, Diana and Unity Mitford, T. E. Lawrence, Heidegger, Paul de Man.

III

By 1928 Lawrence had abandoned his 'leadership' fantasies of the mid-1920s. There is a well-known letter of March 1928 to Witter Bynner, a New Mexican friend.

> I sniffed a red herring in your last letter a long time: then at last decided it's a live sprat. I mean about *The Plumed Serpent* and the 'hero'. On the whole I think you're right. The hero is obsolete, and the leader of men is a back number. After all at the back of the hero is the militant ideal: and the militant ideal, or the ideal militant, seems to me a cold egg. We're sort of sick of all the forms of militarism and militantism, and *Miles* is a name no more for a man. On the whole I agree with you, the leader-cum-follower relationship is a bore. And the new relationship will be a sort of tenderness, sensitive between men and men, men and women, and not the one up one down, lead on I follow, *ich dien* sort of business. So you see I'm becoming a lamb at last, and you'll even find it hard to take umbrage with me.[17]

He then describes his new novel, *Lady Chatterley's Lover*. So the new book coincided with a softening of political outlook in the face of militarist power.

There are several probable factors which helped this change along. These include his residence in Italy, a fascist state which raised his political hackles, and his visits to England in 1925 and 1926 which led him to re-examine his career and think again about English themes. In 1926 he revisited the mining country of his birth and witnessed the effects of the General Strike. *Lady Chatterley's Lover* was written from these circumstances which are evident too in many of the late essays he wrote after 1925. These essays stress 'Insouciance' (the title of one of them) and an impatience with questions of power and social problems which are beyond individual experience. In other words, there is a return to the political focus of 'Democracy'. This insouciance is mirrored in the argument and narrative direction of *Lady Chatterley's Lover*, which takes its protagonists away from mainstream society.

Nevertheless, *Lady Chatterley's Lover* is engagedly political: a critique of English intellectual-political life in the mid-1920s during conditions of heightened industrial militancy, on the one side, and the temptation among the owners of land and industry to reach for ultra-rightist solutions to the crisis on the other. Frequently referred to as a 'pastoral' (having in mind the eloquent eroticism of the woodland scenes), in fact the book seems a pastoral reversed, an English country-house poem written from outside the estate at one of England's fiercest political moments. It identifies the country house, and the culture it supports, as a leading element in the damaged politics of the 1920s.

That *Lady Chatterley's Lover* was written in the wake of the General Strike was first remarked by Raymond Williams in 1970. The idea has never been examined in much detail,[18] though in fact the political dimension was present from the beginning. In the first version Parkin (the original Mellors) was a communist organizer, and until very late Lawrence wished to conclude the novel with a return of the gamekeeper's political commitments (which is the narrative destination of *The First Lady Chatterley*). In his study of the novel's evolution, Michael Squires prints some cancelled passages from the letter from Mellors to Connie with which the final version ends. These call for the rejection of leadership cults and the reform of priorities in the distribution of wealth, thus echoing the letter to Bynner and adding a thoughtful concern for the 'provisioning' systems of English society.[19] Also, despite the shifts of political emphasis, *Lady Chatterley's Lover* does break from Lawrence's by now habitual narrative resolution, escape by travel or emigration. Mellors and Connie talk of moving abroad; but at the close he is working on a farm which breeds pit ponies, and is thus half in the industrial world, noting the rising militancy of his fellow workers. He is also, of course, half *out* of that world, too; just as his relationship with Connie is poignantly balanced between communication (letter writing) and no contact (they are apart); between separation and birth (Connie is expecting their child). The mood is nicely adjusted to their socially precarious state and the tentative ideological optimism they represent.

However, Lawrence *did* cancel those passages and retrench from the political explicitness of the first version; and for some the alterations damage Lawrence's political perspective. Several critics, noting Lawrence's interest in the General Strike, for instance, have been unhappy with the apparent elimination of class issues and the determined proposal of individualist solutions to the social crises of the 1920s.[20] Yet if Lawrence cannot throw his weight behind working-class militants, he does engage in a thorough critique of their class opponents. In any case we have seen how Lawrence consistently works on ultra-individualist premises (the gains and losses of which we have described), and it would have been surprising indeed if he had suddenly opted for socialist collectivism. The force of Lawrence's attention, in all versions of the novel, is all the other way – towards satisfactions and attainments reached in the private life *first*. Other kinds of general benefit may follow but are not imagined, which is perhaps damaging for our culture but hardly unreal. Lawrence's intelligence, as we have seen, remains a *critical* one; that is, his political interests are expressed in their most interesting way in opposition to other ideas, sometimes to other elements of the dissident culture of his times, but principally in a sensually-based critique of the politics of the industrial state. It is this political object Lawrence has in view in *Lady Chatterley's Lover*.

Lady Chatterley's Lover recommences Lawrence's satirical critique of the British intellectual élite. The portrait of Clifford Chatterley's 'cronies' gassing away at Wragby recalls Breadalby in *Women in Love*. Both novels identify the aristocratic country house as central to the intellectual-political culture of the period, and both expose this culture as sham and shamefully complicit with the ravages of the industrial state to which it may think itself opposed. After all, both Clifford Chatterley and Gerald Crich, members of these sets, are coal barons. The cronies at Wragby talk of a worsening world; and one of them, Tommy Dukes, is sometimes taken as Lawrence's 'voice'. However, the inert criticism and dismal incapacity which characterize the cronies' talk are the central feature, and the whole is clearly intended to be satirical. The half-perceiving Tommy Dukes stands forlornly for class reconciliation (as his name suggests), but he has withdrawn from fulfilling personal relations and retreated into the army. The rest are petty and mean-spirited intellectual 'types'. Again, Lawrence carefully notes the connection between this gentry-bred culture and the English bohemianism within which Connie and her sister were raised. The passage between the hegemonic and the supposedly dissident in England remains for Lawrence as smooth as ever, and the position of the Irishman Michaelis, who is definitely not Clifford's 'sort', makes this point in a different way. This culture is also gender-divided, and it is Connie's marginalized perceptions which are to the fore. Lawrence sees very clearly the structures of dependency which characterize this anxious male world.

> Yes, she sat there! She had to sit mum. She had to be as quiet as a mouse, not to interfere with the immensely important speculations of these highly-mental gentlemen. But she had to be there. They didn't get on so well without her; their ideas didn't flow so freely.[21]

Lady Chatterley's Lover, then, exposes an intellectual culture which fails to satisfy even those who participate in it.

The condition of the late-Edwardian intellectual world is a central concern of several late essays also, most strikingly the well-known piece on 'John Galsworthy' which is an attack on the social-realist, social-problem fiction produced by Galsworthy's generation. For Lawrence, Galsworthy's social criticism is made only from within the ideology of bourgeois experience. Forsyte rebels can imagine no other horizon: 'About every one of them something ignominious and doggish, like dogs copulating in the street, and looking round to see if the Forsytes are watching',[22] and clearly this is relevant to Lawrence's sexual renegades. But *Lady Chatterley's Lover* also takes issue with the literary conventions within which Galsworthy worked. Whereas Victorian and Edwardian social-problem fiction posits social and class reconciliation through the readjustment of personal relations, *Lady Chatterley's Lover* posits the unspeakable disruption of them; whereas much of this fiction posits a change-of-heart as the mechanism of such reconciliation, *Lady Chatterley's Lover*'s mine owner becomes only a bitter ideologist. At every point, Lawrence's novel subverts its literary antecedents. The country-house poems of the seventeenth century celebrated (sometimes wryly) the inmates of the estates and the social coherence they offered; Jane Austen mocked these inmates with corrective purposes, but remained in support of the social functions of the great house; even in late nineteenth-century novels like Eliot's *Daniel Deronda* or Meredith's *The Egoist*, though the brick may crumble and the irony become bitter, the point of view remains within the estate. That is not the case in *Lady Chatterley's Lover*, whose perspective is harshly and scathingly outside.

This is indicated in several ways, most obviously in the freely drawn, and frequently noted, symbolic opposition between wood, park and mine. Less frequently noted, however, is the specific social and cultural engagement of these oppositions, for the tendency (especially in criticism dominated by Practical or New Critical premises) has been to assume that *Lady Chatterley's Lover* has little to do with the social world, and more to do with universals; or when reference is made to that world, attention tends to be directed from the estate to the rather unfocused industrial landscape, as in Leavisite criticism.[23] In fact *Lady Chatterley's Lover* is bitingly of its period.

In Chapter 13 Sir Clifford chugs in his mechanical bath-chair into the wood to survey his covers. As is often noted, the incident counterposes the deformed mechanical world with the healthy natural world, but it also counterposes an English gentleman's sense of his estate with that same natural world – that is, property with commonality. For the wood is a remnant of the common-land Sherwood Forest, and references to the oppositional political legend of Robin Hood are frequent. This, though, is not simply a matter of the ownership of acres. Also at stake are narrowing cultural definitions associated with the stuffy Edwardian Englishman Sir Clifford is rapidly becoming. The incident is not simply an attack on 'the mechanical', but on Edwardian notions of English cultural and political identity. Sir Clifford breathes in the spring:

> 'You are quite right about its being beautiful,' said Clifford. 'It's so amazingly. What is *quite* so lovely as an English spring!'
>   Connie thought it sounded as if even the spring blossomed by an act of Parliament. An English spring! Why not an Irish one? or Jewish?
>
> (pp. 191–2)

Clifford's trite manner before natural beauty is a character point; but there is a cultural point, too, in the English appropriation of it, especially as a major part of the literary culture of the period.

Clifford's speech patterns are carefully observed. As they become more awkwardly stilted, they include more and more quotations from a Palgrave's

Golden Treasury world of literary commonplace by which he preserves his sense of ideological belonging, and keeps at arm's length any real human contact. He proposes that Connie has a child to continue the dynasty:

> Connie looked up at him at last. The child, her child, was just an 'it' to him. It . . . it . . . it!
> 'But what about the other man?' she asked.
> 'Does it matter very much? Do these things really affect us very deeply? . . . You had that lover in Germany. . . what is it now? . . . They pass away, and where are they? Where . . . Where are the snows of yesteryear?'
>
> (p. 45)

Again, she gives him violets:

> 'Sweeter than the lids of Juno's eyes,' he quoted.
> 'I don't see a bit of connection with the actual violets,' she said.
> 'The Elizabethans are rather upholstered.'
>
> (p. 94)

His apprehension of the woodland, too, is of this kind.

> '. . . this is the old England, the heart of it; and I intend to keep it intact.'
> 'Oh yes!' said Connie. But, as she said it she heard the eleven-o'clock hooters at Stacks Gate colliery. Clifford was too used to the sound to notice.
>
> (p. 44)

The irony here does more than expose a shallow and conventional sensibility. For not only is Clifford unconsciously covering up the damage his mining interests have done to the natural world (the woodland is shrinking), he is also covering up his social role as a mine owner at a time of recession (the heart of England is in the wood, not in the pit villages to which he is oblivious), and finally he is participating in a shift in English cultural perception whose effects are felt today. I mean the construction of an English literary culture in the Edwardian period as the approved and ruling version of the national self-image.[24]

It seems clear that Lawrence has these things in mind, for his perception of the ideological beliefs of his ruling-class characters does not end with Clifford's witless remarks. There is also the crusty paternalism of Squire Winter, and, most importantly, it is just these assumptions about the world which Connie has to shed. This is evident in her sarcasms at Clifford, but it is also the real psychological action of the famous car ride through Tevershall, often quoted simply as evidence of Lawrence's rejection of industrialism. Of course Connie is in recoil from industrial squalor, but this issues in a more thoughtful reflection that the 'old' England, 'the illusion of a connection with the Elizabethans' (p. 162), is just that – an illusion sustained by wealth. She arrives at her destination.

> Leslie Winter was alone. He had adored his house. But his park was bordered by three of his own collieries. He had been a generous man in his ideas. He had almost welcomed the colliers in his park. Had the miners not made him rich! So, when he saw gangs of unshapely men lounging by his ornamental waters – not in the *private* part of the park, no, he drew the line

there – he would say: 'the miners are perhaps not so ornamental as deer, but they are far more profitable.'

(p. 163)

This is a clear-sighted perception of a class culture overlaying material interests and disguising them, and a political point, in a novel about a new tenderness, which concerns the habit of regarding men, even in jest, as equivalent to game or a mere source of profit. 'This is history. One England blots out another,' thinks Connie. In terms of class or era this perception remains valid.

Lady Chatterley's Lover, of course, attacks the cash culture on both sides of the class divide, and is as antagonistic to the unionism of the barely-glimpsed miners as it is to the mine owners' arid self-delusion. But it truncates Lawrence's politics to see him as having only industrial spoliation in mind. He sees very clearly that the culture at large is complicit with this spoliation in all its reaches. There is much talk in the book of class issues, and Clifford talks at length, in a way puzzling and irritating to Connie, about his class mission and political role. By the close he has a clearly articulated position which in part follows Lawrence's earlier anatomy of the industrial magnate's power obsession in *Women in Love*. But Clifford's politics also spring from ideas widely discussed in Britain in the 1920s, especially after the General Strike, by the authoritarian right, which offered radical social-discipline solutions to the crisis based on firm perceptions of class role, national – and racial – purpose, and the need for a Caesarist leader for England.

It is now clear that these groups formed a significant part of the political culture and that the problems in the coal-mining industry were a point of growth for them (as were the Empire and Irish questions, the splits in the Conservative Party in 1922, anti-bolshevism, and the importation of the ideas of Continental fascism).[25] Lawrence, in drawing Clifford the way he does, is both revising his own 'leadership' commitments and attending to existing political reality. Rightist politics were embraced by prominent Edwardian literary intellectuals (for example, Belloc, Chesterton, Sayers, Rider-Haggard and Kipling, not to mention sympathetic outsiders like T. S. Eliot or, for that matter, Churchill) who were drawn to causes like anti-bolshevism. Mussolini's success – and initial plausibility – in 1922 drew in others, like G. B. Shaw (surprisingly).[26] The country-house network was a centre for these beliefs and features (with different levels of commitment) in the work of rightist writers until after the Second World War – for instance in Yeats's reverence for the 'Great Houses' of the Anglo-Irish Ascendancy, Eliot's *Four Quartets*, and the novels of Evelyn Waugh and P. G. Wodehouse. In Wodehouse's *The Code of the Woosters* (1938) the villain Roderick Spode – the leader of the Black Shorts – is a satire on the country-house fascist.

Clifford Chatterley has a career which was rather typical, and in this way Lawrence was right to insist on his representative quality: an army past, literary interests following youthful bohemianism, a country seat with paternalist social responsibilities, and a substantial stake in heavy industry. Significant features of this career were shared, for instance, by Alan Ian Percy, the 8th Duke of Northumberland (1880–1930), who led the mine owners during the 1926 strike. Percy, like Chatterley, was a writer and a substantial land and mine owner. He was also a publisher and press baron, and a prominent figure among the ultras who took the severest line on social questions. (Like many of his contemporaries with his views, he was also anti-Semitic, which gives a further edge to Connie's sarcasm on the 'English spring' mentioned above.) In *À Propos of Lady Chatterley's Lover* Lawrence said that he wanted Clifford to be representative, to stand for a certain situation. My point is that this situation was not just a generalizable one about a nebulous condition of 'industrialism', as it so often seems from the criticism the novel receives, but was clearly pointed towards a specific state of affairs in the political life of contemporary England. Clifford's political beliefs (see, for instance, the argument with Connie which takes up the bulk of Chapter 13) are specifically relatable to a historical reality.

Lawrence wrote *Lady Chatterley's Lover* after visiting England in 1926 and whilst living in Italy, a fascist state which, unlike many of his contemporaries (and fellow exiles in Florence), he detested.[27] And it is important to register how his 'tender' mood of this late period is related to his response to fascism. An essay like 'Insouciance', for instance, which recommends an unfretted response to nature and the rhythms of life in a characteristically 'Lawrencian' manner, proceeds from overhearing two English ladies discussing Mussolini. This is also evident in his travel book *Etruscan Places*, written between the second and third versions of *Lady Chatterley's Lover*. Just as the novel identifies the ultra-rightist drift of English political life in the 1920s as a central target, so *Etruscan Places* juxtaposes Etruscan civilization with the Caesarist militarism and bullying of Rome. Mussolini's Roman Empire is then identified (as indeed it identified itself) with ancient Rome, and for Lawrence it therefore means yet more power-hungry expansionist bullying, further wreckage in a terrible time. It is Clifford Chatterley, not Lawrence, who looks to the *England* of Nero: 'The masses were always the same, and always will be the same. Nero's slaves were extremely little different from our colliers or the Ford motor-car workers' (p. 190). But it is Lawrence who looks to the burning of that world.

Notes

1 Mark Spilka, 'Introduction' to the 'Twentieth-Century Views' volume, in M. Spilka (ed.), *D. H. Lawrence: A Collection of Critical Essays* (Englewood Cliffs, NJ, 1963), 1.

2 Michael Bentley, 'Lawrence's political thought: some English contexts, 1906–19' in Christopher Heywood (ed.), *D. H. Lawrence: New Studies* (London, 1987), 59–83. See also Emile Delaveney, *D. H. Lawrence and Edward Carpenter: A Study in Edwardian Transition* (London, 1971) and Graham Holderness, *D. H. Lawrence: History, Ideology, and Fiction* (Dublin, 1982).

3 Lawrence's commentary on Russell's lectures is quoted substantially from the manuscript sources by Paul Delany, *D. H. Lawrence's Nightmare: The Writer and His Circle in the Years of the Great War* (Hassocks, 1979). Delany's is an excellent account of the controversy with Russell.

4 Lawrence to Russell, 14 July 1915. *The Collected Letters of D. H. Lawrence*, ed. Harry T. Moore (London, 1962), I, 353–4 (*The Letters of D. H. Lawrence*, Camb. edn, II, 365–6). (Hereafter abbreviated to *CL*.)

5 ibid.

6 Bertrand Russell, *Portraits from Memory and Other Essays* (London, 1956), 104–8.

See also Ronald W. Clark, *The Life of Bertrand Russell* (London, 1975), 265–6 for comment on why Russell delayed until 1956 before going public with his opinions.

7 In the 'Autobiographical Sketch' of 1929, Lawrence himself interpreted his experiences in these class ways. He contrasts himself with H. G. Wells and J. M. Barrie, also from 'the common people', who made a successful 'rise in the world' through their writing. Lawrence could never do this because of his class origins. He could not transfer to 'that other thin, spurious mental conceit which is all that is left of the mental consciousness once it has made itself exclusive' and which was characteristic of middle-class intellectual life. It would mean the forfeit of 'my old blood affinity with my fellow men'. (*A Selection from Phoenix*, ed. A. A. H. Inglis [Harmondsworth, 1971], 18). Little has been made of this class perspective, though Lawrence's friend, the novelist Anna Wickham, in a well-judged early assessment, also made these kind of points (see 'The spirit of the Lawrence women', *The Writings of Anna Wickham*, ed. R. D. Smith [London, 1984], 355–72); and Raymond Williams stressed it in the late 1950s with, it seems to me, just the right nuance (see *Culture and Society 1780–1950* [Harmondsworth, 1958], part 3, ch. 1). See also Graham Martin, 'D. H. Lawrence and class', in Douglas Jefferson and Graham Martin (eds), *The Uses of Fiction: Essays in the Modern Novel in Honour of Arnold Kettle* (Milton Keynes, 1982), 83–97, which comments on the way critics have persistently obscured the class elements and perspectives in Lawrence's work, and the essay by Jeremy Hawthorn in this volume.

8 Edward Carpenter, *My Days and Dreams: Being Autobiographical Notes*, 3rd edn (London, 1921), ch. 5. Details of the Bolton Whitman Club are given on p. 250. For details of the 'Progressive Association', see Phyllis Grosskurth, *Havelock Ellis: A Biography* (London, 1980), 60ff.

9 *Selected Essays*, ed. Richard Aldington (Harmondsworth, 1950), 78. Hereafter page references to this essay will be given in brackets following the quotation.

10 For illuminating comment on the powerful apocalyptic strand in Lawrence, see Colin Clark, *River of Dissolution: D. H. Lawrence and English Romanticism* (London, 1969) and Frank Kermode, *Lawrence* (London, 1973).

11 Bertrand Russell, *Roads to Freedom: Socialism, Anarchism and Syndicalism* (1918: London, 1966).

12 Williams, *Culture and Society* (see note 7).

13 W. H. Auden, 'The prolific and the devourer', *The English Auden: Poems, Essays, and Dramatic Writings, 1927–1939*, ed. Edward Mendelson (London, 1977), 402–3.

14 'New Mexico', *Selected Essays*, 180–8.

15 *Kangaroo* (1923: Harmondsworth, 1954), 15–16. The joke has a personal resonance, perhaps indicative of how distant Lawrence felt himself to be from his origins in the mid-1920s. 'Torestin' was the name of his sister's house in Ripley, Derbyshire (*CL*, 952; Camb. edn, V, 592).

16 *Movements in European History*, ed. James T. Boulton (Oxford, 1981), 307–21.

17 *CL*, 1045

18 Raymond Williams, *The English Novel from Dickens to Lawrence* (London, 1970), 186; Adrian Mellor, Chris Pawling and Colin Sparks, 'Writers and the General Strike', in Margaret Morris (ed.), *The General Strike* (London, 1980), 338–57; Holderness, *History, Ideology, and Fiction* (see note 2), 220–7; Cambridge Alternative Video Group, *D. H. Lawrence and the Culture Industry* (Cambridge, 1985).

19 Michael Squires, *The Creation of Lady Chatterley's Lover* (Baltimore, 1983), 184–5.

20 Graham Holderness, for instance, one of the most interesting of recent Lawrence critics, is unhappy in this way, as are Mellor, Pawling and Sparks (see note 18). See also Martin, 'D. H. Lawrence and class' (note 7) and Peter Scheckner, *Class, Politics, and the Individual: A Study of the Major Works of D. H. Lawrence* (London, 1985), ch. 4.
21 *Lady Chatterley's Lover* (1928: Harmondsworth, 1961), 37. Hereafter page references to this text will be given in brackets following the quotation.
22 *Selected Essays*, 223.
23 Julian Moynahan's influential essay of 1959 – '*Lady Chatterley's Lover*: the deed of life' (reprinted, for instance, in Spilka (ed.), *D. H. Lawrence: A Collection of Critical Essays* – is representative of the former approach. F. R. Leavis's repeated quoting of the drive through Tevershall became a notorious indication of the latter.
24 Paul Fussell, *The Great War and Modern Memory* (Oxford, 1975), esp. ch. 5; Martin J. Weiner, *English Culture and the Decline of the Industrial Spirit 1850–1980* (Cambridge, 1981); Brian Doyle, 'The hidden history of English studies', in Peter Widdowson (ed.), *Re-Reading English* (London, 1982); Chris Baldick, *The Social Mission of English Criticism, 1848–1932* (Oxford, 1983); Robert Colls and Philip Dodd (eds), *Englishness: Politics and Culture, 1880–1920* (London, 1986).
25 Colin Holmes, *Anti-Semitism in British Society 1876–1939* (London, 1979); Kenneth Lunn and Richard Thurlow (eds), *British Fascism: Essays on the Radical Right in Inter-War Britain* (London, 1980); Richard Griffiths, *Fellow Travellers of the Right: British Enthusiasts for Nazi Germany 1933–39* (Oxford, 1983); Mary Langan and Bill Schwarz (eds), *Crises in the British State 1880–1930* (London 1985); G. C. Webber, *The Ideology of the British Right 1918–1939* (London, 1986); Richard Thurlow, *Fascism in Britain: A History, 1918–1985* (Oxford, 1987).
26 Holmes, ch. 13; Griffiths, 13–25; Webber, 19, 58; Thurlow, ch. 2. (See note 25 for full references.)
27 For details of British support for Mussolini, see Griffiths and Webber (note 25) and Denis Mack Smith, *Mussolini's Roman Empire* (Harmondsworth, 1976), 11–12, ch. 6.

14 Envoi: the genie in the second-hand shop

Jane Davis

It is nearly sixty years since Lawrence died, a prophet and seer whose works had been publicly reviled and declared obscene. I am glad if for many he still seems hard to read. He feared gaol, he wrote to Catherine Carswell, as the 'final insult – with a little vague sympathy in the far distance'.[1] In the event it turned out perhaps rather worse: we, that 'far distance', are offering not 'vague sympathy' but canonization, that recognition which means that one's ideas and feelings have probably lost their power. Being taken into the academic and literary fold is not far from being put in gaol: the authorities now have him, and will do with him as they think fit.

It is not enough to be willing to accept Lawrence as an important author. Lawrence demands acceptance as a man, as a thinker, and as an example. It is this that makes him hard. He is not like the dignified men of modern literature: Eliot, Pound, Joyce, even Yeats, who it could be claimed are difficult to understand. No, Lawrence is difficult to take. Think of Ursula, entering college:

> There was in it a reminiscence of the wondrous, cloistral origin of education. Her soul flew straight back to the mediaeval times, when the monks of God held the learning of men and imparted it within the shadow of religion. In this spirit she entered college.[2]

We may laugh at Ursula's naive expectation of her training college, her desire to connect a modern institution with the 'cloistral origin of education', but our laughter turns sour when by her second year Ursula has gained a cynicism to match our own, and is seeing the college for what it is.

> During this year the glamour began to depart from college. The professors were not priests initiated into the deep mysteries of life and knowledge. After all, they were only middle-men handling wares they had become so accustomed to that they were oblivious of them. . . . The life went out of her studies, why, she did not know. But the whole thing seemed sham, spurious; spurious Gothic arches, spurious peace, spurious Latinity, spurious dignity of France, spurious naivete of Chaucer. It was a second-hand dealers shop, and one bought an equipment for an examination. . . . It was a little apprentice-shop where one was further equipped for making money.

> (*The Rainbow*, 484–5; Camb. edn, 402–3)

'Spurious Lawrencian Studies', Ursula might add if she were at college today, when canonization can seem no more than a life sentence in the second-hand shop. For Lawrence is most vulnerable now not to the vagueness of our sympathy but to its superficiality. To overcome this we need, as modern readers, to be careful that we don't lose the vitality of response he knew was so important to real knowledge. We've got to take him at first-hand.

Conversely, if it isn't to be a nod at Lawrence's notional greatness that we're offered, it is also worth remembering that anyone can do a hatchet job on Lawrence: his rawness and integrity render him particularly vulnerable to thuggish critics. The best reader Lawrence's books could have would be a person who genuinely wanted to know what kind of man Lawrence was, what he thought, what he felt, what he saw. A reader prepared to step outside the mental confines of any institution, to read for his or her own sake. Lawrence would say that anything else was 'sham, spurious', that one would be doing nothing but buying 'an equipment for an examination'. How can modern readers bring Lawrence alive and kicking, like some bottled Genie, out of the 'second-hand dealers shop', if that is where they happen first to have met him?

It may be that as readers we too need something of the naivete and idealism which Ursula started out with. She was naive to believe the professors might be 'priests initiated into the deep mysteries of life and knowledge', and she was naive to be shocked at the realization that they were only 'middle-men handling wares they had become so accustomed to that they were oblivious of them'. But the shocked cynicism which follows disillusionment is not here portrayed as sophisticated adulthood, nor can it be seen as intellectual integrity. It is, as Lawrence's vulnerably disappointed language shows, a degeneration. Lawrence makes naivete the primary and, as it were, decent state, at least to start from: cynicism is one with disappointment, and it depends on lost ideals.

> While a man remains a man, a true human individual, there is at the core of him a certain innocence or naivete which defies all analysis, and which you cannot bargain with, you can only deal with it in good faith from your own corresponding innocence or naivete. This does not mean that the human being is nothing but naive or innocent. He is Mr Worldly Wiseman also to his own degree. But in his essential core he is naive.[3]

Lawrence always gives the chance of new life; the belief that the 'core' of a human being is 'a certain innocence or naivete' is a profoundly optimistic and generous one. For this is to say that we all have at centre a youthful self unmarked by time, unhardened by experience, and blind to all the necessary evils and compromises of adult life. A ridiculous and vulnerable core in some respects, but powerfully free of the shopkeeping world.

From this core of naivete comes the power to envisage things other than the world-as-it-is. A reader might have the innocence to envisage a real education, for example, and that vision would come in good faith; even though, as Lawrence says, 'he is Mr Worldly Wiseman also to his own degree', and knows that institutional education is sometimes 'a sham' and can only be improved by careful strategies. Mr Worldly Wiseman knows what's what, but the core of naivete knows what might become.

There is no bargaining with Lawrence, who wants to deal with us in 'good faith'. This is not to say that we must swallow him whole, any more than naivete in a man means he is nothing but naive. The problem is not which parts to keep and which to reject, but rather the attitude with which we decide. Our faith when reading rests in the belief that Lawrence is a man trying to do his best in terms of truth, and if this seems simplistic, perhaps it has to be so, to understand its difficulty. Humanity, individuality, innocence, naivete, good faith: these are not attributes generally built up by our institutional educations.

Ursula's faith in education was destroyed because the college could come up with no matching naivete, no 'corresponding innocence'. If we are cynical, this will seem to be Ursula's failing: she should have been more realistic. Lawrence himself as a young man at college was amazed to find the English teacher rejecting his unconventional piece on autumn and demanding a 'proper essay' instead:

> 'I know it isn't an ordinary essay,' he said; 'it wasn't meant to be, and I thought she'd have the wit to perceive it. But I'll give her the kid's stuff she evidently wants,' he concluded in chagrin. I was surprised to see him so hurt at this reception of his essay – after all, what else could he expect?[4]

The older Lawrence knew what to expect but still refused to be merely realistic, in the lowest sense of that word.

*

Lawrence's best work will make naivete like Ursula's a challenge to more dignified but deadened responses:

> The two women looked at each other. Ursula resented Hermione's long, grave, downward-looking face. There was something of the stupidity of a horse in it. 'She's got a horse face,' Ursula said to herself, 'she runs between blinkers'. It did seem as if Hermione, like the moon, had only one side to her penny. There was no obverse. She stared out all the time on the narrow, but to her, complete world of extant consciousness. In the darkness, she did not exist. Like the moon, one half of her was lost to life. Her self was all in her head, she did not know what it was, spontaneously to run or move, like a fish in the water, or a weasel on the grass. She must always know.
> But Ursula only suffered from Hermione's one-sidedness. She only felt Hermione's cool evidence, which seemed to put her down as nothing.[5]

Here in *Women In Love*, 'Woman to Woman', Lawrence puts Ursula's naive unconsciousness in opposition to Hermione's passion for 'knowing'. From a realistic report of the look between the two women he draws out the emotional and psychological conflict which is his real subject matter. Ursula is resentful and sulky, clearly the less sophisticated; her thought, 'She's got a horse face . . . she runs between blinkers', is the sort of ungracious observation one would not always care to claim publicly as one's own, but rings horribly true. But Lawrence joins in on Ursula's side with his sentence. 'It did seem as if Hermione, like the moon, had only one side to her penny.' And by the time we reach 'She must always know', we understand that Lawrence sees Hermione as a deformed creature, twisted into a peculiarly narrow shape by constantly living in the 'narrow' confines of 'extant consciousness'. Ursula may have escaped this fate, but still suffers from 'Hermione's one-sidedness'. Made to feel little, stupid, insignificant, worthless by Hermione's assumption of superiority, Ursula is not worldly-wise enough to carry her naivete in the world with strength. Lawrence, who knows the necessity for such a combination from direct experience, here both sees the situation freshly, making it quite his own, while also bringing insight from beyond the situation he creates.

In writing this scene Lawrence does what Ursula, living it, can't: he combines the naivete with a personal strength which allows him to see Ursula, for all her gaucheness and sulkiness, as a fuller and more interesting human being than the intellectually sophisticated Hermione. Like Alvina in *The Lost Girl*, he believes that 'life itself is something bigger than intelligence.'[6] The touchstone here as everywhere is emotion not reason, and Lawrence's ear for the emotional tone of any scene is generally almost perfect.

In Lawrence new experience is raw experience. But to be polished imposes a deadening veneer. Hermione is based in 'cynicism and mockery', but she is cultured and knowing and beside her Ursula only looks vulgar and feels awkward.

> When she got outside the house she ran down the road in fury and agitation. It was strange, the unreasoning rage and violence Hermione roused in her, by her very presence. Ursula knew she gave herself away to the other woman, she knew she looked ill-bred, uncouth, exaggerated. But she did not care. She only ran up the road, lest she should go back and jeer in the faces of the two she had left behind. For they outraged her.
>
> (*Women in Love*, 382; Camb. edn, 301)

It is Hermione's 'presence', her sense of self which drives Ursula madly into 'exaggerated' forms of her self. But she does not care how she seems to Hermione, and it is right that despite realizing that she seems 'ill-bred, uncouth, exaggerated', Ursula is prepared to give more weight of meaning and truth to her feeling of outrage than to the exaggerated response Hermione's 'shallow cleverness' (p. 378; Camb. edn, 297) produces in her. Her main desire is not to hide shamefully but to 'jeer in the faces of the two she had left behind'. This jeer is characteristic of Lawrence himself in certain modes, particularly in his non-fiction.

A similar clash of worn-out and new attitudes occurs when Birkin goes to ask Ursula to marry him, and talks to Will Brangwen.

> 'I suppose,' said Brangwen, 'you know what sort of people we are? What sort of a bringing-up she's had?'
>
> '"She",' thought Birkin to himself, remembering his childhood's corrections, 'is the cat's mother.'
>
> 'Do I know what sort of a bringing-up she's had?' he said aloud.
>
> He seemed to annoy Brangwen intentionally.
>
> 'Well,' he said, 'she's had everything that's right for a girl to have – as far as possible, as far as we could give it her.'
>
> 'I'm sure she has,' said Birkin, which caused a perilous full stop. The father was becoming exasperated. There was something naturally irritant to him in Birkin's mere presence.

'And I don't want to see her going back on it all,' he said, in a clanging voice.

'Why?' said Birkin. This monosyllable exploded in Brangwen's brain like a shot.

> (*Women in Love*, 334–5; Camb. edn, 257)

A social conversation turns Ursula into a raging fury; a mere monosyllable blows Will Brangwen into pieces. Ursula, daughter of Will and soon to be wife to Birkin, combines both the necessary disconcertedness in the face of the question 'Why?' and the innocent insouciance that so provokingly must ask it. No less is required of Lawrence's readers.

*

Why, you might ask, bother with him at all, if he's going to be so difficult, if he makes himself hard to take? Lawrence is a very unusual modern: he takes on the problems of modern being without completely despairing of life. When he finds things meaningless, that's the beginning, not the end of the story:

> 'And we've got to live for *something*, we're not just cattle that can graze and have done with it,' said Gerald. 'Tell me,' said Birkin. 'What do you live for?' Gerald's face went baffled.
>
> (*Women in Love*, 107; Camb. edn, 56)

Like Birkin, Lawrence would be glad to confront, even to frighten us. If he makes us angry it is often because we prefer anger with Lawrence to the fear he provokes in us. And if we are baffled by him it may be that we are in reality baffled by things which are there whether we choose to notice them or not. It may be that Lawrence-the-realist is making us see things we might otherwise ignore or forget.

As *Women in Love* is in part a response to the First World War, so the work of Primo Levi is a result of the Second. Levi writes of a dream which troubled him, after returning home from the German prison-camps, for the rest of his life:

> It is a dream within a dream, varied in detail, one in substance. I am sitting at a table with my family, or with friends, or at work, or in the green countryside; in short, in a peaceful relaxed environment, apparently without tension or affliction; yet I feel a deep and subtle anguish, the definite sensation of impending threat. And in fact, as the dream proceeds, slowly or brutally, each time in a different way, everything collapses and disintegrates around me, the scenery, the walls, the people, while the anguish becomes more intense and more precise. Now everything has changed to chaos; I am alone in the centre of a grey and turbid nothing, and now, I know what this thing means, and I also know that I have always known it; I am in the Lager once more, and nothing is true outside the Lager.[7]

Reading Levi's moving account of his survival of the Lager, I was struck by the feeling that however dreadful life inside the camps seemed, it was not simply separate and different from life outside or life afterwards. The very twinning of the dream blurs the distinction, not simply for Levi but for all of us.

The social experiment of the camps showed human life, he writes, not unnaturally but as if under a magnifying glass. And that terrible close-up vision which is the life of the camps, where to be human at all is a massive achievement, is closer to all of us than we might want to think.

Lawrence still makes us aware of both sides of this twinned dream. Thus the Ursula of *The Rainbow* faces an 'outer darkness' completely alone, and finds a sort of strength in it.

> She could see the glimmer of dark movement just out of range, she saw the eyes of the wild beast gleaming from the darkness, watching the vanity of the camp fire and sleepers; she felt the strange, foolish vanity of the camp, which said 'Beyond our light and our order there is nothing', turning their faces always inwards toward the sinking fire of illuminating conscious-ness, which comprised sun and stars, and the Creator, and the system of Righteousness, ignoring always the vast darkness that wheeled round about, with half-revealed shapes lurking on the edge.
>
> (*The Rainbow*, 488; Camb. edn, 405–6)

Where before we have seen Ursula as naive, here it is the sophistication of the world of consciousness which is paradoxically made over-simple. Yet because the camp is proclaiming itself as right (and Righteous), this is not simple naivete but 'foolish vanity', the limitation of intellectual pride which is more damaging than the want of experience which makes Ursula naive. The 'camp' seems big enough, with its '*consciousness*, which comprised sun and stars, and the Creator', but beyond it the darkness of the unknown is 'vast' and is filled with unknown life, for Ursula sees the 'glimmer of dark movement just out of range', the 'half-revealed shapes lurking on the edge'.

Between these several worlds, the world of terror epitomized by the Lager, the world of peace epitomized by friends and family, the world of the vanity of the camp fire, and the world of fear of the unknown, human beings must somehow mark out a path which will be wide enough to encompass all that we are, and all that we are capable of being. To take Lawrence seriously today, we must take him in the context Levi maps, of real human degeneracy and real corruption, close to all civilized beings. We need to take him as dedicated humanist revolutionary and we have to understand that what he is out to change is not 'society' but us. To many modern readers it is exactly this that makes Lawrence so hard to take. And even if we can take it, change is always difficult, and can feel damaging. *Women in Love* is an account of modern people, Birkin in particular, who feel 'damned and doomed to the old effort at serious living' (p. 383; Camb. edn, 302).

The very heart of the land, London, is portrayed as a centre of degeneracy and even death:

> Gudrun hated the Cafe, yet she always went back to it, as did most of the artists of her acquaintance. She loathed its atmosphere of petty vice and petty jealousy and petty art. Yet she always called in again, when she was in town. It was as if she had to return to this small, slow, central whirlpool of disintegration and dissolution: just to give it a look.
>
> (*Women in Love*, 471; Camb. edn, 380)

Lawrence's task as a realist in the modern world was partly to name areas of 'disintegration and dissolution' when he saw them, just as he reported that Hermione was essentially dead, 'a leaf upon a dying tree' (p. 373; Camb. edn, 293). This is not unusual in itself. What marks Lawrence out from most of his contemporaries is that he is not prepared to name it all as 'petty' and then to accept it, as Gudrun, the modern artist, does: 'Gudrun hated the Cafe, yet she always went back to it'. Lawrence won't go back. He pushes on, and will push us too. Thus Birkin contemplates Gerald's final journey into death:

> Gerald might have found this rope. He might have hauled himself up to the crest. He might have heard the dogs in the Marienhutte, and found shelter. He might have gone on, down the steep. . . .
> He might! And what then? The Imperial road? The south? What then? Was it a way out? – It was only a way in again. . . .
> 'God cannot do without man.' It was a saying of some great French religious teacher. – But surely this is false. God can do without man. God could do without ichthyosauri and the mastodon. These monsters failed creatively to develop, so God, the creative mystery, dispensed with them. In the same way the mystery could dispense with man, should he too fail creatively to change and develop. . . .
> It was very consoling to Birkin, to think this.
>
> (*Women in Love*, 579–80; Camb. edn, 478–9)

Might, might, might. Gerald 'might have' lived but, Lawrence insists, did not, perhaps could not. For what would a return to life have been for Gerald? No more than Gudrun's self-defeating return to the Cafe society she despised. Through Birkin here, Lawrence tries to outline the enormity of the big modern problem: *What happens when there is no answer to the question 'What do you live for?'* Grant the premisses behind that demand, and Lawrence offers only two alternatives for humanity: to 'change and develop' or to die. And though this is experienced as a deeply personal and individual problem (Gerald dies, Birkin does not), yet Lawrence also wants to tell us that it is more than personal, and not entirely under personal control. Thus humanity is classed with ichthyosauri and the mastodon, as if the problem were biological or evolutionary. We can do so much – face the questions, pose them – but a point comes where it is not quite up to us anymore. 'God *can* do without man.' There is something bigger and more powerful than human will, but something harder to identify. In his essay 'Benjamin Franklin' Lawrence writes,

> We are only the actors, we are never wholly the authors of our own deeds and works. It is the author, the unknown inside us or outside us.[8]

'It' in us is both something we have to discover and something which can only be revealed to us. *Women in Love* manages to show us this movement of 'it' in human lives, even as it shows the difficulty of incorporating 'it' in a modern life. In the chapter called 'Excurse' Lawrence shows us Birkin and Ursula struggling with themselves, each other and the difficulty of relationship. When we see Ursula stalking off, or flinging disgusted words at Birkin, we are bound to think they'll never sort it out and manage to be together. *They* can't do it. But Lawrence, powerfully certain of 'it', brings them together like two new people, quite fresh despite the ugly scene.

'See what a flower I have found you,' she said, wistfully holding a piece of purple-red bell-heather under his face. He saw the clump of coloured bells and the tree-like, tiny branch; also her hands, with their over-fine, over-sensitive skin.

'Pretty!' he said, looking up at her with a smile, taking the flower. Everything had become simple again, quite simple, the complexity gone into nowhere.

(*Women in Love*, 392; Camb. edn, 310)

Something has happened and quite what 'it' is remains a mystery. But it is also true that this is simply a lover's tiff and nothing much has happened. Yet something has shifted the perspective – 'the tree-like, tiny branch; also her hands, with their over-fine, over-sensitive skin' – making Birkin see with a new and innocent clarity. It isn't the flower which makes everything simple, nor even Ursula's 'wistful' way of showing it to him. 'Everything had become simple again, quite simple, the complexity had gone into nowhere.' It is not Birkin and it is not Ursula who did it, they are both passive at this point: neither of them brought the simplicity, it simply 'became'. But they had to get stuck in the argument, feel the desperation and violence even, become quite lost in the complexity, before such a peaceful and accepting resolution could come about. Birkin's rawness, Ursula's naivete, their joint complexity, deserve to 'become simple again'. 'Look, we have come through!'

*

If educational institutions are infamous for their power to deaden interest, and if canonization means a thoughtless nod of recognition, should Lawrence be studied in schools and colleges and universities? Oh yes. Because if he provokes us, we shall get het up and begin to care more deeply, or feel more strongly and think more carefully about what we are doing. We may get stuck in the complexity he insists we face – 'Might! And what then?' – but not to face it would be to die much more slowly and far more ignobly than Gerald. A course on Lawrence threatens to make him a commodity, but if he is being read at all, it seems to me the man could easily break out of academic gaol, and then he'll have us.

Notes

1 'Letter to Catherine Carswell, 12.8.1929', in *The Collected Letters of D. H. Lawrence*, ed. Harry T. Moore (London, 1962), II, 1177.
2 *The Rainbow* (Harmondsworth, 1981), 480 (Camb. edn, 399).
3 'John Galsworthy', in *Phoenix*, ed. Edward D. McDonald, 2 vols. (London, 1936), I, 540–1.
4 Jessie Chambers – 'E.T.', *D. H. Lawrence, A Personal Record* (London, 1965), 79.
5 *Women in Love* (Harmondsworth, 1982), 372 (Camb. edn, 292).
6 *The Lost Girl* (Cambridge, 1981), 283.
7 Primo Levi, *The Truce* in *If This Is A Man, and The Truce* (London, 1987), 379.
8 'Benjamin Franklin' in *Studies in Classic American Literature* (Harmondsworth, 1971), 26.

Index